BISHOP'S CASTLE

Portrait of a Country Railway

by
John Scott Morgan

IRWELL
PRESS

The Lion in its Lair. In between trips to the Great Western's Wolverhampton works Carlisle , as its predecessors, was kept going through extraordinary local effort. Its earlier four wheel tender had a wooden weatherboard, built by the venerable driver, Whittaker (see text), the six wheel tender appearing after about 1924. Whittaker, and his successor as 'driver-fitter', would gather together the platelayers and the engine would be lifted on screw jacks and packed with wooden sleepers. The wheels could then be got out and sent to the GW to be turned up. Work as fundamental and protracted as firebox patches was carried on in this tumbledown gloom.

The late Dr. I.C. Allen.

Early Morning Encounter

The church clock was striking five, as the young lad in overalls stepped along the path, past fields of long grass, on his way to locomotive shed. It was bitterly cold and a north wind was blowing across the slumbering town; not a lamp or light in sight, he crunched his way up the cinder path and across the yard to the shed, picked out by the moonlight glinting across its roof.

Reaching the entrance, he opened the door slightly, a billow of black sooty smoke emerged from the top and drifted out into the early morning air, like a last gesture from yesterday, heralding the new dawn. Cajoling the doors fully open and securing them, he walked through the spooky darkness to the oil stove, where he began to prepare for the coming day, lighting the old tilly lamp, its glare seeming suddenly to illuminate the old timber building and its multitude of nooks and crannies, casting long dark shadows across the joists and beams.

There, in the cold darkness before the first grey light of dawn, stood the aged but proud warhorse, a relic from a time long dead and even forgotten. There in the long shadows in the weak yellow light stood graceful lines of forged iron and beaten brass, that once helped to build railways such as that from Aston to Birmingham. Her copper capped chimney showed a dull glow in the strange yellow light. After checking the gauge glass and boiler water level, the lad clambered on top of the old tender, a survivor from days long ago when she had gone for overhaul to the Great Western works at Wolverhampton.

He lifted the filler lid and found the tender full to the brim. Now he could prepare the fire – a collection of oily rags would be needed, some wood and best steam coal. After preparing the fire he lights a large oil soaked rag on a shovel, depositing it through the fire hole into the cavernous copper firebox. The fire gently crackles and spits as it grows in heat and intensity, throwing a rich, bright yellow-red light across the whole back end of the shed. Steadily the needle of the steam pressure gauge nudged from 0 as steam started to bring the old weary frame to life, and a plume of soft grey smoke gently drifted out across the yard into the cold air of morning.

With a small ball of cotton waste he began to rub down the boiler cladding sheets, revealing a shiny dark Great Western green livery, under a thin coat of sooty grime. The town clock struck six as he finished polishing the safety valve cover. There was a sound of boots crunching outside. Presently the figure of an elderly man, clad in light blue overalls appeared at the door; after a brief morning greeting he set about oiling up the ancient beast, with an old and dented oil can.

The lad was by now preparing the lamps and oil cans for the 0-6-0's first journey of the day, while the dawn was groping up behind the eastern hills. Six thirty, and the old driver was standing in the small cab, polishing the copper pipes and taps with a small piece of rag and emery cloth. Opening the regulator slowly, with steam gently coursing through her cylinders and valves, she moved out into the grey light, beams of weak wintery light glinting across her slender boiler and wheels, as she rolled across the yard past a line of derelict carriages and wagons. Her creaking progress ends only on reaching the limit of shunt board. The young lad jumped down from the cab and after switching roads the engine is dropped back down to the station platform, to couple up to two time worn four wheel carriages. An old ex-Great Western four wheel brake van brings up the rear.

Down at heel, but possessed of a human charm, with its striped paint work, Bishop's Castle station was in every sense a true leftover from the mid-Victorian age. Its thickly panelled doors, short awning and large sash windows were not unlike buildings on the early Cambrian, and Potteries, Shrewsbury and North Wales Railway. The ancient slotted signals with their wooden arms at drunken angles, almost always ignored by the footplate staff, protruded from the lineside like giant, thin, iron bean poles.

It was now seven and as the church clock chimed the hour, last packages and boxes were being loaded into the brake van; a last passenger hurriedly booked a ticket and ran for the train, jumping in the third class compartment of an old four wheeler, with its musty worn out material and sagging old seats.

A sharp toot from our engine and we are off at last, through the yard past the brick goods shed, past the dilapidated engine shed, more like a lean-to shack out of a Western film set, out into the fresh air of the morning. A trail of white steam drifts across the fields, on the way to Lydham Heath where, after 'Carlisle' runs round its gypsy train, she will proceed to Craven Arms, past the trees and hills of green grass dotted with sheep and cattle. Following the river Onny through Eaton, Plowden and Horderley the train picks its way between the river bank and clusters of broad leaf trees forming a green roof over the valley floor; crossing the river at several locations its silvery waters rush over rocks and stones below the bridge abutments.

Then onward to Stretford Bridge with its timber platform keeping a lonely vigil, for the few trains and passengers that have cause to stop there.

Finally to the junction and Craven Arms, where the 1860s finally met the present impersonal world; 'Carlisle' proudly coasts into the large LNWR station with its late Victorian iron and glass roof, past a Great Western Dean 0-6-0 goods, heading a train of eight plank private owner wagons.

There under the early morning winter sun, the optimistic mid-Victorian world met the uncertain post-Great War world. The driver, fireman and guard group together and chat for a short while, before taking the train into the large goods yard, to make up a return working.

Many years later, after the line had closed in 1935, a forlorn ill-kempt 'Carlisle' and demolition train left Bishop's Castle for the last time, ripping the iron rails up behind her, never to return. She slowly went up the Onny valley taking all after her, rails, bridges signals and all manner of iron fittings.

It was December and snow covered the rents in the old road bed, left behind after the demolition men had done their deed. The white stuff covered their methodical, destructive work, as if to cleanse the landscape of this final act. The bridge abutments stood empty now, mute witness to the once colourful past, and only empty, ghost-like station buildings along the line bore witness to the railway.

They took 'Carlisle' down to the bottom of Craven Arms yard and cut it up; 'No.1', the ex-Great Western tank, was scrapped where it stood at Plowden. They smashed the ancient four and six wheel carriages to pieces, and they broke the wagons up for firewood and scrap iron. In the name of progress.

Carlisle at Craven Arms.

Craven Arms joint station about 1906, with Great Western 0-6-0 No.453 shunting on the main line.

Roger Carpenter.

Great Western steam railmotors (No.74 leading, on the Much Wenlock service). To the left is No.1, the ex-GWR 0-4-2T delivered only after the Bishop's Castle cheque was safely cleared.

Roger Carpenter.

Chapter One
Courthouses and Closures

The story of the Bishop's Castle Railway is an extraordinary one by any measure, a triumph of hope over expectation; a Will Hay script that ran for decades only to expire, funnily enough, as his gentle comedies began to popularise precisely the sort of undertaking represented by the Bishop's Castle Railway. That even Colonel Stephens should turn it down is perhaps the keenest measure of its limping decrepitude. Yet it draws us still, a concern so beset by financial and legal difficulties, and overall impecuniousity as to beggar belief. A railway moreover, with the Receiver as 'proprietor' through more or less the whole of its existence, a railway that eluded both the Grouping and the bemused attempts of the Board of Trade to make it conform to something like recognised operational standards. The mightiest of British Railway companies, some amongst the greatest business operations in the world, fair jumped and rattled at a missive from the Board of Trade; the Bishop's Castle usually shrugged its shoulders. To the comprehensive improvements usually demanded by an aghast Board of Trade Inspector, figuratively the BC pulled out the linings of its pockets. They were barren and holed.

The 'Castle' of the title had its origins in long-ago wars with Wales, a few miles distant; the wild Celts had not prevailed and the railway occupied a jewel-like piece of England. For this and the peculiar *Land that Time Forgot* quality of the town, we owe an early attention to its railway. E.C. Griffith published a book on the line, the first edition as early as 1948 and it has attracted sporadic attention ever since. Closed in 1935 its last splutterings occupied much of the following year, surely the most closely documented dismantling of a line ever.

The Bishop's Castle was an unintended remnant of a through route across Shropshire and Montgomeryshire; extraordinarily, it even contrived *three* termini, for Bishop's Castle itself was but a *branch* off the 'through' route, perhaps the only passenger-carrying line in Britain (excluding Ireland perhaps) to combine vestige and appendage.

This account seeks to present a photographic record of this strange line and through Ordnance Surveys and Board of Trade archives (hitherto little aired) bring a fresh treatment (long overdue perhaps) to the line. Nestling in the ghostly weeds of its trackbed (they chopped fresh boughs from the lineside for sleepers, so fresh legend has it, they *sprouted shoots*) a new look at the line, half a century or more on, is appropriate. It is made possible in good part through the S.H. Pearce Higgins Collection now with the National Railway Museum. Pearce Higgins was enamoured of the line and took many photographs as well as copious notes. His interest however ranged much wider than the Bishop's Castle. The catalogue alone of this single collection, the donated material of one individual, is a bulky volume in itself and a tribute to the painstaking, scholarly care which typifies the work of the National Railway Museum. Collections come to it in all conditions, from shoeboxes upwards and are transformed into worthy historical records.

The most comprehensive published work on the subject of the Bishop's Castle probably remains that of E.C. Griffiths, published privately in 1948 and subsequently in enhanced form. It is particularly good on the promotion of the railway and its operations but this account, it is hoped, will be able to shed some further light, in the use of various archive extracts and the Ordnance Survey, as well as further photographs. Closing so long ago, in a district pretty isolated even now, it is necessary to be somewhat archaeological in any pursuit of the Bishop's Castle. S.H. Pearce Higgins' notes, so meticulously cared for, allow an 'eye witness' aspect, for which we must be particularly grateful; other primary sources comprise principally material kept at the Public Record Office.

In the 1850s and 1860s the district knew little of and was little interested in the affairs of the world outside. Bishop's Castle lay at the centre of a tract of country where railways ran only at the periphery. By this time the idea of towns entirely shunning the railway was largely over and the various notables, butchers, bakers and candlestick-makers soon organised themselves into A Campaign. The idea from this early time was quite sensibly for a line *through* the district from the Cambrian (then the Oswestry and Newtown) at Montgomery to the LNW and GW Joint (then the Shrewsbury – Hereford) line. Griffiths entertainingly records the usual tale of local infighting, culminating in a home-grown attempt at excommunication on the part of the local vicar!

A Bill received Royal Assent in June 1861, for a line between the two railways with a Bishop's Castle branch from Lydham Heath. The usual problems with money and landowners slowed events and time slipped by alarmingly, with no work begun. In a gloomy portent of what was to come, the company was forced to pursue its contractor into Chancery in the summer of 1864 and a start was finally made on the line later that year. By October 1865 the section from Stretford Bridge (where the line attached itself to the GW and LNW Joint, a little north of Craven Arms) to Lydham Heath, and the 'branch' to Bishop's Castle itself was complete. Montgomery was yet far off indeed and it was felt it could wait awhile. The great undertaking would open as it was....

Firstly, before any service could begin, there was the awkward matter of the Board of Trade ... Celebration of an almost pagan intensity greeted formal opening on Tuesday 24th October 1865 but the purely incidental detail of Government Inspection and Approval had not been attended to. Colonel Yolland duly attended on 13th December, penning his report (after getting over the shock perhaps) a few days later. The outcome was suitably chastening:

OUR LOCAL EXPRESS
Bishop's Castle

The poor old Bishop's Castle, reduced to a post card joke. The Observer remarked in 1903 'that the pictorial post card craze has invaded Bishop's Castle and Clun' though this is doubtless not what it had in mind. Despite the fun poking, in 1914 the paper was quite sniffy about the railway taking Christmas Day off. The cheek of it. The company was always wrong in any case: "a good deal of annoyance and inconvenience was caused to travellers on Friday at Craven Arms, owing to the lateness of the trains in the afternoon and evening. That scarcely anybody knew of the alteration, for very few people take the trouble to stop and read little handbills. Why don't the Castle Co. advertise such things properly?"

Stretford Bridge Junction on 14th June 1936. The boundary between the BC and 'the railway proper' is more marked than ever. Approaching engines simply whistled to gain the attention of the signalman and in the cleared ground on the left, amongst sidings and huts said to have been built in the first years of the line, a turntable was rumoured to lurk. Higgins could find no-one to recall it in use after the 1890s.

Approaching Horderley, facing Bishop's Castle on 14th June 1936. Emmanuel Beddoes was the last contractor for the line, and served for 28 years. He and his men maintained all the bridges, buildings, carriages and wagons and painted much of the stock as a matter of routine. They even built one or two wagons: 'a van, possibly No.21 as I recall, and a coal wagon, No.64, I think' an elderly Mr. Beddoes recounted in 1960.
Roger Carpenter.

Plowden with its stock, including No.1, on 14th May 1936. The collection included the more modern Bishop's Castle carriages, 1 plank opens 58 and 60, guards van No.1, covered steel vans 23 and 24, and carriages 2 and 3, with the bodies removed.

W.A.Camwell.

Bishops Castle Railway – Inspector's Report – I have this day inspected two junctions of the Bishop's Castle railway viz; from the junction with the Shrewsbury and Hereford Railway about a mile north of the Craven Arms station to Lydham Heath, a length of seven and a half miles and from Lydham Heath to Bishop's Castle, a length of two miles 17 chains. The line is single throughout with sidings at some of the stations and near the junction with the Shrewsbury and Hereford Railway, but the land has been purchased and the over bridges and steel work of the under bridges have been constructed for a double line if hereafter required. The width of the line at formation level is 10 feet for the single and 29 feet for the double line, the gauge is 4 feet 8 and a half inches and the width between lines where there are two is 6 feet. The permanent way consists of double headed rail that weighs 75lbs per linear yard in lengths of 10, 21 and 24 feet, fixed in cast iron chairs that weigh 28lbs each by means of wooden keys, the chairs being secured to transverse sleepers each by two wrought iron spikes. The sleepers are of half turned timbers 9 feet long by 10 feet by 5 inches length placed at intervals, average distance of 3 feet apart from centre to centre. The joints of the rails are secured by fishplates, the ballast is of gravel and is stated to be 14 inches deep below the bottom of the sleepers. The sharpest curve is of 15 chains radius and the steepest gradient is 1 in 80. There are four over bridges and 13 under bridges crossing roads and streams. The over bridges are of stone with brick arches, transverse timbers on iron girders carrying the superstructure, the largest span being 29 and a half feet on the skew. Some bridges have stone abutments, mostly with

iron girders and timber platforms but there are a few small culverts with timber tops, The largest span is 44 feet, the masonry is good and the bridges are sufficiently strong and no unusual deflections were found. There appears to be one unauthorised level crossing at 13 miles 10 chains and I do not know if it was originally proposed as a level crossing and disallowed by the House of Parliament or not and it is not even protected by signals.

There are several matters to be attended to before the line can be opened for traffic. No turntable has been provided at the Craven Arms station from which the Bishop's Castle trains are to run and the turntable at Lydham Heath station is not yet in position. The Craven Arms station requires some shelter, the two platforms should be lengthened and one of them raised as it is not above a foot high – and additional sidings off the up and down lines should be provided in order to accommodate the traffic of the Shrewsbury & Hereford Joint Line, the Knighton Railway, the Central Wales Railway and the Bishop's Castle Railway. An additional signal at the station is wanted for the Knighton Road.

There are also two level crossings on public roads between the junction and the Craven Arms station which require the protection by signals in each direction; the signals on the Bishop's Castle line should be connected with a distant and repeating signal worked from the junction and the repeating signal should be removed to a greater distance from the junction. The curve of the down sidings at the junction and at Plowden Station should be eased off; they are too sharp at present. The platforms at several of the stations are too low and must be raised. The station buildings

are incomplete at Plowden and are only now wooden huts at Lydham and Bishop's Castle. A footpath is required to be made to allow persons to reach the Lydham Heath station from the turnpike road. A complete double junction should be made at Lydham Junction with a double line of way and up and down platforms, so as to fit it for the accommodation of the main and branch line traffic. The line requires lifting and packing in places, particularly at the ends of the under bridges and there are a few spent bolts through the fishplates which should be removed. The Bishop's Castle company are to make a line parallel to the S&H from the junction to the Craven Arms station and in doing this will have to construct over bridges over two public roads and for that purpose they propose to run their line at such a distance from the S&H line as would admit of the slope up the road coming out of the existing land of the Shrewsbury & Hereford. Now this should not be done but the opportunity should be embraced by the S&H of getting rid of their Level Crossings altogether, of which one, if not both, if I recollect rightly, are not authorised by Parliament – by making the line close alongside of the Shrewsbury & Hereford Railway and then making the overbridges to cross both railways by one arch – the S&H Rly Co. contributing to the cost of these bridges.

I should also recommend that the working of mineral traffic (coal) should be commenced with as little delay as may be practicable as it will assist in consolidation of the line. I must therefore now report that by reason of the incomplete works the opening of the Bishop's Castle Railway for traffic cannot be sanctioned without danger to the public.

I have your honour to be ...

The gulf between achievement and reality runs throughout the story of the Bishop's Castle. Earlier in the year, before the unfavourable Board of Trade report, so bouyed up with future prospects were the directors and shareholders that borrowing powers and the rest of the legal paraphernalia had been arranged and an Act secured for yet a further branch northwards. The 'main line' to Montgomery was still no more a few scraps of paper (and so it remained) and this second branch would secure more direct access to Shrewsbury. The sense of unreality is sharpened by Griffiths' detailed and delightful description of the opening celebrations, with bands, feast, general Bacchanalia, fulsome toasts and speeches, on Tuesday 24th October. To the local Reverend it was hardy less than the second Coming, though as we have seen, the aftermath of Board of Trade Inspection was a descent surely into pure bathos. There were after this some desultory tinkerings with the 'main line' and various improvements and additions to the existing works allowed a public service proper (in BC terms at least) to begin on Tuesday 1st February 1866.

A nautical imagery was employed in one of the glowing opening speeches, as recorded by Griffiths; the chairman and directors were a bold 'ship's crew', on 'a three year voyage and meeting nothing but storm and tempest'. If this was so then the Bishop's Castle vessel, barnacle encrusted with tattered sail, foundered long before a kind harbour or even before a safe embarkation. By the end of the year unsuspected financial shoals found the infant railway bankrupt. From hereon the company's long life under the Receiver began. Not for the last time bailiffs descended upon the line and whilst the train service carried on, more or less, most of the assets were knocked out at a sale in Shrewsbury, to be rented back thereafter. From *The Worcester Herald* of 2nd February 1867:

On the 23rd ult; a sale of rolling stock took place at the George Hotel, Shrewsbury. The stock was the property of the Bishop's Castle Railway Company, whose line running from Craven Arms to Bishop's Castle, with a projected continuation to Montgomery, was lately seized by the Sheriff, and the Company being unable to satisfy the claims of the suing creditors, their available property was ordered to be sold by auction. The catalogue enumerated 61 lots, comprising 25 strongly built goods waggons, with break, built by the Birmingham Waggon Company; 14 cattle trucks with spring buffers and break, built by the Midland Waggon Company; 5 coal waggons, 5 enclosed goods vans, with spring buffers and break; composite carriages, 4 third class carriages and 2 passenger vans, all built by the Midland Waggon Company; a tank engine, and a powerful six-wheel locomotive engine.

There was a large attendance in the auction room; but, as might be expected, only a few was present with the intention of becoming purchasers. The first lot put up was one of the goods waggons, which starting with a bid of £20, was ultimately knocked down at £31. The buyer in this case elected to take the whole of the waggons at this price, and his example was followed by the purchaser of several other distinct classes of stock. The cattle trucks which was stated to have cost £80 each, brought £50; the composite carriages, original cost £250, sold at £123 each; the third class carriages first cost £170, went for £57 a piece; the tank engine, built at a cost of

Carlisle on a mixed train at Bishop's Castle. Trains ran chimney first up to here, or rather as far as Lydham and tender first down to Craven Arms. On the day of 'The Big Fair' at Bishop's Castle trains of up to twenty cattle wagons would be run, coming up on loan a day or two before and loaded by the ever resourceful and versatile platelayers.

£900, realized £410; and the 'powerful six-wheel locomotive engine with tender in good working order', was knocked down for £470. The stock, with the exception of the locomotive, was guaranteed to be equal to new, and it was stated that some of the carriages and waggons had never been used. The total sum realised was £3,522. A gentleman from Birmingham, stated to be the representative of the Midland Waggon Company, was the principal purchaser.

'The Midland Waggon Co.' (and the de-benture shareholders) apparently was con-vinced of the line's possibilities and was content for the line to operate as before, only now under the icy profit and loss direction of the Receiver, who *hired* back the stock. Years later in 1903 Jasper More the MP was to recall that new debentures were raised in 1872 to pay off the Midland Waggon Co, and other liabilities. Though 'the public probably didn't know', these debentures overode all others, taking whatever profit was available. The his-tory of the Bishop's Castle after this is princi-pally one of court cases over debts and other wrongs, and the decline and dilapidation of the railway. In this the Receiver, it was widely suspected locally, played a less then wholly protective role.

Certain of the company's lands were siezed during 1867 and in 1869 the Railway Clearing House emerged as another Bishop's Castle creditor. That august body wrote somewhat despairingly to the GWR/LNW Joint Com-mittee, on 8th July 1869: it had obtained a judgement against the Bishop's Castle for £621 4/9d 'principally on through traffic with GW/LNW'. The judgement having been obtained the matter was placed in the hands of a Sheriff, 'who, however, could find no property to seize…' The Clearing House then tried suing shareholders 'who had not fully paid up their shares, but this course also was not attended with any satisfactory result. One person who appeared by the Register to be the most promising turning out upon inquiry to be a man of straw'. Solicitors had advised 'let the matter rest', but the GW/LNW were asked to 'bring any pressure to bear' if they could. Both wisely kept out of the business, having early on learnt to get the cash in advance from the Bishop's Castle. The Railway Clearing House seemed a bit of a soft touch – by 1886 it was owed £1,258.11.0!

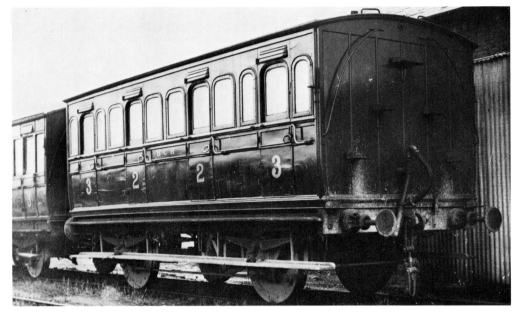

Ex-Brecon and Merthyr coach at Bishop's Castle and (below) Carlisle , in a sadly faded view, taking its leave of Bishop's Castle. One of Beddoes' home grown wagons, based upon an LNW vehicle, which he had measured up in the yard, was condemned and barred by the LNWR. It required a trip to Earlestown for Beddoes to plead his case. Rubber, in place of laminated springs on drawgear, was not something The Premier Line approved of – according to Beddoes that is.

Carlisle at Craven Arms about 1910. The Bishop's Castle bay behind it was later known as the Wenlock bay and much later, as the layout altered, as the 'Knighton siding'. W.H. Smiths had the Craven Arms bookstall by the 1880s and a Shrewsbury firm ran the Refreshment Room. A lad toured the platform crying 'Banbury cakes, port wines and sherry' and a ticket collector rang a bell five minutes before a train was due off.

Roger Carpenter

Chapter Two

More of the Same

Getting cash in was no easy matter and the autumn of 1867 was more or less typical; 'the fifth and final call' of £2 shares went out on 21st October and was payable by 16th November. In the case of shareholder No. 187 this involved ten shares, a total of £20, accompanied by this note:

Secretary's Office
Montgomery, 21st October 1867

Sir,

The Directors of this Company having made a Call of £2 per share, on or before Saturday, the 16th day of November next, I have to request you to pay the amount of such Call, in respect of the Shares registered in your name, to one of the undermentioned Bankers, viz:-

The North and South Wales Bank, Bishop's Castle.
Messrs Beck Downward & Co. Welshpool.

Interest at the rate of £5 per cent. per annum will be charged on all Calls in arrear from that day.

I am, Sir,

Your Obedient Servant,

W. Wilding
Secretary

The Bishop's Castle Receiver was curiously impervious to any demands for money it would seem and the line operated hereafter strangely immune to judgment or regulation. It was not a member of the Railway Clearing House for a start and declared this so in an early tussle with the Board of Trade:

9th September 1876; Secretary of Bishop's Castle Railway to Board of Trade:

Sir,

Explosives Act 1875

In reply to your letter of the 31st August, I beg to state that this Company is not a member of the Clearing House.
I have however forwarded your letter and enclosure to the General Manager Mr. John Craston, requesting his observations on it. I may however state that the length of this Company's line is so short viz: 9 miles, with a good Turnpike Road running the entire length of it, that the Carriage of explosives by Railway may be wholly dispensed with.

Yours,

We can only be thankful that gunpowder never rattled its way along the line. To make sure, a by-law was issued to the Bishop's Castle Company prohibiting just that.

The line was to become notorious for its closures, and the most celebrated, arising out of a rent dispute, coming in 1877; a meeting of the Debenture holders, preference shareholders, and 'others interested in this Company' was held at 53 Victoria St. Westminster on the 15th February 1877, 'at Noon', to discuss the claims upon the railway. James Ashbury M.P. was in the Chair and 'the motion of the Chairman, seconded by Mr. Hadley, was unaminously resolved. A Committee was to be formed, of three Members of each class of Debenture, preference and ordinary shareholders *with a view to secure the assents necessary to raise the sum sufficient to complete the Railway and consider existing liabilities and to treat both with the representative of Dr. Beddoes as regards his claim and other creditors, and with a contractor who is willing to undertake the execution of the Works and generally to consider whatever may be deemed necessary for continuing the use of the Railway as at present, and for completing the original scheme – and to report to a subsequent meeting.* This committee was to consist of Mr. Ashbury M.P., Mr. Fraser ('for Mr. Finney') and Mr. Hadley for the debenture shareholders; Mr. Francis Tothill, Captain Foot and Mr. Ommaney for the preference shareholders; Mr. Whalley, M.P., Mr. Farmer and the Midland Wagon Co. for the ordinaries. On the motion of Mr. Whalley M.P., seconded by Mr. Hadley, 'It was unaminously resolved ... that Mr. Ashbury be requested to communicate with Mr. Richard Marston of Ludlow as regards the claim of Dr. Beddoes representatives requesting him to

Carlisle stabled near Plowden on demolition work, on 14th May 1936. Higgins paid several visits about this time and records mournfully the activity of 22nd April: "there were white clouds rolling across a blue sky as the train pulled slowly away from Plowden, and without effort gathered speed on the falling gradient along the embankment just below the bridge over the road; a memorable and pleasant sight, which seemed a momentary revival of former days"
W.A.Camwell

allow time for the Committee to make arrangements for meeting his claim.

The legal wording makes it all difficult to follow but its meaning is plain to anyone (who will feel a familiar chill) who has ever been near a court case – the Bishop's Castle was in Queer Street. There next followed the familiar and much recounted saga of the Bishop's Castle's second major confrontation with bailiffs...

Dr. Beddoes had died, never having demanded payment for slices of land taken by the railway: his relatives thought otherwise and pressed for the money. The outcome (no cash coming forward) was that bailiffs took possession of the line, on 27th February 1877. They descended, laying siege to the isolated Bishop's Castle community, legend has it, by choking off its railway lifeline (actually essentials got through by road with little ill-effect). The incident richest in railway lore concerns the duping and thwarting of the bailiffs, preserved in *The Advertiser* of 22nd February 1901:

How a Railway Circumvented the Lawyers! (A true Railway Narrative)
By W. Beddoes, Traffic Superintendent, Waterford, Limerick and Western Railway.

It is not often a railway gets so deeply into the meshes of the law as to be in the hands of the bailiffs...

Some years ago, when Mr. Frank Beddoes (master of the United Pack of Fox Hounds) living at Longville, Salop, died, the settlement of his estates came into the hands of the family lawyers. The Bishop's Castle Railway ran through his land, for which he had had never been paid, and, being a liberal minded landowner, had allowed things to slide, taking the broad view that the railway was a public convenience, and the loss to him of a few acres of land not much one way or another.

When he was gone the lawyers thought differently and were not long in closing on the railway, and getting a judgment for payment or possession. Money not being forthcoming, the bailiffs swooped down on the railway near the village of Horderley, and, after taking out a couple of rails and so blocking the line, sat down on the embankment, lit their pipes, and waited developments.

Matters continued so for about a week, with famine staring Bishop's Castle in the face, coal at starvation prices, and things generally looking 'blue' in the district served by the line. To make matters worse, there were a lot of London and North Western Railway waggons blocked in, and these were lying idle. As things were growing desperate, a certain coal merchant, now dead and gone – some of whose trucks were also 'in pawn' – called a secret council

of war in the back parlour of the well known hostelry at Craven Arms, where the London Estate coaches used to call, before the Shrewsbury and Hereford line was made. The 'council' decided to make a bold bid, and after the shunting engine at the 'Arms' had been very busy, every truck labelled for the Castle was ready for a journey. In the meantime a couple of men had crossed the line near Horderley, where the faithfull 'bums'* were keeping watch over the vacant spaces in 'the iron road' and took pity on them on their cold and lonely job. The visitors suggested a drink at the 'village pub' and thither the bailiffs went.

A gallon or two of mulled beer, tempered with a drop of gin, was served out in front of the blazing fire. This seemed to suit the bailiffs better than watching out in the cold and as they thought there was no fear of the railway men being about at that time of the night, they made themselves comfortable in the chimney corner of the 'Lion Inn'. There was no lack of beer, and as the time wore on, each of the company became jovial. In the meantime a gang of men, by the aid of dark lanterns had placed the rails back in position, and soon after, an engine with all the empties crept quietly down from Bishop's Castle into Craven Arms, picked up a train load of goods and coal, and steamed off hard as she could 'pelt' for the beleaguered town. The bailiffs, however, by this time had recovered a little, in fact, sufficiently so to hear the snort of the engine, and reeling out of 'The Lion'

shouted and waved their lanterns and tried in vain to stop the train as she sped by, but repentence came too late. They were outwitted, and the goods and coal were safely landed at Bishop's Castle, much to the delight of everyone. The lawyers threatened the manager with arrest, but he was able to prove alibi. Terms were afterwards arranged, and once more the Castle Railway was allowed to pursue the even tenor of its way, unmolested by hard hearted lawyers, and the public appreciated the advantage of again being able to get from Bishop's Castle to Craven Arms for 1/3d, instead of hiring a road conveyance for half a sovereign, as will once more be the case if the line is again closed.

In the conclave of local notables that followed the Beddoes/bums episode, the first mutterings against the management of the Receiver are heard. Various notions also surfaced, for a takeover by the GWR for instance, and a revival of the original aims to open through to Montgomery. The problem of the Beddoes land was solved through a rental arrangement and yet another 'celebratory opening' was possible, on 2nd July 1877. *The Railway Fly Sheet and Official Gazette* of that month found the whole thing highly odd, very much to its nineteenth century sense of humour:

This wording did indeed cause some concern but to one's relief turns out to be a now little-used term for an arresting bailiff – 'from touching the debtor on the back'.

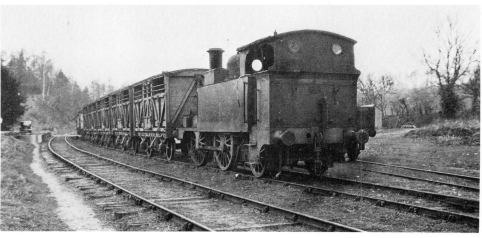

No.1 on a train leaving Bishop's Castle and (below) standing out of use with its 'rake' of derelict cattle wagons, at Plowden, in May 1936.

Re-opening of a Railway

The Bishop's Castle Railway, which has since the month of March been 'locked up' from all traffic, has again been opened to the public. The line was forcibly taken possession of in the beginning of the year by the legal representatives of the executors and heir of the late Mr. W. Beddoes, who were creditors to the company for a large amount. Some of the rails were removed, and all communication with Bishop's Castle was cut off, the line being 'blocked' for some months. The greatest inconvenience was felt by the inhabitants of the whole district through which the railway runs, and coals and other articles rose to fabulous prices. The permanent way for miles has grown into what appears a long level grass field, and where the 'iron horse' was wont to rush to and fro the road has been taken possession of by rabbits. Exertions were made at Bishop's Castle to bring this state of things to a termination and last month arrangements were made by which part of the money was paid, and the line is to be worked under a receiver in Chancery. The reopening of the line and the appearance once more of the train was welcomed with no small amount of satisfaction by the whole district from Bishop's Castle to Craven Arms.

Shutdowns bedeviled the railway throughout its life, to a greater extent, probably, than has heretofore been recognised. On 11th April 1883 for instance, a letter arrived on the desk of the The Secretary, Great Western Railway. It is hilarious not only for the fact of the BC resorting indignantly to law, but for some of the antics it hints at … "Sir, As you may be aware the Bishop's Castle line was closed at Easter by the Receiver. On the 7th inst. on our application on behalf of Mr. Plowden of Plowden Hall, Mr. Justice Bruce made an order appointing Mr. Thomas Cartright of the Wrexham, Mold and Connah's Quay Railway Receiver and Manager of the Bishop's Castle with full powers to reopen and work the line and to make all necessary payments. The engine hitherto in use had it appears *been taken to pieces* [author's italics] by the late management and Mr. Cartwright sent one over from the Welsh line but we were informed by telegraph today that it is blocked at Craven Arms and one cannot understand the reason. The Bishop's Castle Railway pays a good rent to the Joint Committee for the use of Craven Arms station, besides giving them the benefit of the Bishop's Castle traffic: we are at a loss to know by whose authority the engine is blocked. If it has been done by the Station Master at Craven Arms we trust you will at once instruct him to withdraw the block. From whatever source the obstruction arises we hope it will be speedily removed as our client and also the Debenture Holders whom we represent are considerably damaged to say nothing of the great inconvenience caused to the neighbourhood. We are writing a similar letter to the London & North Western Railway. Yours, Slaughter and Colegrave, Solicitors, The Strand, London."

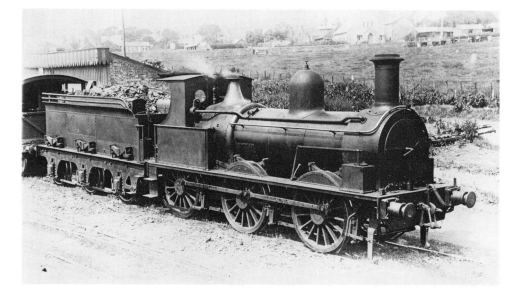

Delightful portrait of Carlisle at Bishop's Castle. It enjoyed a productive and ancient lineage; a dignified loco, well kept and ordered under difficult, often primitive conditions. Tubes leaked and burst soon after its delivery in 1895 and many were replaced at Bishop's Castle. On the firebox wearing thin, two slabs 4ft. by 2ft. were simply cut out and replaced.

No.1 with a Bishop's Castle train at Craven Arms on 8th October 1931 – trains could be arranged, it is clear, in any disposition, with carriages at front or rear.
Roger Carpenter

Horderley in 1932, reminiscent of a particularly down at heel 'native' railway, in some remote corner of Empire.

Bishop's Castle vehicles in 1928. The new stock was long overdue; Cartwright, the Manager and Receiver, had asked Beddoes after the Great War to do them up but the contractor, even then, declared them 'past it'.

Chapter Three
'I Have Never Seen in England or Elsewhere a Railway in such a Bad Condition'

In 1878 a typical Bishop's Castle saga had begun, the railway falling foul this time of the local Highways Board. There are many such *Titfield Thunderbolt*-like instances in the annals of our minor railways. The Corris for one, suffered similar persecution; it was as if the Highway people, perceiving all railways as enemies, saw in these decrepit undertakings a target for once their own size. The Board was worried about the declared proximity of the line to the road north of Plowden station. Its somewhat peculiar proposition was that the train would alarm horses on the road. 'Screens' would be required! The Bishop's Castle would have none of this and through a combination of inactivity and bluster fobbed off the Board for several years. It returned to the offensive on 31st December 1886:

…the Board apprehend danger to the passengers on the Highway leading from Plowden station to Eaton … in consequence of there being no shields or screens erected and owing to the non-existence of such shields or screens horses may be frightened by the sight of the engines or carriages travelling upon the railway.

By the following year even the Board of Trade had been dragged in and Major Marindin, unimpressed, took a trip to the line in March 1887 … *at a place about half a mile west of Plowden station the road is fenced by post and rail. There is more or less growth of brushwood between the railway and the road. I was met by the Bishop's Castle Secretary, Manager, and one of the Directors and by the Vice-Chairman, Clerk and Surveyor of the Highways Board.* This group of worthies, shuffling in the March chill, heard that there had been no accidents in 22 years, and only one complaint to the railway. Engine drivers (though they would be expected to give the right answer) had 'never seen a frightened mare'. Marindin plainly thought the whole thing a storm in a teacup and suggested 'a belt of spruce'. The Highways Board could be relied upon to reject this and in June was still demanding a screen. The Bishop's Castle simply pleaded poverty and ignored all further correspondence.

Eluding the clutches of the Highway Department fairly easily though its practice (which it was to perfect) of doing nothing, the Bishop's Castle next found itself in rather deeper trouble, with the Board of Trade. There appears to have been an accident or a complaint at least to bring the Inspector in and this is his (fairly damning) indictment of 24th September 1878:

Report on the condition of the Railway.

I have inspected the Bishop's Castle Railway with reference to its fitness for public traffic. The Bishop's Castle Railway is a single line (which was opened in the year 1866) nearly 9¾ miles long commencing with a junction with the Shrewsbury and Hereford Joint Railway about a mile north of Craven Arms Station from whence it runs to Lydham Heath a distance of 7½ miles. From this a branch nearly 2¼ miles long connects it with Bishop's Castle. The line was originally intended to join the Cambrian System at Montgomery. Its funds having failed the line between Lydham Heath and Montgomery has never been constructed and in consequence of this it is stated, and of excessive expenditure on the construction of the open portions of the line, the financial condition of the railway has never been satisfactory. It has been for some years in the hands of the receiver and I have been given to understand, it has been difficult to obtain the necessary means for the proper maintainance of the line.

The permanent way as originally constructed consisted of double headed iron rail (75lbs per yard) in 18, 21 and 24ft lengths, fished at the joints – secured by outside keys in cast iron chairs, weighing 28lb each. The chairs were secured to the sleepers by two iron spikes in each; the sleepers were of half round timber 9ft by 10ins x 5ins, placed at an average distance of 2ft from centre to centre. The ballast is of gravel.

The sharpest curve has a radius of 15 chains and the steepest gradient is 1 in 80.

There are 4 bridges on the line and 13 under it, crossing roads and streams – of the latter one is constructed of masonry, 10 are constructed of masonry abutments spanned by wrought iron girders with wooden cross girders; (largest span 44ft). The remaining two (spans of 9ft) have stone abutments and timber tops. The fencing is of post and rail.

With reference to the state of the permanent way I found that the rails are generally in good order; many of them have been turned and there are few which require renewal. The condition of the fish bolts is anything but satisfactory. I counted no less than 1100 deficient ones, there being in many cases only two instead of four to a joint, in many of the joints the bolts were quite loose and had evidently received no attention for a length of time.

The state of the wooden keys securing the rails to the chairs is also very defective – owing to the line being in many instances overgrown with grass and in many others the ballast being close to the top of the outside of the rails, it was impossible fully to ascertain the condition of the keys, but between one third and one half of the keys are either deficient or broken, this being the case not only in the straight portions of the line but also on the outside curves where proper keying is most important.

The state of the sleepers is also very unsatisfactory. It would have taken a much longer time than I had at my disposal to have examined most sleepers for they, like the keys, were in many cases so covered with weeds and ballast that it required a considerable amount of labour to get at them, but judging from those which I did examine I should estimate the number of decaying ones at least a third of the whole. There is no great deficiency of ballast but it was allowed in many cases as I have before remarked, to be overgrown with weeds and the line requires lifting and relaying to a great part of its length.

The state of the timber in the tops of many of the bridges wants immediate attention, wallplates, crossgirders or longitudinals being in large numbers more or less decayed.

The number of men employed for the maintenance of the line (1 Inspector and 6 platelayers) would not be sufficient for the purpose were it in good order, as there should be at least 9 platelayers or one man per mile, but looking at the state to which the line has been allowed to get, it is now far too few.

In conclusion, I feel it my duty to report, in consequence of the defective state of the Bishop's Castle line as regards the sleepers, keys and fish bolts, the lack of proper attention to the packing of the rails and the condition of the timbers on the tops of many of the bridges, I consider that the public are exposed to constant danger in travelling on the line…

Thus the fourth major closedown (probably to passengers only) was visited upon the Bishop's Castle. Throughout that winter its men (whether expanded to the levels suggested by the BoT or not) set to it and the Inspector was (fairly) pleased in June the following year:

Re-inspection of the Bishop's Castle Railway. 27th June 1879.

The state of the main line from the junction to Lydham Heath is now very different to what it was when I went over it in September last – the defective sleepers have been replaced to the extent of about 4000 or one third of the total timbers, the keys have been almost entirely renewed and the deficient fish bolts supplied; the ballast has been cleaned and the rails levelled and repacked; the decaying timbers have been removed from the tops of under bridges and safe timbers substituted.

There is consequently no reason why the restriction as to the speed of trains between the junction and Lydham Heath should not be removed.

As regards the branch between Lydham Heath and Bishop's Castle, the deficient fish bolts have been supplied and some of the defective keys removed and the wooden tops of an underbridge repaired, but there is still a good deal of work to be done on the branch in respect of the keys and sleepers and ballast and until this is reported complete the existing restriction should remain in force.

The work proceeded fitfully; Craston of the BC for instance writes to the Board of Trade on 3rd October 1878, asking for permission to resume passenger traffic ... "On Monday morning at the latest, as the present stoppage is a great inconvenience to the neighbourhood and a considerable loss to our revenue, I am at present working the goods traffic with one train to and fro daily and you may be satisfied that I shall not fail to have the Line perfectly safe for general traffic before Monday as I am determined to run no risk."

Traffic 'had been resumed' from 7th October and by January 1879 Craston could declare that the whole length of line had been 'cleared of weeds and undergrowth'and please could he up the speed limit to 20, 'or even 15mph'. Slow running 'was complained of by passengers' but the Board would not relent.

Soon after this proposals emerged to alter the whole of the arrangements, a revivification of the line to Montgomery together with new ideas involving *the abandonment* of the Bishop's Castle 'branch'. Needless to say nothing came of the proposals. The local vicar no doubt threatened all manner of hellfire and damnation.

In 1889 the Board of Trade was seeking to implement the various terms of *The Regulation of Railways Act* of that year. It was to be largely frustrated in the case of the Bishop's

Castle ... On 23rd December 1889 Mullens & Bosenquet, solicitors to the London Bankers Association, and representing ultimately the railway, wrote somewhat plaintively to the BoT. There was it seems little need for the Act, with its provisions regarding continuous brakes, the block system and interlocking, and comparable fuss, to press too heavily (or at all) upon the Bishop's Castle...

"With reference to the Bishop's Castle Railway, owned by this company. All the stations on the line have but one platform so that there are no points which require interlocking. Only thrice trains a day are run each way and the traffic is very light in both passengers and goods. Each train consists of two composite (first and second class) carriages and third class with the brake. The mixed trains have also four or five ordinary goods wagons. There is only one tender engine in steam at a time and all the carriages have Clark Webbs chain brake.

All the trains are run at low speed, never exceeeding 20 miles an hour. The whole line is but a few miles in length and is carried on under the control the Chancery Division of the High Court of Justice, which has appointed a Receiver. The line, though worked with great care, has to be carried on in the extreme of economy consistent with efficiency, as the receipts only just cover the expenditure and any increase of expense might necessitate the closing of the line."

'Craving the consent of the Board of Trade', Mullens and Bosenquet offered to

adopt a staff and key for all points into sidings, which would meet the requirements of the Act. The running of passengers and goods separately did not take place, 'through insufficiency of traffic', the solicitors declared, arguing against any requirement for continuous brakes. Mixed trains of two or three carriages braked throughout with Clark Webb chain and 'an average of four or five working goods wagons' appears to have been a typical train . They were in any event 'very light'.

The BoT stuck out for the block system however and the argument ran on through to February 1892. Costs were of course the root of the problem, again. A further extension of time was asked for; affairs being in Chancery, tolls all went to the Receiver. The line it was argued supplied the needs of a purely agricultural district and the receipts after paying expenses of working did not even allow of the Receiver paying rent charges to which the landowners over whose land the line runs were entitled (we have heard this before).

The rolling stock did not belong to the company but was hired from the Midland Waggon Company. 'Under the circumstances' it appeared quite impossible to provide the funds 'to carry out at once in their entirety the works referred to in the order of 20th November 1890' but it might, Mullens & Bosenquet hinted, just be possible to carry them out by degrees, 'the outlay thus spread over a longer period'.

The solicitors mentioned that the traffic of the company 'is in part carried over the line of the Shrewsbury and Hereford Railway at its junction at Craven Arms and we have at the present time to meet extraordinary expenditure occasioned by alterations in the signal arrangements now being made at that point.' The line had been worked for a great many years with the greatest care and without accident and 'very serious inconvenience would be occasioned to those living in the district if it had to be closed in consequence of your Board insisting upon its requirements being immediately met. I should also mention that the company never has more than one locomotive engine in steam at a time and that as it only runs one train backwards and forwards between Craven Arms and Bishop's Castle there is no possibility of any accident occuring which would be prevented by the use of block signals. Trusting that under the circumstances you may feel justified in granting some substantial indulgence to the company that I have the honour etc...'

Colonel Yorke finally inspected the 'interlocking' and reported on 24th May 1895.... At Horderley he noted a siding loop and a public road level crossing. The loop was provided with safety catch points and the connection worked by single levers (one at each end of the loop), locked and unlocked by an Annett key attached to the train staff by a chain and shackle. The level crossing was protected in both directions by signals fixed

Bishop's Castle, despite its general air of decay and neglect, was nevertheless the centre of activity for the working of the line; all carriage and wagon work (also buses — see the goods shed lean-to) and locomotives of course. Note No.1 up on blocks.

about 200 yards from the gates and the signals and gates interlocked by means of a key 'in such a manner that the signals must be at danger before the gates can be opened.' But this arrangement, although fairly satisfactory in itself was rendered absolutely useless by the practice (the BC blokes didn't think even to put on a bit of a show for the Colonel – it was just the way they *always* did it...the wrong way) 'of leaving the signals permanently at danger and *permitting the driver to pass these when in this position.*' Eyes bulging by now, Yorke found at Plowden a loop siding, the points worked and interlocked as at Horderley. 'At Eaton there is a dead end siding and a public road level crossing. The arrangements are similar in all respects to those at Horderley.' At Lydham Heath ('a reversing station') there was a loop siding and a single junction between the two sections of the line and at Bishop's Castle a loop for running the engine round the train, with a siding connection on the main line. At both places, the points were worked by single levers locked and interlocked

by the key on the staff. Colonel Yorke was unable to report that the arrangements were satisfactory and demanded that the following requirements be satisfied, before the hapless company could be said to comply with the Order (with regard to interlocking) served upon them under the Regulation of Railways Act 1889, viz:

1. The key must be rigidly attached to the staff so that it cannot be separated from it.
2. The facing points on the main line must in all cases except at the far ends of the loops at Lydham Heath and Bishop's Castle be provided with (a)gauge ties (b)facing point locks.
3. The signals for the protection of the level crossings must be brought into regular use and the most dangerous and improper practice of running past signals at danger must be stopped.

Although compliance would meet the obligations imposed upon the company Yorke felt it his duty to declare that the permanent way of the line, 'so far as I saw it, is in such a

condition as to be unsafe for traffic, the sleepers are so decayed and the rails so much worn that it is a matter of surprise that the trains ever reach their journey's end, and I have never seen in England or elsewhere a railway in such a bad condition'. This was the Board of Trade on its hind legs for sure.

Yorke confined his remarks to the track in the immediate vicinity of the stations but considered it likely that the whole line was in similar parlous state. Aware of the receivership, he had no wish to add to the company's embarrassment....

Cartwright, reliving Craston's *travails* of 1878, reported some three months later, after what must have been some pretty frantic work, that 'all Colonel Yorke's requirements had been carried out'. Yorke reinspected and in a Report of 17th July 1896 declared matters as fit as probably they ever would be. He had not seen all the line, though he presumably travelled over all of it, but was assured by Cartwright that every effort was being made to put it in proper order.

Plowden on 28th June 1936; the truck on the right contains No.1's chimney (W.A.Camwell). Below is Bishop's Castle station in 1928; it is typical that the closed station is hardly different, in any marked way, from the open one. The carriage shed had been renewed about 1903/4, corrugated iron in place of corrugated zinc.

Carlisle *in all its glory, around 1932.*

The BC before demolition. Near Horderley (on the Craven Arms side), this scene was very close to conditions throughout the line's life and not too far, no doubt, from those which so unnerved the BoT Inspector. Carlisle and No.1 were always off the road and latterly trains seemed to be sailing through a ploughed field, grass waving before its passage and clods of earth and water spray flying up.
W.A.Camwell

Chapter Four

Year of the Wasp

Bishop's Castle Advertiser, 22nd August 1901: It will undoubtedly be handed down to posterity in the pages of history, that the Salopian wasps of 1901 excel all others for size, numbers, and ferocity...

So there had been more to endure than the attentions of the Board of Trade, as if it wasn't enough coming after the Beddoes affair. 1901 saw another bout of crisis and though the line was to survive a further thirty years or so, it was only on a lurching, limping, basis. The would it/wouldn't it? question of closure became an almost annual event. The Bishop's Castle survived the marauding financial wasps of 1901 but the year cast a shadow over the rest of the line's existence that could grow only darker. The *Advertiser* was in the thick of things and there were heroes and villains at every turn:

An interesting reminiscence. Is the Bishop's Castle Railway to be stopped? This is the question which is at present occupying the attention of all the inhabitants of the ancient borough and the neighbourhood. There are a certain few in the town who would for curiosity sake be pleased to see the line closed for a short period, but we are of the opinion that their curiosity would soon be satisfied, if such was the case. Bishop's Castle can never be styled a flourishing town but the little trade and development it has made during recent years is certainly owing to its railway service, which, although not of the best and most convenient, is fully appreciated by everyone. Therefore, it is to be hoped the line will not be closed, and that every possible effort will be made to influence the 'powers that be' in this direction. A greater blow to the town and trade of Bishop's Castle could hardly be conceived. Trade in all directions and of all kinds would be crippled, the price of food, coal, gas and every other necessity of life would be increased, indeed everything would be at 'famine price'. Such is the picture that confronts the inhabitants of Bishop's Castle. Surely the influential men of the town and neighbourhood can use their power in this crisis, which it must be admitted, will affect the poorer classes far more than others.

Everyone is on the tiptoe of excitement, each waiting for any fresh development that may occur. The rumour that the line was to be closed was made known in the town during the latter end of last week and all sorts of rumours were afloat. It was said a letter had been received from Mr. Plowden, and that he was going to close the line for three months. We are in a position to state that Mr. Plowden is most desirous that the line should keep running, and a perusal of the copy of the letter, which that gentleman sent to the Town Council, will bear this out. The Mayor received the letter, and called a special meeting of the Town Council together on Monday morning. A good many of the Corporation members turned up, as did also the representative of this paper. By a clever little manœuvre on the part of one or two of the more 'influential' members, however, the meeting resolved itself into committee, which was a polite way of informing our reporter that his presence was not desired. Of course, he withdrew, after making an apology, but the action of these members, in keeping from the public of the town, a matter which is of the greatest public importance, will be resented by every rate payer. Therefore, we are unable to give details as to what was said by 'the representatives of the town.'

Mr. Plowden was extremely agitated over the action of a certain Mr. Fraser, a London accountant representing the first debenture holders. Mr. Fraser had, for some time, insisted upon his right 'to almost the whole of the annual surplus of income from the working of the line.' Now Plowden was owed 'a very considerable sum for arrears of rent', apart from the loss of the selling value of the land in question. It had almost become, it seems, ungentlemanly to want one's money out of the line. 'It is entirely due to me' Mr. Plowden declared, 'that the line is not only working, but owing to my persistent exertions (or effected on my behalf), eventually leading to legal proceedings, resulting in my obtaining the appointment of Mr. Cartwright as Receiver and Manager, that it is in a state of efficiency never before known'.

Plowden was more than a bit put out, considering that under the circumstances, if anyone was entitled to some payment, it was him. It is easy to see his point. He had offered Mr. Fraser (he said) 'the most liberal terms' rather than a resort to taking back the land; Plowden was exasperated and upset, he had suffered loss in order to see the railway carry on and it was even more frustrating for him to take action that endangered it. Blame, he was anxious to point out, should be apportioned rightly, which in his estimation, meant Mr. Fraser, who had insisted ... 'upon taking something like fourteen – fifteenths of the profits, to which I cannot assent.'

The Bishop's Castle Railway was due in the Chancery Court again on Friday March 1st 1901, though postponements gave some weeks grace. Traffic in coal and provisions rose enormously on the threat of the line being 'stopped up' again and 'nearly all the tradesmen' according to the *Advertiser* had 'ordered large consignments of goods in case'. The paper looked forward to a great sale in the event of the line remaining open. There was nothing like looking on the bright side. Rumour flew in the air – the town apparently was 'full of commercial travellers of a sudden' (hard to work that one out) and a representative of 'a big Birmingham firm' was supposed to have paid a clandestine visit to the area; ominously he 'was well pleased with the road from the Castle to the Arms' for motor cars. Mr. R. Jasper More M.P. was taking a great interest in the matter and was 'in daily correspondence with the leading men of the town'. He was in an awkward position, representing of course both shareholders and users and wrote from the House of Commons on 26th February with some peculiar, if novel ideas. Death apparently had it in for the Bishop's Castle:

My policy was to try to get the district beyond Bishop's Castle selected for Army Manœuvres, which would bring such an influx of visitors into the neighbourhood, that the extension of the railway, probably in these directions, would soon follow. A well-known chairman of a Board of Guardians told me to-day, he was surprised to see how little this policy was appreciated.

I thought it might appeal to local feeling if it was proposed to use the same ground for the training of our Army that was used with such effect by Caractacus against invaders so many years ago. Several attempts to complete this railway have been frustrated by the death of someone. First of all Mr. Bussey, who had arranged to extend the line to Minsterley, the year before his death; then of Mr. Ashbury, who died the week after he had arranged to have it completed. Between these, Mr. Pring offered to complete it if Mr. Fynny's interest could be bought out. Then by Mr. Adams, the chairman of the Newland Waggon Company, who had the ground surveyed and put the money down to complete the line to the Snailbeach line, which they declined. And latterly a syndicate at Manchester, who have considered it, have been inconvenienced by the death of their chairman, Sir J. Maclure, M.P. But I don't abandon a difficult problem.

Jasper More had an involvement with the line going back to the 1860s, when he had been asked (he apparently declined) to act as Chairman of the railway. He had known Fraser (who Plowden so complained of) for 25 years and defended him foremost. Fraser was by now ill, a reason perhaps for his wanting his money and Jasper More chided Plowden for his words. 'The neighbourhood' the MP declared was greatly indebted to Fraser 'for the introduction of capital to make the line'.

The *Advertiser* on 15th March 1901 was able to summarise events on 15th March 1901; some of the heat had gone out of things after Mr. Plowden's sabre-rattling and the Emergency seemed to be fizzling out...

We are informed on very good authority that there is very little possibility of the Castle Railway being stopped for several weeks to come, as the Chancery proceedings in the High Court are not yet down in the list. The date of the nearing of the case is very uncertain, and may not be before another month. The case will be made more complicated by the entrance of Mr. Beddoes, who possesses land through which the line runs. The traffic on the line still continues to be as great as ever. Should the line close at any time, it would seriously affect the postal arrangements, a fact which seems to have been overlooked by many. At present mails are taken away at nine in the morning, and the afternoon delivery of letters always relies on the afternoon train, so the difficulty would be great.

We have received the following interesting particulars from an authoritative source: The Bishop's Castle Railway Act is

Ch. 103, 1861. An Act for making a railway from the Oswestry and Newtown Railway, near Montgomery, to Bishop's Castle and other places in the county of Salop. Capital £180,000, in 18,000 £10 shares. The first directors of the company were William Minton Beddoes, master of the United Pack, William Edmonds, of Pentre, Churchstoke, Jasper William Johns, uncle of Mr. Humphrey Owen, M.P., William Henry Francis Plowden, and Dr. John Powell Wilding, of Church Stretton. A clause was inserted to prevent any part of the line which was to run from Montgomery to Wistanstow parish to be opened till a branch was opened to Bishop's Castle. As the land of the Rev. Arthur Oakeley was not first obtained, the negotiations for this, and a law suit between the contractor and Mr. Fynny, the largest debenture holder, delayed the line. The successors of two of the original promoters are now taking proceedings, one of whom, Mr. Plowden, enjoys a rent charge of £224, whilst the nephew of Mr. Beddoes, is also taking proceedings in order to secure a rent charge.

Latest advices from London are to the effect that the case will not come on for hearing until after Easter.

The strict accuracy of the foregoing seems to have suffered somewhat in the journalistic process: the name of the Reverend John Bright, apparently, was omitted (the *Advertiser* corrected this in its next issue) and William Francis Plowden, son of the Plowden deemed an early promoter of the line, plainly doubted the 'authoritative source', producing letters to demonstrate that his father had actively *declined* any involvement with the line or its construction. But the *Advertiser* had made its point, that those originally involved with the line had all been local men. 'Consequently the success of the early pioneers of the line 40 years ago should be appreciated as their efforts for the good of the neighbourhood with respect to the completion of the line'. The paper went on to lament the loss of this local involvement. Early meetings had been held in Bishop's Castle but following public apathy to the completion of the line (the general yeomanry, I'm sure, had always had a more hard-nosed view of the railway) the meeting place had drifted first to Craven Arms and then even further abroad.

The threat of closure revived all the old ill-

The two locos viewed (unusually) together – almost certainly a favour to the photographer though about four times a year there were two engines in steam, according to Emmanuel Beddoes. The passengers went off first, to Lydham Heath, the cattle following. (Below) No.1 with the older four wheelers.

feelings of being 'left out' of the railway system (though the inhabitants of Bishop's Castle traditionally delight in their isolation). The district needed more railways not less – hows this for a prospectus, a marvellous exercise in unreality:

NEW RAILWAY SCHEME FOR BISHOP'S CASTLE AND DISTRICT

Just What is Wanted!

About a month ago, the inhabitants of Bishop's Castle and the neighbourhood were startled by the report that the only railway which connects their ancient town with the outside world, was to be stopped owing to complications which had arisen between two parties interested in the line. What was done by the tradespeople in the way of laying up provisions, etc, has been fully reported, and it was well-known that in case the Castle line was stopped, the town would be in a state of siege, as the nearest railway is some 12 or 14 miles away. Therefore, any scheme which is put forward to alter the existing state of affairs, and which is calculated to develop the mineral, agricultural, and industrial resources of Bishop's Castle and the rest of South-West Shropshire, and which will open up the country generally will be read with interest by all. We have no doubt, that many of the more influential gentlemen of the neighbourhood will only be too willing to give their hearty support to such a scheme if it is considered desirable. For many years Mr. R. Jasper More. M.P., has been advocating and agitating for a railway which would open up the district, and it is mainly through his good offices that we have been favoured with a copy of the report of Mr. Percy Justyne, the well-known consulting engineer of Manchester. In his report on the advantages and prospects of a railway for Bishop's Castle and district, he says:-

Between the populous and busy market town of Shrewsbury in the north, and the rich agricultural district of Clun in the southwest of Shropshire, there is one of the most beautiful and interesting tracts of country in the kingdom. From Shrewsbury to Clun, a distance of about 23 miles, there is no railway communication from east to west. From Church Stretton and Craven Arms to Montgomery, a distance of 16 miles, the only railway is a branch line from Craven Arms, which terminates at Bishop's Castle and is, therefore, entirely dependent on the traffic between that small town and the important junction at Craven Arms. The area of country thus unprovided for by railway communication represents roughly 370 square miles, and embraces a region of great mineral wealth, of most remarkable scientific interest, of many historical associations, of abundant pre-historic relics, and a natural beauty unsurpassed by any county in England. To the great mass of tourists this district is almost inaccessible. To the geologist it possesses singular attractions – indeed a world-wide fame has the district, where the most ancient sedimentary rocks of the earth's crust are tilted up to the surface and exposed. Sir Roderick Murchison studied here the Llandeilo or Lower Silurian strata, which enabled him to write his famous work on the Silurian system.

But although in these days of cheap popular excursions, the traffic of pleasure seekers is one of the most profitable to railway companies, it is by no means the most important argument in favour of the construction of a railway through a district like South-West Shropshire. The development of the mineral and industrial resources of the country should be the first consideration. Facilities for the cheap and quick transit of agricultural produce to large and ready markets is also an object of vital interest.

Carlisle *running round at Lydham Heath in 1932, 'spick and span in its bright green livery' as H.C.Casserly noted at the time.*

H.C.Casserley

We cannot fairly measure the possible traffic by the present slow process of horse and cart.

New wants, new activities and increased population quickly result from a railway, especially in a country rich in heavy materials, ore and stone, which can be profitably carried to suitable markets by other means. Yet admitting the exceptional attractions which would be opened to the tourist and excursionist, and admitting a great possible development of the extraordinary mineral wealth of the country, and allowing liberally for the general awakening of local agricultural and commercial enterprise by a well-managed railway, it is nevertheless absolutely necessary to look for something more than local traffic to assure the financial success of the undertaking.

With this in view I have examined the country to ascertain in what direction a small local system of railway might act as feeders to existing main lines, and secure a fair amount of through traffic north, south, east and west. The Great Western Railway from Shrewsbury through Church Stretton to Craven Arms runs along the east, and thence on to Hereford, Monmouth, and Cardiff, and the London & North Western Joint line to Welshpool, with the Cambrian to Montgomery, on the extreme west of the district, opens up a direct route for the populous and favourite watering places and ports of Cardigan Bay, including Aberystwyth, as well as to Tenby, Milford Haven, and Pembroke further south. North of the district there is a line from Minsterley to Shrewsbury, and on the extreme south the London & North Western runs from Craven Arms through Hopton Heath and Knighton, to Llandovery, Carmarthen and Swansea. The Bishop's Castle Railway, for want of through communication, is practically of little value.

Carlisle *in its earlier guise, with Whittaker's weatherboard and four wheel tender, at Bishop's Castle in 1909.*

21

I regard it as essential to a successful scheme to acquire this line on fair terms and extend it from Lydham Heath to Hyssington, Church Stoke, Chirbury, and Montgomery, where it would join the Cambrian system. From Bishop's Castle an extension to Hopton would put the district in direct communication with Carmarthen and Swansea. From Hyssington, I propose to make a line through the great mineral districts between Corndon Hill and Linley Hill, passing the Shelve Mines, the Bog Mines, Tankerville Mines, etc, to Snailbeach, where the line would join the Minsterley line to Shrewsbury.

I recommend a single line of the ordinary 4ft 8½ins gauge, and the total length of the line to be constructed would be approximately 32 miles, at a cost of about £4,000 per mile – £128,000. There are no engineering difficulties to be overcome, and no exceptional gradients. The acquisition of the Bishop's Castle line would give us a junction at Craven Arms, and the acquisition of the narrow gauge railway which joins the Minsterley line and the Snailbeach Mines would also give us a junction on the line to Shrewsbury. Seeing that the proposed lines would act as feeders to the London & North Western, Great Western, and Cambrian lines, increasing their traffic without in any way competing with them.

I do not anticipate any difficulty in arranging with those great companies for junctions at Hopton Heath and Montgomery respectively. It is probable therefore, that the undertaking will not be burdened with the usual heavy Parliamentary costs. The financial position of the Bishop's Castle Railway Co. and the Snailbeach line (which latter would have to be reconstructed to standard gauge) encourage me to believe that these properties may be acquired on favourable terms. The 17 miles of road belonging to these companies are not included in the above estimates of mileage and cost.

Lead, galena, blende, and baryte are to be found in great abundance, and although numerous and extensive mining operations have been carried out in the past, and only ceased owing to the difficulties of carriage, the low price of ore and the absence of those methods and appliances which have added so materially to the profitable character of modern mining, there still remain enormous stores of mineral wealth in this district, awaiting the capital and enterprise, which cannot be encouraged without railway facilities.

The completion of this great undertaking together with the construction of a railway should awaken this wealthy district from its long sleep and make it one of the industrial centres of the country. Of the area of 370 square miles of country, which would be served by the proposed railways, about 60,000 acres are under cultivation, and 120,000 acres form pasture for sheep and cattle. The agricultural produce may be roughly estimated as follows; wheat 16,000 acres, barley 28,000 acres, oats 19,000 acres, rye 450 acres, beans 950 acres, peas 1,100 acres, hay 50,000 acres, root crops and green vegetables 18,381 acres.

There are numerous fairs, cattle sales and markets which would be rapidly increased in number and importance if the present horse and cart conveyances were supplanted by railway communication. The stock sales held at Craven Arms every alternate Monday, the horse and cattle sales at Bishop's Castle and Clun would be especially benefited, and from all parts of the district cattle and produce would be sent to the greatest shows and markets of Shrewsbury, if more direct railway facilities were provided. I have interviewed many cattle breeders and large farmers in the rich agricultural districts about Chirbury, Montgomery, Bishop's Castle and Clun, who all concur in the belief that the suggested railways would be of enormous advantage, rendering it possible to send produce to distant markets at present quite inaccessible.

The holiday and tourist attractions of this beautiful and interesting country opened up by the proposed railway are unique. Cordo Hill at 1,166 ft, Brown Callow 1,200 ft, Stapeley Hill 1,300ft, the famous Stiperstones, 1,600 ft and the Longmynds from 1,400 to 1,600 ft, form a panorama of the most varied and picturesque grandeur. The historical associations are of the deepest interest. There are many most remarkable and well preserved Druidical circles of great antiquity, notably the Hoar Stones, near Stapeley Hill, the Whetstones, and Michell's Fold. In the neighbourhood of Chirbury, there are several ancient encampments and barrows, while the line of retreat of the brave Caractacus before the Roman Army, is marked by well-defined remnants of defensive earthworks. The remains of Roman villas and Roman mining works are to be seen. The Town and ruined castle of Montgomery are extremely interesting, and near Chirbury there is a deep and exquisitely beautiful ravine, called Marrington Dingle, which is a notorious and favourite resort of pleasure parties. But the extraordinary attractions within the district immediately served by the proposed lines convey but a limited idea of the possible excursion traffic – for it must be borne in mind that many places outside the district now involving by road and rail a long and tedious circuitous journey, will be brought within a comparatively easy run. Aberystwyth, Barmouth, and other charming and popular watering places on the Welsh coast will be easily accessible. The distance by railway from Craven Arms to Aberystwyth and Barmouth will be reduced by 30 miles – and this means that Birmingham and all the great industrial populations of Worcestershire will be within measurable distance of a direct route to the Welsh coast, saving about 30 miles, and avoiding numerous and inconvenient changes. Montgomery and all places on the Cambrian system will be brought not only 30 miles nearer to Craven Arms, but the whole district from Minsterley in the north, to Hopton Heath in the south, will be in direct and easy railway communication with every part of the kingdom.

Carlisle *again, in more prosperous times – note the timber and the Beddoes wagon – the name interweaves the story of the Bishop's Castle like no other.*

This part of Shropshire then, was second only to Eden in its delights and the fever spread. All these lines could even be electrified! This last notion came from Mr. Percy Justyne, who managed to take time off from a scheme to supply Manchester with underground electric railways. We know what happened to that... Jasper More was enthusiastic, though he was still banging on about bringing soldiers to the district. He had harangued the 'seven leading officials' of the Great Western and LNWR about the need to extend the line. They were unmoved. The reaction of the locals to 20,000 squaddies rampaging through the fields was muted, to say the least.

The great day came, 25th April 1901. The petitioner, William Francis Plowden, had allowed (as we have seen) the Bishop's Castle occupation of certain lands at a rental and had received judgements already, in 1880 and in 1893 'appointing a manager or receiver and directing an inquiry of what was due to him' as well as other impenetrable legal consequences. His current campaign 'at the instance of Thomas Cartright, receiver and manager' was for a series of directives as to how monies now in the court (some £1500) could be disbursed. Apparently the peculiar status of the Bishop's Castle necessitated this recourse. There were a brace at least of King's Councils involved and even the *Advertiser* account reads like a legal text. A comment of the Judge, Mr. Justice Kakewich, lightened proceedings...

We can try that question. We do not expect everything to be straight forward. I never heard a Bishop's Castle railway case that was. (Laughter).

"The facts with regard to Mr. Plowden were as follows: On 21st July 1880, the Bishop's Castle Railway Company were in possession of his land wrongfully and on that date Mr. Plowden recovered judgement in ejectment. That judgment was in the ordinary form. It was decided that plaintiff should recover possession of the land and premises, and receive a sum of £1,345 16s for mesne profits."

Mr. Plowden had obtained the right of possession but on 24th July 1880 he made an agreement with the railway, withholding the execution of his rights on certain terms. The learned counsel referred to this at considerable and impenetrable length. In January 1893, a writ had been issued claiming a sum amounting to £3,276 6s 1d. This ended up as rent from the railway charged at £224 6s a year.

In February 1893 Mr. Plowden obtained judgment for the money, which was owing to him by the Bishop's Castle. "It was in consequence of that payment that the applicant presented a petition under the Railway Companies Acts. Previous proceedings had been taken by debenture holders in the action of Griffin against the company; on 17th April 1893 Mr. Cartwright was appointed receiver of the company, since that time the rest of the

judgment debt had never been paid, nor had any interest ever been paid also." There was now something like a thousand pounds payable in interest alone...

There was much more, including an amusing digression by his Honour concerning his experiences acting for the London Chatham and Dover 'an extremely impecunious company' – this would have equipped him ideally for the Bishop's Castle. The judgment was involved and naturally enough, highly legalistic, the Judge making the point that he could only offer up his findings in the matter of the Companies Act 1867. Beddoes 'must be left to take such course as he might think desirable' nor was there much in it for Plowden:

The arrears are not outgoings which can be paid in priority to the claims of the debenture holders, and he has no jurisdiction to order possession of the land to be given to Mr. Plowden; but he gave him leave to bring such action as he might be advised to recover possession of the land.

Rumours continued to abound in the town: 'a good many expect the railway will close on Thursday' (the case was originally to be heard on the Wednesday). The following week 'great relief' was expressed that the line should not be 'stopped up' and it 'remained to be seen' what Mr. Beddoes and Mr. Plowden might do. Surfacing for the first time, and probably unique amongst our lesser branch lines, or any lines for that matter, was an organisation for the defence of the railway. By 1904 it had become the 'Defence Trust' but in May 1901, it was the 'Bishop's Castle Railway Defence Scheme' – 'members met in private on Wednesday but what took place is not known'.

All the furore had got a lot of talk going as to the extension of the line (again) and great hopes were pinned to Mr. Percy Justyne, who would descend when ready and weave his spell. 'When he does visit the Castle' a report runs obscurely ... 'it is to be hoped he will not be left the same as the War Office Official was a short time ago'. Beddoes and Plowden it was said were both to bring further actions to recover their land ...

By August (confidence had returned in the line's future, now it was clear that no closure was possible without recourse to the Judge)

Justyne was 'on the stump' in the district, enthusiastically supported by the MP Jasper More. Justyne was 'pushing forward the arrangements of his railway schemes for Bishop's Castle and the neighbourhood'. He would shortly be calling meetings and confidence was high, Justyne having received 'plenty of support from influential gentry and landowners'.

'Sundry gloomy minded pessimists' prophesied the closure of the railway on September 1st 1901 according to the *Advertiser* though it does not betray its reasoning. Councillors, it was said, 'generally discredited the rumours'. Jasper More found his correspondence on the matter increasing so much that in August he acquired a typewriter...

Talk of closure now fades and the major stir to round off 1901 – the year of the wasps – concerned the fate of another Bishop's Castle institution, Driver Whittaker. He had served his apprenticeship at Crewe on the LNWR, moving on to Craven Arms. In May 1875 he had assumed 'full charge' of locomotive work at Bishop's Castle and on November 20th 1901 received a letter from Mr. Cartwright, the receiver and manager which was nothing if not blunt: "Having regard to your state of health, the uncertainty thereby entailed of your being able to satisfactorily and efficiently fulfil your duties; also your age, it will be necessary to make a change, and I am sorry I shall have to part with your services in 14 days from this date, that is Thursday, December 5th"

'The intelligence has created some indignation in the town' declared the *Advertiser*, the hapless driver having resided in the town for some 28 years; his son immediately resigned his own position on the railway and the paper earnestly hoped that pressure would be brought upon Cartwright to reconsider his action.

This was all good stuff, faithful retainer badly done by and all that; fireman Whittaker left for Stourbridge on the GWR the following year and his dad moreover was reinstated 'to his old place on the footplate ... which has ... occasioned widespread satisfaction in the town and district'. Which was a nice enough end to the year of the wasp.

The delightful No.1, already 'of an obsolete type' when sold to the railway back in 1905.

Venerable figures, human and mechanical, in the yard at Bishop's Castle in 1909. This is a fine illustration of the level of work carried out, much of it, quite obviously, in the open air. The whole place is a workshop, with trestles, benching and the engine with various bits off it. The BC staff incidentally, were famed at one time for the smartness of their uniforms, but they gradually degenerated, through the indigence of the company, to 'civvies'.

Carlisle with four wheel tender and staff. The BC was one of the few railways where a member of staff, 'liking his lotion' overmuch, could be disciplined by being forced to 'sign the pledge'. Ale was afterwards served up, covertly, in a teapot. This is a useful illustration, incidentally, of Carlisle's odd feature – the absence of balance weights.

Chapter Five

Pride before Fall

Threats to the railway came more or less all the time. It was peculiarly vulnerable of course through its odd legal position; inheritors of the shares and interest and debts incurred from the 1860s did not look on the line as indulgently as their fathers. Court cases and the threat of them were ever present, or rumour of them was, which amounted to the same thing. It also made for interesting reading, so closure, though salvation through 'Light Railway' status appeared sporadically on the horizon, hung like smoke in the air. W.F. Beddoes was again in court in February 1902 attempting to take possession of certain of his lands. Practically speaking his application was granted but he required additioanal leave for proceeding further. The Town Clerk Mr. E. Griffiths arranged a counsel to oppose Beddoes' application 'on behalf of several parties locally interested'. 'something must certainly be done' wailed the *Advertiser* 'We must now possess our souls in patience a little while longer and watch closely the next move in the matter'. This move didn't seem to come, drifting away as many matters connected with the Bishop's Castle – like the new line, which Jasper More the MP still claimed to be 'developing into a reality' in January 1903. Lack of enthusiasm locally ('the lethargic attitude of the community') was deplored, not for the first or last time. Heightening the unreality still further, by February *cutting the first sod* of the line to Montgomery was confidently expected. The Bishop's Castle, 'even at present', according to Jasper More was profitable, making some £2000 in 1902 and more than a thousand the year before. Since 1891 there had been an average annual profit of over £700.

Extension to Montgomery including the purchase of the Bishop's Castle was being actively discussed by the MP in London though a more attractive alternative had surfaced. Suggested by the Reverend Prebendary White, vicar of Church Stoke, this envisaged a continuation from Lydham to Montgomery but *via* Kerry and Newtown. 'Emancipation day is coming' was the clarion call in the *Advertiser;* 'the railway problem is still on its upward grade; it is authoritatively stated Bishop's Castle will not be a sparsely inhabited isle much longer'.

On 13th March 1903 it was revealed ('this gratifying intelligence') that all litigation was at last at an end, and the Bishop's Castle Railway, now free of legal entanglement, was already the object of a 'syndicate sitting in London'. It would purchase the line and extend it either to Montgmery to Welshpool or to Newtown via Kerry. Great things were predicted...

**IMPORTANT
ANNOUNCEMENT.**

In spite of drawbacks the line, thanks to able management, and the support it derives from Bishop's Castle, makes a good profit annually. In Blakeridge Woods at the present time there are 32 acres of falling timber, and in other parts of the district timber in smaller quantities awaits transit. From this source alone, a railway extension scheme is within realisation at an early date ... Whatever is done will be effected from outside that is perfectly certain, judging from events but the general public will be grateful, if, in the end, the borough is brought into more direct touch with the outside world, after such a long period of suspense and agitation.

A measure of how far all this got out of hand comes in an announcement of March 1902 – hydros, golf links, and Carnegie public library and reading rooms were sure to follow and 'the present locomotive carriages and rails will form the nucleus of a museum in the town for future generations to gaze upon with wonderment and awe'.(!) The new line to Montgmery would be electric.(!!)

Mr. Jasper More died at the end of November 1903 and this signalled an end to much of the active campaigning for extension of the line. His 'indefatigable efforts to promote the prosperity of the district' were alas at an end.

The spectre of the courtroom returned and the Bishop's Castle Railway Defence Trust seems to have come into proper being in 1904. How it operated is unclear, but local worthies seem to have clubbed together to cover whatever debts were in question. Further ideas for extension on to Montgomery spluttered into being about 1912, sparked by the notion of Government grants but these went the way of all the previous hares started in various directions out of Bishop's Castle. The Montgomery *idée fixe* staggered on through the early 1920s, the Great Western sensibly fending off an attempt by the Council to get it interested in the 'direct Montgomery' route.

The Bishop's Castle, bankrupt and unwanted (its peculiar legal status would probably have gummed the works of the Grouping Bill) remained on its own despite the establishment of the Big Four in 1923. The Grouping seemed to render the Bishop's Castle even more plainly an anachronism and it was not long before the next closure crisis, in 1930/31. In the House of Commons the new Ludlow Member, Col. Windsor Clive, who did not have quite Jasper More's attachment to the typewriter, asked the Minister of Transport Herbert Morrison (it was MacDonald's second Labour Cabinet of 1929-1931) if he proposed to take any action on a resolution of the Bishop's Castle Borough Council, that the

Great Western should take over the line. Shuffling his papers no doubt, Morrison (later Home Secretary in Churchill's War Cabinet) had naturally consulted with the GWR (or rather his minions had), who upon 'careful consideration' (of course) didn't want to know. Morrison 'did not propose to promote legislation for the compulsory transfer of the railway.'

The 'Bishop's Castle Railway Users Committee' emerged in 1931 following an unsuccessful attempt at a Government grant. It was presumably the lineal descendent of the 'Defence Scheme' and the 'Defence Trust' and though it was not a club of monied benefactors it was able to put some pressure on the Receiver/Manager. In turn it drifts from the scene after a couple of years or so. The Defence Trust was still in existence, presiding over dwindling funds, so the Bishop's Castle is probably unique again, first in enjoying *two* co-existing support organisations and second in their failure.

By now the closure threat had become perennial and all dreaming of extensions to Montgomery or elsewhere a thoroughly dead duck. *The Shrewsbury Chronicle* reported the latest moves in its issue of 26th May 1933 – remember this was at the end of the worst Depression in living memory (though perhaps not the worst in agriculture) and the Bishop's Castle in a way had done well to survive this far. The council at a special meeting in May 1933 expressed 'the profoundest apprehension and dismay' at the latest threatened closure; it would raise the price of all 'the necessities of life', inevitably cause further unemployment, handicap farming locally, possibly kill off altogether the local cattle market and bring further rural depopulation. A dismal prospect altogether.

Through all the threats and upsets, closure stalking the line throughout its life, there was always hope, almost an assumption that somehow things would work out. From the early 1930s this changed and a feeling of inevitability, a resignation to closure, took hold. The last two or three years had a 'death row' quality about them with regular appeals and reprieves, each less convincing than the last. Jasper More's £700 a year profit had long vanished and a Master in Chancery (these legal figures haunt the Bishop's Castle story like no other) ordered the closing of the railway. Oddly enough it seems to have been the final decision of the Defence Trust: The End was fixed for Saterday 20th April 1935. 'Road transport has given the railway its death blow' *The Shrewsbury Chronicle* declared. Funds of the Defence Trust were exhausted, it continued, and the trustees could do nothing but withdraw the receiver. This they duly did on 8th April, to be afterwards confirmed by the Master in Chancery...

The famous junction of the Bishop's Castle – Stretford Bridge in 1906. The neat halt platform seems to have appeared sometime in the 1880s or 1890s, a characteristically Quixotic gesture on the part of the BC. The company was surely the most litigious (in relation to its mileage) in the country, a situation forced upon it, no doubt, by its dire financial condition. Documents from 1888 reveal something of the nature of life at the junction; the joint committee had complained on 2nd July that the BC "has no block telegraph or communication of any kind from their line to the junction with the Joint Line at Craven Arms. The engine merely whistles. It should also be mentioned that it has been pointed out to the Bishop's Castle that there is a set of points on their line about 270 yards from the junction which are worked by an ordinary lever on the ground, and they were asked to agree to these being connected with, and worked from, the Junction Signal Cabin but it would appear … that they are disinclined to do this." Well, this was strong stuff and a Mr. Wilding, from 'The Manager's Office, Bishop's Castle' responded to the Board of Trade on 19th July 1888 … "I really cannot see that anything has arisen in the working of our trains over the Shrewsbury and Hereford line with Craven Arms down the long time this railway has now been opened to necessitate the alterations and larger outlay of money suggested … is incorrect to say the signalman has no indication of the approach of the BC train … at a distance of 1400 yards or over ¾mile from the signalman's cabin the engine shuts off steam and whistles twice for the Distance Signal which is placed 650 yards from and worked by the joint Signalman. If the arm of that signal is not dropped the train proceeds thence slowly and can pull up and come to a stand between that point and the Junction, which is also protected by the home signals … The Bishop's Castle trains are very light, there are only four in the summer and three in the winter and with the exception of a month or two work in daylight the whole of the year; they pay a heavy rental for running into Craven Arms…

Chapter Six

'The Last Parliamentary in England'

Closure provoked a number of fond recollections of the line. T.R. Perkins wrote to *The Wellington Journal* in September 1936 describing his startlement on coming across this unsuspected railway – the engine he said, gave 'an uncouth cry': *Latterly the old locomotive has been the smartest-looking feature of the BCR, as it was kept very clean, with its profusion of brasswork, well polished. It is a pity that so interesting a relic cannot be secured for the Railway Museum at York, as its long record of service deserves a better fate than the scrap heap.* 'Over Seventy' wrote in the same issue:

Your recent article on the Bishop's Castle Railway was most interesting ... I have a vivid recollection, as a small boy, of a momentous occasion when I was given a ride on the footplate of the 'Plowden'. This engine had a very large dome over the firebox and no protection whatsoever was provided for the enginemen from the weather. The third class carriages were open from end to end, and furnished with plain wooden seats. Many times have I seen the train pushed by the engine from the 'terminus' at Lydham Heath to Bishop's Castle, to save shunting. The porter at Bishop's Castle was named Beadles, and the guard of the train known as 'Tommy'. I am not quite sure if the driver's name was Shuker or not. Water was sometimes brought in the tank of a spare tender from the River Onny at Plowden. I have seen minnows swimming in the water as the tender lay in Bishop's Castle station, and tried to catch them.

Amongst the most amusing observations was a series of comments in the *Express and Star Wolverhampton*. It is quoted in full by Griffiths but this, from Mrs. Sherwood, (see also Higgins' account later) the Horderley 'stationmistress', is my favourite ... 'I want you to understand, that some of the tales that are told about the train are untrue. The train never stops to enable passengers to pick mushrooms. Its nonsense!'

Mr Tom Dolby wrote to the *Wellington Journal* in October 1936:

It is very interesting to read the correspondence that has appeared in the Journal respecting this railway, but I have not noticed the engine, 'Perseverance', mentioned. This engine was in use at the time the 'Plowden' was running. I well remember as a boy and being a favourite with the driver, stoker and guard, Messrs. Whittaker, John Shuker, and John Broom, going sometimes on the footplate and other times in the guard's van to Craven Arms. In those days a Mr. Craston was manager and Mr. James stationmaster at Bishop's Castle. An unusual incident once happened, for some obliging individual uncoupled the carriages, unknown to the driver, evidently thinking the engine was going to the front. On this occasion they were pushed and when at the Bishop's Castle side of the Lea Bridge, the engine brakes were applied, the carriages, to the amazement of both driver and stoker, went careering ahead leaving the engine far behind, whistling furiously to attract the guard's attention. This fortunately occurred, thus giving him time to apply the brakes in the van and prevent the carriages running into the embankment at the end of the platform.

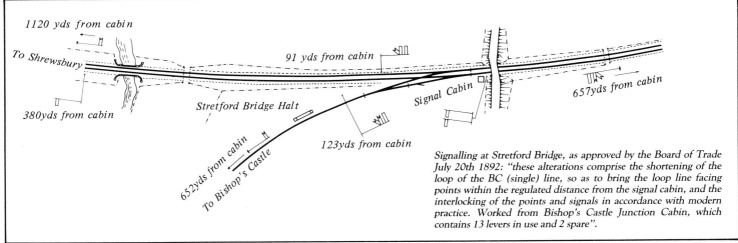

1120 yds from cabin

To Shrewsbury

91 yds from cabin

380yds from cabin

Stretford Bridge Halt

Signal Cabin

657yds from cabin

123yds from cabin

652yds from cabin

To Bishop's Castle

Signalling at Stretford Bridge, as approved by the Board of Trade July 20th 1892: "these alterations comprise the shortening of the loop of the BC (single) line, so as to bring the loop line facing points within the regulated distance from the signal cabin, and the interlocking of the points and signals in accordance with modern practice. Worked from Bishop's Castle Junction Cabin, which contains 13 levers in use and 2 spare".

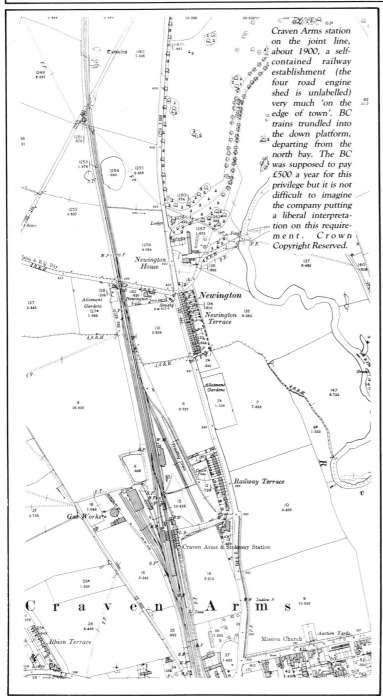

Craven Arms station on the joint line, about 1900, a self-contained railway establishment (the four road engine shed is unlabelled) very much 'on the edge of town'. BC trains trundled into the down platform, departing from the north bay. The BC was supposed to pay £500 a year for this privilege but it is not difficult to imagine the company putting a liberal interpretation on this requirement. Crown Copyright Reserved.

Churchward's bargain, No.1, at Craven Arms with The Train, about 1932.

Roger Carpenter

The Stretford Bridge Junction – compare with the pristine condition of pages 26/27. 'Bishop's Castle Junction' box was rebuilt around the turn of the century – see opposite; the boundary of maintenance (grass versus ballast) is a vivid demonstration of the different permanent way standards in force on the BC and the GW/LNW joint line.

'The Last Parliamentary in England'

Being a record of visits to the Bishop's Castle Railway by the late S.H. Pearce Higgins. Reproduced by permission of the Head of the National Railway Museum, York.

Tuesday 14th April 1931

My First Visit to the Bishop's Castle Railway.

The junction of this line with the LNW and GW Joint is protected by a GW pattern signal (2 arms; the 'distant' having been painted yellow, and an orange colour glass replaced the former red glass; what I presume was the old red glass lay broken nearby).

In the car, we followed the line up the valley, through magnificent scenery, here and there the line crossed the river on iron or steel bridges, and in one place the road ran beneath the railway. The signal below Horderley was photographed and all the signals as far as I noticed were of the same pattern. This was in a dilapidated condition and did not seem to have experienced much use lately; the red glass (I do not recollect a green) was broken.

At Plowden there was a fairly extensive building, which had the appearance of a village school; in the goods yard (perhaps more accurately a siding) there were one or two coal wagons. At Eaton the buildings were on the north side of the line whereas those at Plowden were on the south. Eaton seemed to be without goods accommodation (this actually was not so).

At Bishop's Castle we found the lion in its lair. 'Carlisle', an 0-6-0, with two carriages, a guard's van (BCR No.1) and a modern covered iron van (BCR No.21). The last two were at the front of the train and in that order. 'Carlisle' was comparatively 'Great Westernized' with a species of copper chimney and GWR safety valve cover, also a raised round-top firebox. The tender was six-wheeled with springs above the framing and rails acting as coal guards; presumably an old GW tender. The name was stamped on the beading of the centre driving wheel splasher. The two carriages were apparently painted dark brown but might have been anything. Beneath a dilapidated dejected and derelict shed was a rather smart carriage having I think 6 wheels and painted red; the numerals on the doors were in gold, with black shading. This carriage had 'First' class accommodation its general appearance reminding me of the prolific LNW six-wheelers when repainted in LMS red. A number of timber bolsters were in the yard being loaded up.

At the booking office I brought a ticket, a '1st Class Parliamentary Single' to Lydham Heath.

26th March 1932: My first ride on the BCR.

When I arrived at Craven Arms the little train

Craven Arms about 1910 with GWR train on the main line. How smoothly modern and efficient it must have seemed to the wheezing BC!

Roger Capenter

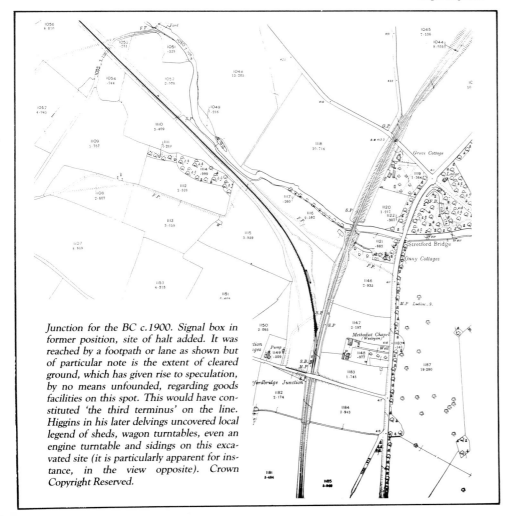

Junction for the BC c.1900. Signal box in former position, site of halt added. It was reached by a footpath or lane as shown but of particular note is the extent of cleared ground, which has given rise to speculation, by no means unfounded, regarding goods facilities on this spot. This would have constituted 'the third terminus' on the line. Higgins in his later delvings uncovered local legend of sheds, wagon turntables, even an engine turntable and sidings on this excavated site (it is particularly apparent for instance, in the view opposite). Crown Copyright Reserved.

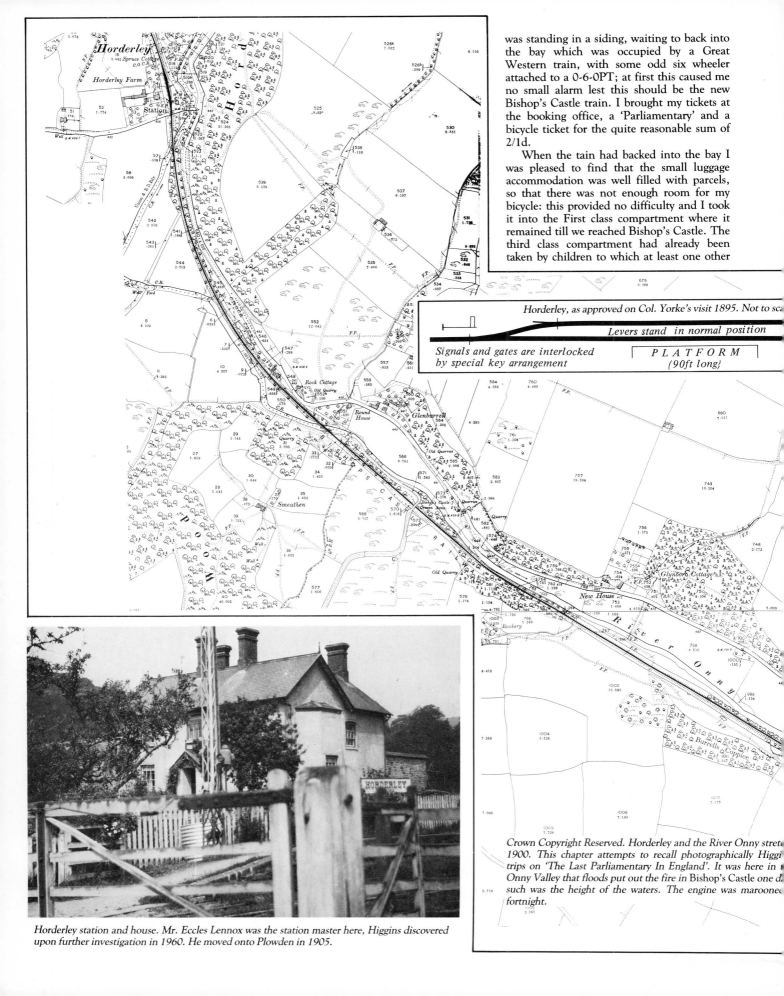

was standing in a siding, waiting to back into the bay which was occupied by a Great Western train, with some odd six wheeler attached to a 0-6-0PT; at first this caused me no small alarm lest this should be the new Bishop's Castle train. I brought my tickets at the booking office, a 'Parliamentary' and a bicycle ticket for the quite reasonable sum of 2/1d.

When the tain had backed into the bay I was pleased to find that the small luggage accommodation was well filled with parcels, so that there was not enough room for my bicycle: this provided no difficulty and I took it into the First class compartment where it remained till we reached Bishop's Castle. The third class compartment had already been taken by children to which at least one other

---

Horderley, as approved on Col. Yorke's visit 1895. Not to sc[...]

Levers stand in normal position

Signals and gates are interlocked by special key arrangement

PLATFORM (90ft long)

Crown Copyright Reserved. Horderley and the River Onny stret[...] 1900. This chapter attempts to recall photographically Higgi[...] trips on 'The Last Parliamentary In England'. It was here in [...] Onny Valley that floods put out the fire in Bishop's Castle one d[...] such was the height of the waters. The engine was marooned[...] fortnight.

Horderley station and house. Mr. Eccles Lennox was the station master here, Higgins discovered upon further investigation in 1960. He moved onto Plowden in 1905.

passenger was added before we started: another passenger occupied one of the seconds and a rustic chose the company of my bicycle in the first, until he got out at Horderley (it may have been Plowden). He remarked that there were two men on the footplate in a way that suggested this had not always been so, but I gathered he had never travelled on the line before.

Before the train started I talked to a porter and others from whom I was told that the engine can take water at Bishop's Castle but as the pressure is very weak they usually take what they want at Craven Arms. The financial state of the company was very serious, and it seems that the only painting that the engines receive is carried out by one of their men when he had time. I have forgotten now (3rd July 1932) what was the exact loading of the train. 'Carlisle' was in charge, the train being made up of Carriage No 1, a red-painted ex-LSWR vehicle, then I think an LMS wagon, a coal wagon, three small bolsters (1 Midland, 3 Great Western) and a Guard's Van (every appearance of being ex-GW). There may also have been a Bishop's Castle covered iron van.

The watch I timed the train with gained about 1 minute in 24 hours; at a time corresponding to 11.20am on my timepiece, 'Carlisle' whistled and some 4 minutes later we had started and quite well too. Long Lane box was passed at 11.22 and we were now going quite well. Perhaps as well as we ever did on this journey (which was probably like thousands of others on the line). The advantage of the main line track must have helped although there was some surprisingly good running near Lydham Heath in spite of the incomparable inferiority of the track.

Although the train was moving well enough, 'Carlisle' seemed to be making heavy work of it, and judging by the quantities of smoke the firebox must have been receiving a generous supply of coal. As we approached Bishop's Castle Junction steam was shut off and speed reduced, and the heavy panting of 'Carlisle' momentarily ceased. Bishop's Castle Junction was passed 11.24 and 17 seconds am. We lurched round the points and then all those deficiencies which the energies of the LNW and GW platelayer had concealed were suddenly apparent; and we rattled on round Stretford Bridge Junction with at least the footboard brushing past the bushes. Stretford

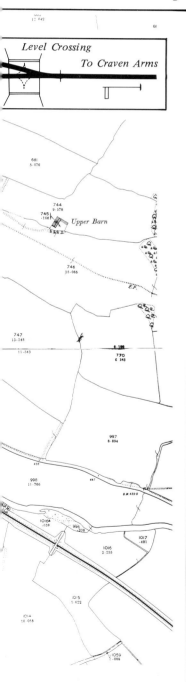

Horderley and its wooded hills. Higgins visited Harry Mullard at Preston in 1960; he had been a fitter at the LNWR shed there and, 'engine mad' had lived near the station at Horderley as a lad. The noise of the train, he mused, had filled the valley and even the closing of carriage doors and the guard's whistle carried on the air.

Dashing figure at Horderley in 1932.

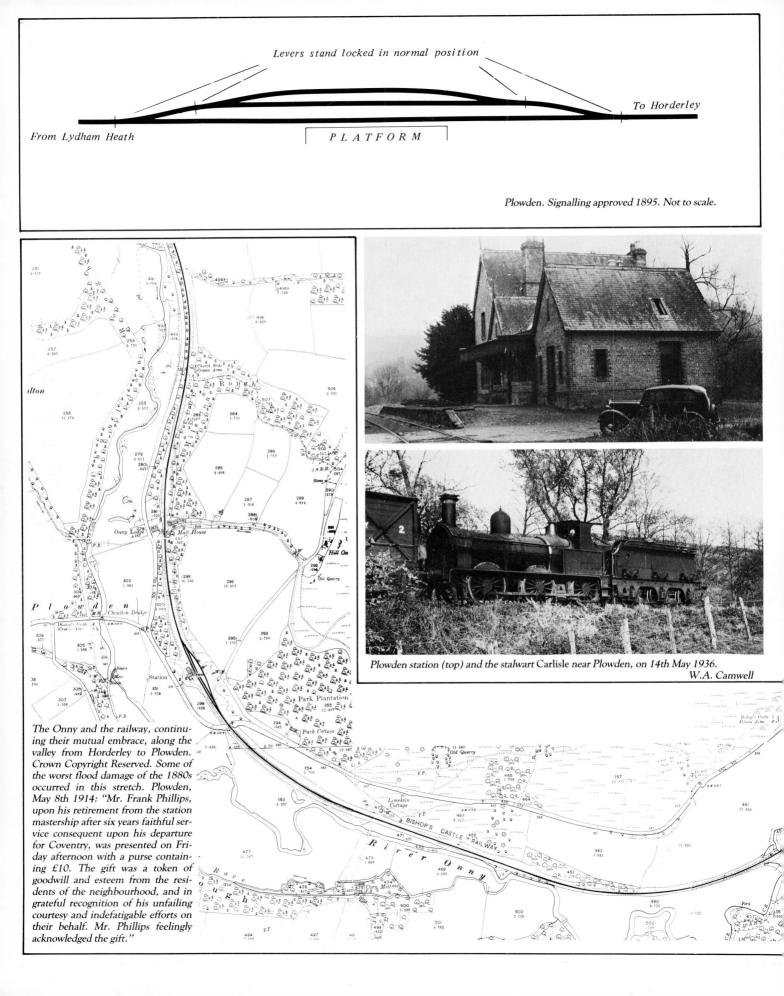

Levers stand locked in normal position

From Lydham Heath

PLATFORM

To Horderley

Plowden. Signalling approved 1895. Not to scale.

Plowden station (top) and the stalwart Carlisle near Plowden, on 14th May 1936.
W.A. Camwell

The Onny and the railway, continuing their mutual embrace, along the valley from Horderley to Plowden. Crown Copyright Reserved. Some of the worst flood damage of the 1880s occurred in this stretch. Plowden, May 8th 1914: "Mr. Frank Phillips, upon his retirement from the station mastership after six years faithful service consequent upon his departure for Coventry, was presented on Friday afternoon with a purse containing £10. The gift was a token of goodwill and esteem from the residents of the neighbourhood, and in grateful recognition of his unfailing courtesy and indefatigable efforts on their behalf. Mr. Phillips feelingly acknowledged the gift."

Bridge was passed and then 'puff puff' again in short animated blasts and the speed was really very convincing (perhaps 12 mph?). There's still much firing, and now we pass a GWR 'distant'. By the right hand side of the track are numerous old and decayed sleepers, having I imagine been replaced by others cut from neighbouring trees, and probably not creosoted.

Speed now dropped to nearer 7 mph (but my estimates are very bad) and we pass under a dismantled over bridge and speed appears to return to about 12 mph, which was maintained to some distance, to the river I think. Crossing the Onny by a girder bridge, the line ascends a slight incline. And so to Horderley where the signal was if anything 'up'.

Arrival 11.33, departure 11.35am. Are three signals at Horderley, a crossing loop, catch points connected up to a lever and a London & North Western notice board.

The start from Horderley is slow and measured, a stern and cautious 6 mph. By a cottage on the right hand side a woman watches our progress, without apparent interest. The heavy 'puffing' of 'Carlisle' begins to take effect and speed increases slightly. Bushes are very close to the carriage, which is running very creditably. Some distance beyond Horderley the scenery begins to open out, sheep scatter and rabbits run as 'Carlisle' puffs her way towards Plowden but chickens seem undisturbed. With heavy beats a steady uphill speed is maintained: heavy

firing too.

Plowden. Two passengers and, I think, a postman got out. Newspapers were put out and there was one wagon in the yard. Is a stationmistress here. Departure was 11.43am, through a narrow cutting and 'Carlisle' still finds it hard work. There was now time to look round the carriage which was upholstered in Dark blue (1st class) with block seats. Beneath the communication cord which I am sure cannot have given any communication with the guard and probably not with the engine crew either, was the familiar warning: "Communication between Passenger, Guard and Driver – To call the attention of the Guard and Driver in case of emergency. Passengers must pull down the chain which will be

Carlisle on the demolition train near Plowden. The prolonged uprooting of the Bishop's Castle drew photographers from far and wide, anxious to record the last work on the line, and indeed sad though it is some of the best pictures of the railway relate to these last months. Carlisle pushed this train along the line. The booty was poor stuff: sleepers were often circular, retaining the contours of the trees from which they had been hewn. Others kept the bark! There were many cases where the sleepers had rotted and cracked under the chairs (almost all dated 1864 or 1865, with a few marked 1889) which sank into the sleepers like a cushion as the train passed over them.

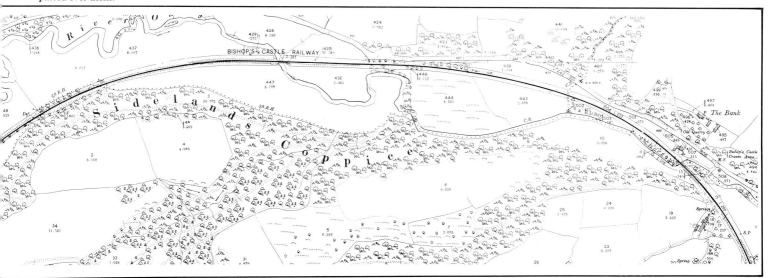

Plowden. Top left is No.1 and its stored wagons, and below left, the station in happier days. The single truck is a typical BC traffic – loads of fertilizer, basic slag and coal to the goods siding of each station, to be carried off during the day by a farmer or trader, in his own cart. Agricultural machinery would come and go at odd times, whilst seeds came in covered vans. Timber for pit props, much of it off the Earl of Powis' land, was very important in the Great War. There were at one time quarter mile posts (but never gradient posts) put in for the convenience of the platelayers. All seemed to have disappeared by 'historical times'.

found inside the carriage over the windows. Any passenger who makes use of the means of communication without reasonable and sufficient cause will be liable to a penalty not exceding FIVE POUNDS. By Order."

The lighting fittings or system was by 'Pintshs Patent Lighting Company Limited'.

At Eaton the signal on the right hand side was down and an old Bishop's Castle van, No. 24, lay in the yard, evidently used as a 'warehouse'. Were three passengers and a child on Eaton station but I am not sure how many got in: Two people out, who had got in at Plowden; some parcels were put out. Between Eaton and Lydham (though writing some years later it is possible that this note about the firing applied to the stretch before reaching Eaton) firing was not so heavy; this was not to last.

We arrived at Lydham Heath a little less than a minute before noon. The station build-ings were painted dull red and light blue and contained a First and Second class waiting room. Two passengers and a child got out. Whether 1st and 2nd class were separated or shared the same room, leaving the 3rd's on the platform I cannot now remember.

This was evidently the 'ticket station' for Bishop's Castle; the guard came round for tickets; I asked to keep mine and before I had taken them out to show him he was pleased to let me save them. Meanwhile 'Carlisle' was running forward to clear the points, round the loop and coupled on to the back of the train which for the rest of the journey was to be the front, leaving the carriage at the back. 'Carlisle' made light work of the rest of the journey, which was surprisingly good when it is remembered that a second hand 6 wheeler at the back of a goods train is scarcely the place to expect the smoothest of running.

Arrived at Bishop's Castle 12.13pm.

The clock was not in use, as a 'timepiece' at any rate. I believe that Lydham Heath, where the clock is inside, is the only station on the Bishop's Castle where the station clock was working. At Bishop's Castle the luggage compartment was emptied and 'Carlisle' prepared for the return journey. A cattle wagon was standing at the entrance to the shed, this she pushed forward into the shed, coupled up and ran round the train with it, then put it at the back of the carriage ready for the return to Craven Arms. After shunting for a short time 'Carlisle' returned to her train and waited. As is usual No 1 was standing at the back of the shed. (In my notes I remarked 'retaining the iron seat on top for the guard — actually this was not quite so much a seat as a board used to reach the oil lamps which had been used on this carriage)

Behind the station buildings I found that one of the old coaches had been converted into a 'garage' for the new bus. I was told that the Traffic Commissioners 'would not licence the old Berliet bus which lay derelict between the station and the goods shed. I was also told that sometime ago the bus had been used instead of the last train because the goods traffic came up on the middle day trip, and it was not worth running the train for the passengers only.

I looked round the wagons in the yard, and also penetrated to the back of the carriage shed, which was more extensive than I had realized: at the very back were two worthy vehicles — old four wheel carriages. No.1 externally reminded me of the very early railway carriages which recalled coaching days. This carriage was painted grey; it may of

No.1 and stock wagons, awaiting sale at Plowden on 14th May 1936. A post-closure scene but hardly distinguishable from a Bishop's Castle train in full flight, or at least what passed for it. Wagons were 'always a lead colour' Higgins discovered from Emmanuel Beddoes long after. The BC paint store was a van body leaning against the carriage shed at Bishop's Castle; there the paint was ground in a small steam mill. The engine's numberplate (and we can all understand this) drew Higgins: 'Monday 15th June 1936. The demolition gang (just two of them) was working just above the small overbridge, a short way beyond Plowden station. For some reason I have not discovered Mathews had very little to say — the only occasion when I can remember conversation being heavy going. This was unfortunate, as I had hopes of arranging to have the numberplate off No.1'; and the moment did not appear favourable in this strange 'heavy' atmosphere. But rapid action was called for, as already an attempt, or attempts, had been made to remove the plate and it was clear that the engine would soon be scrapped so that Plowden yard could be cleared. The plate was firmly secured to the back of the bunker and we had no suitable tools; however mild interest with a screw driver developed into more energetic measures with a crow-bar. Not perhaps the neatest, and certainly not the most convenient, weapon for the work. The bolts securing the plate to the bunker had become so corroded that when the plate was eventually separated from the engine a small piece of the bunker came away with it....'
W.A. Camwell

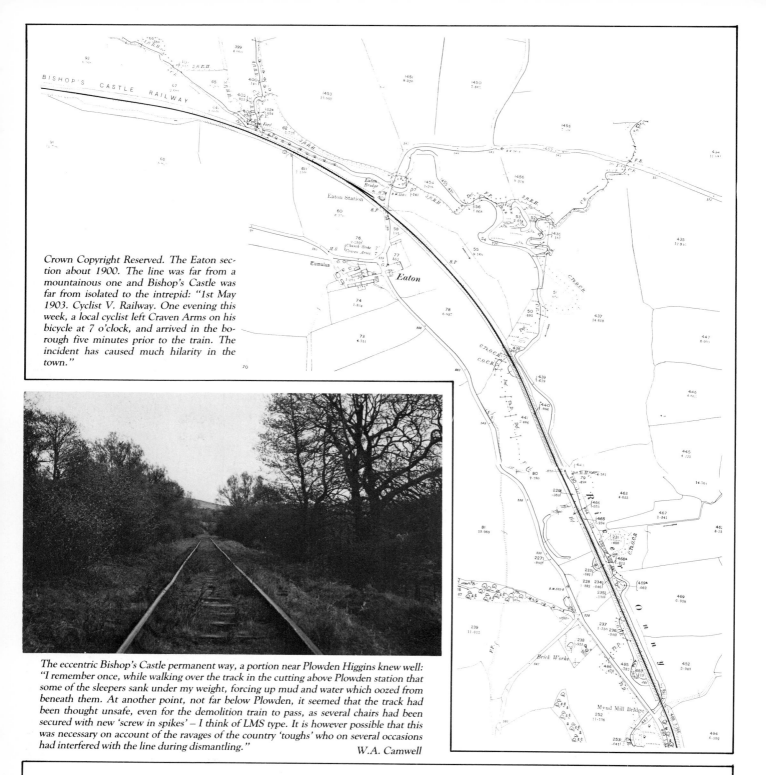

Crown Copyright Reserved. The Eaton section about 1900. The line was far from a mountainous one and Bishop's Castle was far from isolated to the intrepid: "1st May 1903. Cyclist V. Railway. One evening this week, a local cyclist left Craven Arms on his bicycle at 7 o'clock, and arrived in the borough five minutes prior to the train. The incident has caused much hilarity in the town."

The eccentric Bishop's Castle permanent way, a portion near Plowden Higgins knew well: "I remember once, while walking over the track in the cutting above Plowden station that some of the sleepers sank under my weight, forcing up mud and water which oozed from beneath them. At another point, not far below Plowden, it seemed that the track had been thought unsafe, even for the demolition train to pass, as several chairs had been secured with new 'screw in spikes' – I think of LMS type. It is however possible that this was necessary on account of the ravages of the country 'toughs' who on several occasions had interfered with the line during dismantling."

W.A. Camwell

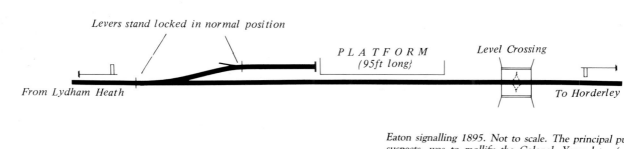

Levers stand locked in normal position

PLATFORM
(95ft long)

Level Crossing

From Lydham Heath

To Horderley

Signals and gates interlocked by special key arrangement.

Eaton signalling 1895. Not to scale. The principal purpose, one suspects, was to mollify the Colonel. Years later (see Higgins' journeys) bits of the signalling littered the ground.

Eaton station. It was similar to that at Horderley and both, as Griffiths points out, were in the charge of ladies – at Eaton, according to The News of the World *of all things, a Mrs. Annie Bason, who in 1931 had been there no less than a quarter of a century.*

Eaton after the demolition train had passed through. The sleepers were supposed to have been sold for £140, and sold on to Rollestons for £235. No-one had enquired properly of their true condition, obviously.

W.A. Camwell

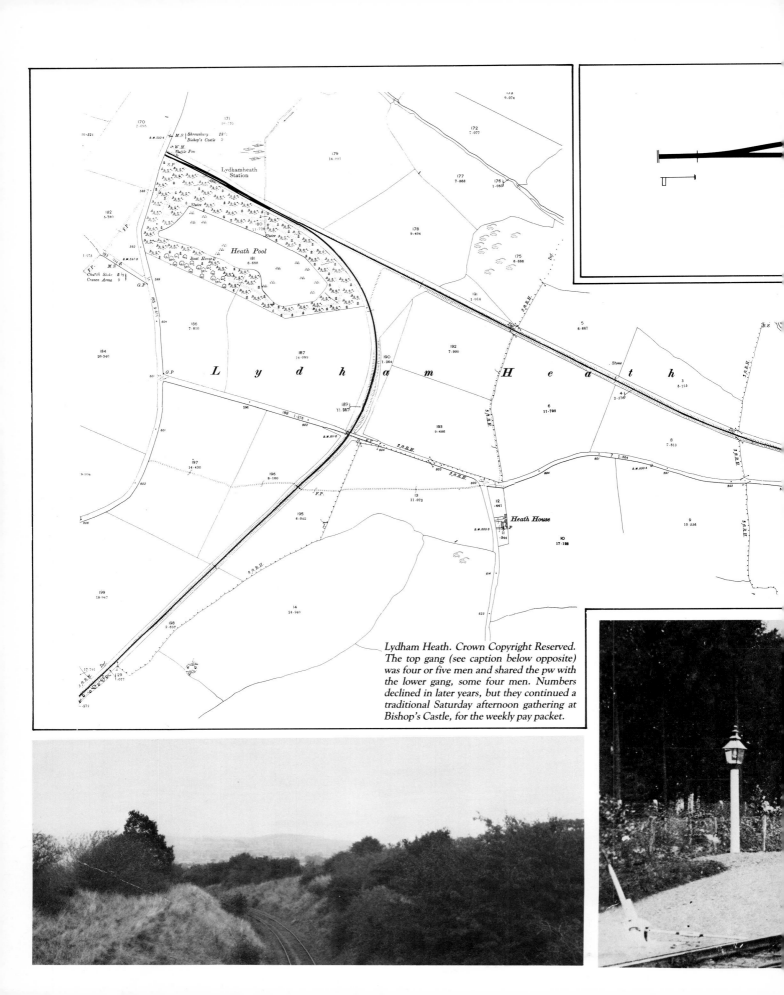

Lydham Heath. Crown Copyright Reserved. The top gang (see caption below opposite) was four or five men and shared the pw with the lower gang, some four men. Numbers declined in later years, but they continued a traditional Saturday afternoon gathering at Bishop's Castle, for the weekly pay packet.

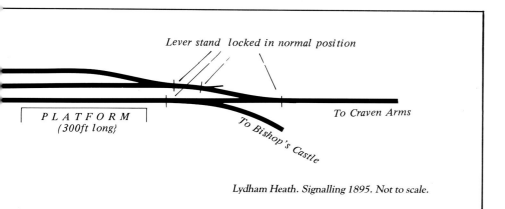

Lever stand locked in normal position

PLATFORM
(300ft long)

To Craven Arms

To Bishop's Castle

Lydham Heath. Signalling 1895. Not to scale.

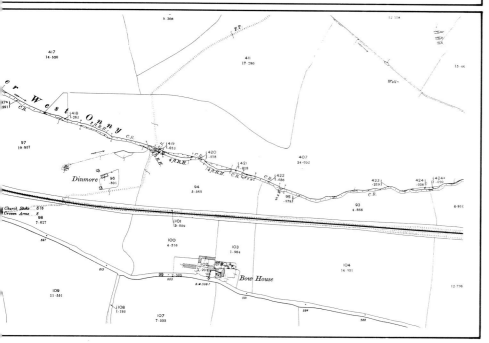

course have been painted quite a different colour, but whatever the colour it had now become grey. There were four compartments, second; first; first; second but as I recall the class was written on the door panels and not put on in numerals. The buffers had wooden ends and there were side chains as well as screw couplings. The second vehicle was No 6; inside it was a brake wheel and a seat for the guard. The compartments were arranged:- Guard; Third Smoking; Third; Third. The windows were a very curious shape, apparently serving two compartments.

In the yard were some fine modern cattle wagons; all had screw couplings and vacuum brake and were 'To be returned to Bishop's Castle, via Craven Arms'. The maker was S.J. Clay, Long Eaton, and the Nos. 51 (tare 7-10-3 tons), 52 (tare 7-10-1 tons), 53 (tare 7-11-1 tons), 55 (tare 7-10-3 tons), and 54 (tare 17-11-0 tons). There were three one plank wagons, Nos 60, 58, and 59 in grey paint and BCR wood van No.21. Carriage No.2 was by the shed, painted red (actually a dark crimson lake) with yellow figures; 3, 2, 2, 3. It had screw couplings and vacuum brake. Carriage No.1 had screw couplings, side chains and vacuum brake, and was in dark crimson.

When I returned to the station after wandering in the yard, I found that almost everyone had disappeared and the station boy was setting out with a barrow of parcels for delivery. The clock still read 20 minutes to 12.

I had previously bought a First class ticket to Lydham Heath, No.208 – Lydham being spelt without the 'h' – 'Lydam'. I bicycled back to Lydham Heath where I talked for sometime with the man in charge of the station. Rain was now falling quite heavily and I waited for a long time, talking about the Bishop's Castle Railway and railways in general. I was given a Bishop's Castle Lydham Heath (24th March 1932) 'Parly' and several 'handbills' of the Bishop's Castle Railway.

And then on to Plowden where I saw the station mistress and the arrival of the 3.20pm from Craven Arms; it was quite exhilarating to see several farm carts arrive to meet it, although they did not collect very much from it. And thus I went after travelling on what surely must be the last Parliamentary train in England and on a line that may well be the most fascinating of all time.

(Far left) the Bishop's Castle in typical guise – a continual struggle against the vegetation, anxious to reclaim its ground. A 'top gang' and a 'lower gang' looked after the track, the chargemen walking the whole of the line every day. On the immediate left is Lydham Heath station, the 'main line station' which became that oddest of places, a 'half way terminus'.

11th July 1932.

I bicycled to Craven Arms; a hurried and not altogether successful visit. It happened to be the day of the fortnightly market and the signalman told me that a certain amount of cattle had come down on the Bishop's Castle train. The train arrived fairly well to time – worked by No.1 (tank capacity 620 gallons?). There was a certain amount of shunting; after this the train waited in the bay. A most interesting visit to the booking office. I had not realized before what an immense variety of stock (including privileges etc) that the

Bishop's Castle Railway had. I also discovered that the 'Parliamentary' tickets were only available by the first train each way. A new arrangement in the ticket line was the issuing of half (child) tickets; these were only issued in Parly and third and not I think in First or Second. Before, what I think was an LNW practice (taking a small piece out of the ticket) had been used. Market tickets (at 2/1d?) are I think issued to Bishop's Castle on Fridays.

13th January 1933.

Once again to that glorious little Railway that

never loses its attractions, however often I see it. Alas! the service is sadly depleted (as I realized before going). On and from December 8th 1932 (Thursday) a Rail and Road combined service is being operated.

No.1 (with her train) was not in the bay by 12.15 but was standing in the yard. I went to the Booking Office again, and was shown an even more amazing array of Bishop's Castle tickets than before: apart from the ordinary series in the rack there were many in the drawers awaiting their turn, which I fear will never come. In the drawers there were also vast quantities of 'excursion' (1st, 2nd and

Lydham Heath. It was rebuilt about 1906 (its former condition and facilities can be imagined); a peculiar little place of limbo, amidst deserted fields, few ever had call or wish to leave its confines whilst Carlisle or No.1 fussed about running round. This was to be the mighty junction as the line swept proudly on to Montgomery.

Lydham Heath on 8th October 1931. The road omnibus above all had reduced the gallant little line to this parlous state. There was no station house at Lydham Heath.
Roger Carpenter

Carlisle *having run round waits departure to Bishop's Castle. This hotch potch of vehicles was the essence of the BC train. Coaches took gas at Craven Arms, from an LNW supply. In earlier times, in the days of the three coach set only two had the chain brake, the third being called 'a runner'. There were spare coaches, but on Fair Days, LNW stock would be borrowed.*

H.C. Casserley

Lydham Heath in its glory.

3rd) and 'Golf Tickets' (1st, 2nd and 3rd), the former to Bishop's Castle, the latter I think to Plowden. It seems that very few of these tickets had ever been issued; in a series of the 'excursion' tickets only one (No. '00' if it existed) had been issued. All these tickets were thick with dust. Each class of ticket had a different colour (the Golf return 'Thirds' were I think vermilion on the one half and green on the other).

I went to the station house at Horderley and was shown the tickets by a girl whom I assume was the station master's daughter; the tickets were kept in a small white wooden hut on the platform which was on the opposite side of the line to the station house. Here one would think that many of the tickets must have begun life with the Bishop's Castle Railway, especially 'Firsts'; very few of the 'first returns' had been issued, while it appeared that no one had ever booked a 'First Class' return to Plowden since the present stock was

printed. The damp in this hut had caused so much mould etc. to form on the First Class tickets that it was difficult to recognize them and if touched would resolve themselves into the layers of paper from which they had originally been formed.

I was told that very few tickets were ever issued at Horderley nowadays and after I had bought a 'Parly' single to Plowden (which the dating machine quite failed to make any proper impression on) we realized that the ticket should not have been issued, as the 1.30pm from Craven Arms, the only regular train to Bishop's Castle, is not regarded as 'Parliamentary' since it starts after 12 o'clock! So the only Parliamentary train now is the morning train from Bishop's Castle to Craven Arms.

I remained talking for some time and was told about a certain gentleman who lived near Horderley and used to travel to Craven Arms from time to time. He always travelled 'Sec-

To Lydham Heath

Levers stand locked in nor

Bishop's Castle. It managed a fair measure of bustle when it had to; witness the various bundles and boxes laid out rather after the fashion of trophies, at the end of a big game hunt. For most of the time the station dozed and dreamed. Fairs and whatever (the Shropshire Light Infantry to camp for instance) brought a temporary crush, such as 200 Juvenile Oddfellows, no less, on August 9th 1901, conveyed to Plowden for 'various games' and a picnic. The Bishop's Castle incidentally did well out of boxes and cases and the local press grew indignant. The Great Western apparently could convey a small packing case 'weighing less than the cwt' the 54 miles from Birmingham to Craven Arms for two shillings whilst the canny (or avaricious) BC extracted no less than 1/4d for the ten miles on to Bishop's Castle.

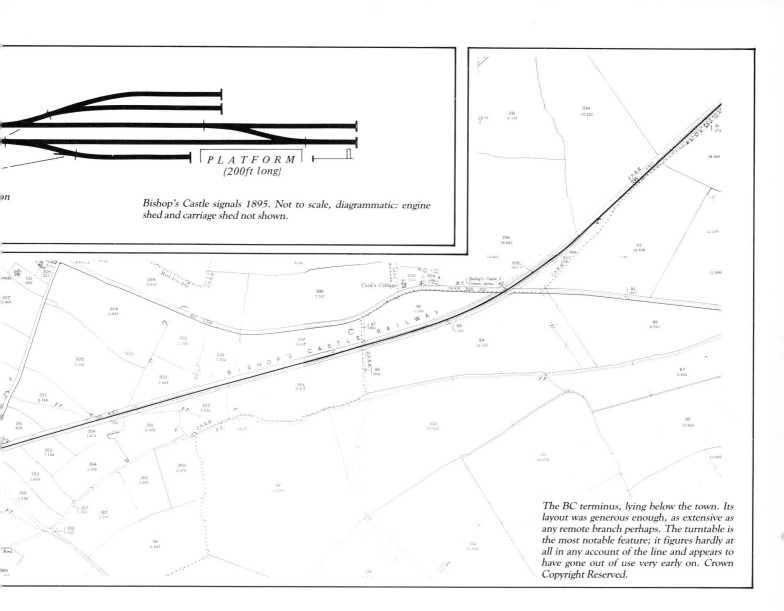

PLATFORM
(200ft long)

Bishop's Castle signals 1895. Not to scale, diagrammatic: engine shed and carriage shed not shown.

The BC terminus, lying below the town. Its layout was generous enough, as extensive as any remote branch perhaps. The turntable is the most notable feature; it figures hardly at all in any account of the line and appears to have gone out of use very early on. Crown Copyright Reserved.

Part of the 'fleet' at Bishop's Castle, when timber was still one the line's thriving traffics – the place after closure indeed became a timber yard, with Charles Ransford the proprietor. A 5-ton crane was available for loading.

ond' and took his dog with him; but from the condition of the second class returns he had apparently not travelled much recently.

I also asked about the signals, and was told that the signal above Horderley was not used as the wire had broken – owing to the frost I gather, and for this reason the signal below Horderley was not being used in frosty weather; these two signals were referred to as 'Distant' signals (although I did not notice anything which suggested this) and were worked by two levers near the crossing gates. The signal on the station had once had two arms, the one had broken off and the other when lowered drops into the post. The crossing gates and signalling arrangements seem to have fascinated a certain master John Dixon (Dickson?) from Church Stretton who used to come over to Horderley about twice a week to open the gates and work the signals. And then came the train well to time and with a very good load, No.1 (it would be Hotchkiss driving still) with a carriage and no less than 8 wagons and vans and Brake No.2.

The track below Hoderley seems to have been 'weeded' and a quantity of the trees felled by the side of the line. While descending the valley to catch the 4.15pm Leominster to Worcester I noticed that the bridges crossing the Onny below Horderley appear to have been built so that a second line could be added later.

6th October 1934.

'Carlisle' had received touches of green paint, sandbox splashers and boiler bands (red edging to them). The train started from the main line platform, 'Carlisle' with (I seem to remember) the LSW six-wheel carriage, a BC van (possibly No.21), two coal wagons and BC guards van No.2. From the booking clerk I discovered there were no longer 'Firsts' and 'seconds' (I put 1st and 3rd in my notes but presumably this was a mistake) They were suppressed by the auditors about July or August and the old Golf Tickets also went. (I think that it is possible no return tickets are now issued). I was also told about the football excursion to Bishop's Castle on Easter Monday: the BC borrowed Great Western carriages and special return tickests were issued – there were 172 passengers.

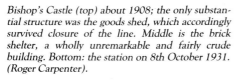

Bishop's Castle (top) about 1908; the only substantial structure was the goods shed, which accordingly survived closure of the line. Middle is the brick shelter, a wholly unremarkable and fairly crude building. Bottom: the station on 8th October 1931. (Roger Carpenter).

Bishop's Castle station in earlier times, before extension of the building (see opposite). Some of the efforts belied its hopelessly Heath Robinson reputation – such as a through excursion to Shrewsbury Fete in August 1903, obviously with borrowed stock ... 'phenomenal enterprise, and many were grateful'.

The museum quality of the BC, as unearthed by a procession of intrepid (and delighted) observers, such as Higgins, in the 1930s.

No.1 *in low sunlight. It took no part in the demolition of the line, languishing at Plowden. It was not used at all, it seems, from the spring of 1933. A chalked inscription 'one weeks work since washed out' survived through these last years out of use.*

Bishop's Castle yard. Fitted up with chain brakes on its arrival after these were done away with vacuum brakes were fitted to the engine. This was thought to have been done at Wolverhampton, though Higgins' delvings revealed a legend at least that Mr. Sinclair did the work. He came as driver and was in charge of loco affairs (the odd BC institution of 'driver-fitter') until 1926.

Taking Stock

In its locomotive stock the Bishop's Castle resembled nothing so much as the odds and ends of a rather battered but well loved train-set, left in a box and forgotten in the loft for a few years. It had to hire locos on occasion and this (of course) led almost immediately to payment difficulties. There was nothing, so far as the Bishop's Castle was concerned, like starting as you meant to go on. Griffiths gives *Bee* as the first engine, an 0-4-0ST used in the construction of the line. It was built by Brotherhoods of Chippenham and was unsuitable for the traffic even then. For the 'pre-opening' (only the Bishop's Castle could open several times) a loco was borrowed off the Mid Wales Railways and the following Mid Wales Board Minutes will have a familiar ring:

30th May 1866 ... as to the claim against the Bishop's Castle Railway for hire of locomotive ... referred to the solicitor.

4th July 1866 ... the Account against the Bishop's Castle Railway Company – for hire of locomotive having been submitted to Mr. Noyes, he reported that the Bishop's Castle Railway Company should be called upon to pay £166, being the proportion from 1st January instead of £314, as claimed by Mr. Broughton on behalf of the Company.

24th October 1866 ... Resolved, that with respect to this account that the same stand over for a month, and in the meantime the Secretary do make a further application for payment of the amount...

By December 1869 the LNWR too, had lent locos, or a loco; the type is not specified but the charges were four guineas a day:

LNWR Loco Construction Handbook Vol. 3; Minute 502; 10th December 1869: Loco Engines Lent on Hire – Bishop's Castle railway – 1 Loco at £4.4s per day.

Griffiths records the second Bishop's Castle-owned loco as an 0-6-0, *Plowden* acquired in 1865. It had belonged to the St. Helens Railway and was got rid of in 1874. P. Higgins uncovered this note in the St. Helens company records, then at Crewe. *15 Scorpion 1381, examined in October 1861. Had new plates in bottom of boiler; new iron tube plate but has been burnt and cracked box. Sold to Mr. Davis, Craven Arms, June 1865.*

The Bishop's Castle bought an extremely altered and very much hand-me-down 0-4-2T *Perseverence* in 1870, duly passing it on in 1887. *Progress*, a 2-4-0, came next, in 1875 and seems gradually to have been ploughed into the Bishops Castle earth. It was finally scrapped after the turn of the century. *Bishop's Castle* was a more or less identical 2-4-0: like *Progress* it was built by George England & Co. arriving, secondhand naturally, on the Bishop's Castle in 1877. *No.1* came next, an 0-4-2T off the GWR. The big company took care, and who could blame them, to see that the cheque was cashed before handing it over; here is Churchward's letter on the matter:

5th August 1905. Loco & Carriage Dept, Swindon.

We have a side tank engine No.567, built at Wolverhampton in 1869 and had a new boiler in 1888. After inspection the Bishop's Castle Railway have offered to purchase it for £700. In view of the fact that the engine is of a type now practically obsolete for our purposes, I should regard its disposal at this price as a favourable transaction for the Co.'

(sgd) G.J.Churchward

The GWR got and cashed the cheque in August before handing over No.567; it became 'No.1' on the BC and was scrapped at Bishop's Castle after final closure in 1936.

The best known of the Bishop's Castle 'fleet' was of course *Carlisle*. It had been built in 1868 by Kitsons of Leeds, works No.1421, and served on a number of important railway contracts, in the ownership of a Thomas Nelson of Carlisle. It began its long life on the Bishop's Castle in 1895. In periodic trips to the Stafford Road Works of the GWR, at Wolverhampton, along with No.1, it lost various original bits and acquired GW chimney and safety valves, six wheel tender and a more generous cab. Both No.1 and *Carlisle* spent most of their BC lives in a GWR form of livery.

Sequence of Locomotive Stock, as recorded in the Hayward Collection, Public Record Office, Kew.

1866-1869 Bee and Plowden 1870-1875 Plowden and Perseverance 1875-1877 Progress and Perseveranve 1877 Progress 1877 Progress and Perseverance 1877-1887 Progress, Perseverance and Bishop's Castle 1887-1904 Progress and Bishop's Castle 1904-1905 Carlisle and Bishop's Castle 1905-1935 Carlisle and No.1

This is the Bishop's Castle 'stock list', as declared to the Board of Trade in December 1895:
"2 Engines, fitted with hand brake,
4 Carriages, fitted with Clark and Webbs Chain Brake, 2 Carriages, no Brake,
10 Cattle Wagons, ordinary Lever Brakes, 5 Covered Goods Vans, ordinary Lever Brakes, 3 Coal Wagons, ordinary Lever Brakes."

Very little is known of the early carriages, though there were six four wheel vehicles, three of which were sold in 1885 to the Golden Valley Railway. The company then purchased a set of three ex-LNWR Clarke and Webb four wheelers, chain brake stock, in

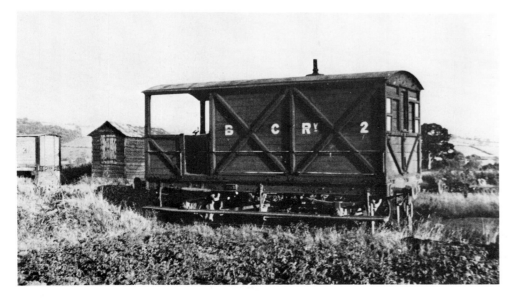

Bishop's Castle yard on 4th August 1935. All the vehicles were much repaired and cannibalised by Beddoes' men over the years (Sinclair's son afterwards worked for Beddoes). Wagon timbers, headstocks, solebars, main bearers and so on were stood in the engine shed; in 1905 timber cost 2/9d a cubic yard.

Roger Carpenter

1900. The BC probably had a spare set of carriages at this time but nothing is known of their origins and background.

The LNWR vehicles served until 1924, when the Board of Trade banned their use. The Bishop's Castle then turned to the GWR for a further three vehicles, deriving in their turn from Grouped South Wales companies. Even then they were second hand and included, of all things, an ex-LSWR six wheel brake third. Off the Brecon and Merthyr, it had a third class compartment, a first and two seconds and a guards compartment. The second vehicle was a four wheel ex-Cardiff Railway brake hailing originally from the Hull and Barnsley. Making up this motley trio was another Hull and Barnsley carriage, a four wheel compo which became on the BC a third, second, second, third. This too had passed through the ownership of the Brecon and Merthyr.

The carriages were painted chocolate brown in early days and dark red latterly, with black running gear, buffer shanks, hooks and so on. At closure these three were the only carriages in use. Some of the chain brake stock was broken up during the mid-1920s but one or two still stood, out of use at Bishop's Castle, in 1935.

The company also had a small fleet of goods wagons including some iron vans of a design not unlike the GWR standard iron minks. There was also a single verandha GW brake van built in the 1870s and often used on passenger trains. There was also a hand crane and runner, probably ex-Midland. The goods rolling stock it is believed, was painted a medium grey with black underframes, brake gear and so on.

"Last stand of the chain brake"

The Bishop's Castle is now the only railway in the Board of Trade Return unequipped with continuous automatic brake. It still has a chain under the vehicles, wound on a drum in the guards van, so as to be kept in tension. Thus tightly wound the chain keeps the brake blocks off the wheels. When the guard unwinds the drum, slackening the chain, or it breaks if the train parts, compressed springs force the blocks against the tyres. When applied a succession of ear-torturing squeakings and groanings arise from under the frame of the carriage.

How else could a Portrait of a Country Railway end?

Variety of Bishop's Castle stock – the vehicles always seemed to litter the yard, rather than standing around, awaiting attention or use, as was the case. 'Midland Waggon Co.' bits such as axleboxes, continued to be oddly and randomly distributed amongst the stock until the end. In all its rambling, ramshackle glory, the railway is now more missed than ever; Harry Mullard, well into his seventies, mused to Pearce Higgins in 1960, in as good an epitaph as any, "I fancy I can hear that shrill whistle yet echoing up the valley."

LNWR
Branch Lines
of
West Leicestershire
and
East Warwickshire

Geoffrey Hurst

First Edition

ISBN 0-947796-16-9

Printed by: Ryton Typing Services, Ryton Street, Worksop, Notts. (Front Cover)
Printed by: BDC Printing Services Ltd., Slack Lane, Derby DE3 3FL. (Text)

Published by: Milepost Publications, 39, Kilton Glade, Worksop, Notts S81 0PX.

Introduction

This book covers the former London and North Western Railway (including the Charnwood Forest Railway) in West Leicestershire and East Warwickshire. The lines featured are - Charnwood Forest Jn - Loughborough (Derby Road); Nuneaton (Trent Valley) - Wigston North Jn; Nuneaton (Trent Valley) - Coventry; Coventry - Leamington Spa (Avenue); Leamington Spa (Avenue) - Rugby (Midland) and Marton Jn - Weedon.

A short local history is given for each line, with selected passenger timetables and a photograph every station (except three halts) is included.

The railways in this book started life in 1844 with the opening of the Warwick & Leamington Union and grew until the final major works were completed in 1914. The LNWR formed part of the LMSR, which was nationalisation to become part British Railways. Passenger traffic was the spur to the building of all but a handful of branch lines. Coal and Granite were major sources of traffic for the railway, but was gradually lost to the lorry, the last colliery closed 1991. Freight traffic is now down to granite from the quarry at Croft and Homefire at Coventry is now the only source

of freight generated locally, and incoming coal to Homefire and LPG to Bedworth.

Charnwood Forest Railway was the first line to lose its passenger service in 1931, the first casualty of the internal combustion engine. After the Second World War, local passenger traffic suffered and closures followed in 1958 and 1959, leaving no passenger trains east of Leamington Spa. Nuneaton, Coventry and Leamington survived until the Beeching cuts and was axed in 1965, reaching a low in 1968 with the demise of local stopping train between Nuneaton and Leicester. However with the reopening of Narborough station in 1970, over 10 years of closures had ended. Inter City reopening Coventry to Leamington in 1977 and local authority support enabled South Wigston and Bedworth to rejoin the passenger network. More are planned but the councils are short of funds. The proposed privatisation leaves a black cloud hovering over local services, will it be a basic 9 to 5 railway as you have in North America or will be more of the same but under a new label. Time will tell.

Acknowledgements

I would like to thank the following people and organisations who have made the production of this book possible. The Leicestershire Libraries at Leicester and Loughborough, Warwickshire Libraries at Nuneaton and Leamington Spa, Northamptonshire Libraries at Northampton, the County Archive Services of Leicestershire, Northamptonshire, Warwickshire and West Yorkshire and to City of Manchester Central Library. The National Railway Museum Library, British Coal, National Power and British Library Newspapers Library. To the photographers - G.Coltas, R.M.Casserley, H.C.Casserley, R.S.Carpenter, Michael Mensing, Michael Mitchell, N.D.Mundy, Bryan Hicks, Steve Turner, G.Biddle, Alec Ford, Horace Gamble and City of Coventry Local Studies Library. Special thanks to Peter Fox, Peter Hall, Jim Slater for the tickets, Glyn Waite and Bill Hudson and Ron Kosys for the extra help they have given.

Geoff Hurst
May 1993

Bibliography

The following newspapers have been used - Leicester Mercury, Leicestershire Advertiser, Hinckley News, Loughborough Monitor, Coalville Times, Coventry Standard, Coventry Herald, Royal Leamington Spa Courier, Rugby Advertiser and Northampton Mercury.

Bradshaws, LMS and BR public timetables and various British Rail working timetables.

Register of Closed Railways 1948-1991, RCH Handbook of Stations 1904 and 1956, Register of Closed Stations by C.R.Clinker, Regional Histories of East and West Midlands, British Locomotive Catalogue Vol. 2B by B.Baxter, An Illustrated history LNWR Locomotives by E.Talbot, and the RCTS Railway Observer magazines 1948-1973.

1. Charnwood Forest Railway

Six local traders - Marmaduke Shield (Whitwick); Major George Thomas Mowbray (Overseal); Joseph John Fairfax Scott (Mountsorrel); Henry Humphreys, Woodhouse; George Louis Vaughan; Henry Hughes; and Edward Handley Weaver (Quorn), met and formed the Charnwood Forest Railway. The aim of the company was bring improved rail communications to the Charnwood Forest area, and prosperity would follow. Mr Maraduke Shield was made company chairman.

The Charnwood Forest Railway would leave the Midland Railway near Coalville, and pass through Whitwick, Thringstone, Sheepshed to join the Midland Railway to the north of Loughborough station. With a short branch from Coalville to Bardon Hill, running parallel with the Midland railway. The railway would skirt the northern edge of the granite massif of Charnwood Forest and use part of the ill fated Loughborough canal. The company had temporary offices in Devonshire Street, Loughborough.

The Charnwood Forest Railway act was passed on 16th July 1874, this enabled the company to build the following -

"1. A railway 1 miles 11 chains commencing in the Parish of Hugglescote by a junction with the Leicester - Burton railway of the Midland Railway, about 40 yards from the signalbox called Coalville Jn, terminating in the township of Swannington, Parish of Whitwick about 165 yards at the north end of fence separating 2 fields belonging to Midland Brick and Terracota Co.Ltd. fields no. 203/204.

2. A railway 10 miles 32 chains, commencing in parish of Whitwick by junction with said Leicester - Burton railway of Midland Railway 90 yards from level crossing of that railway Coalville to Whitwick road. Terminating in the Parish of Loughborough by junction with Midland Railway near place where footpath to Falcon Ironworks is carried by footbridge over last mentioned railway.

The company may raise £135,000 in £10 shares. The railway to be constructed within 5 years. Single line, except double over level crossing the Whitwick - Swannington road and Whitwick - Thringston road.

The main shareholders (promoters) were made company directors."

The Midland railway did not oppose the railway as it would give the company access to another part of Leicestershire as well as keeping out any rival railway. One month after the act was passed, the directors met for the first time.

Later that year the Charnwood company submitted plans to deviate two sections of the 1874 act, it was not successful. The plans were resubmitted in November 1875, and were successful. The Charnwood Forest Act of 24th July 1876, enabled the company to build -

"1. A railway of 24 chains and 70 links in the township of Hugglescote and Donnington in the Parish of Ibstock by junction with Railway 1 authorised by 1874 act at a place authorise crossing railway crosses public highway Bardon - Coalville and terminate in same parish at or near a fence on easterly side of field No.7.

2. A railway of 56 chains and 60 links junction with railway 1 at terminating thereof and terminating in said township of Hugglescote and Donnington by junction with Ashby and Nuneaton Railway (LNWR and Midland Joint Railway) extending from the Leicester and Burton Railway of Midland Railway to Shackerstone at or near a bridge which carries the said joint line over Leicester - Ashby de la Zouch turnpike.

Raise additional capital of £24,000. Construction in 5 years."

The optimism of the Charnwood Forest Railway board was shattered in early 1877, when no contractor would undertake the construction of the first section of line from Charnwood Forest Jn to Whitwick, even though the LNWR said it would contribute £1350 towards the cost. In the year the company decided that it would not be able to build the line in the time aloted in the 1874 Act. They therefore had to apply to parliament for new powers to extend construction time and to deviate parts of the line. As part of the additional LNWR finance, the Charnwood company to cut its links with the Midland railway at Loughborough.

The Charnwood Forest Railway Act of 16th April 1878, authorised the company to -:

"Authorise deviation No.1 - 72 chains commencing in Township of Hugglescote and Donington in Parish of Ibstock, from Railway No. 1 authorised by Act of 1876 at commencement here of public highway leading from Bardon to Coalville, about 12 chains along highway in westerly direction, from the point where same is crossed by the public road from Greenhill to Hugglecote and terminate in Township of Swannington in the Parish of Whitwick at terminus of railway authorised by Act of 1874.

No.2 A deviation - 3 miles 3 chains and 60 links commencing from and

out of railway No.2 authorised by Act of 1874 in Township of Thringstone in Parish of Whitwick, at or near point marked 2 miles 20 chains on the plans deposited in November 1873 and terminate in Parish of Sheepshed by a junction with said railway No.2, at or near point thereof on plans marked 5 miles 10 chains on said deposited plan.

A deviated railway - 42 chains 50 links in length. Commencing from and out of the said railway authorised No.2 at or near point thereon in Parish of Loughborough marked 9 miles on said plans and terminate in same parish at point from southwestern fence of Leicester - Derby turnpike about 130 yards measured in southerly direction along road from culvert carrying that road over Burleigh Brook. Completion in 4 years.

Abandon as much of railways No.1 and No.2 authorised by Act of 1874 and abandon railway No.2.

Extend the time of Act 1876 another 2 years, with all work to be completed by 24th July 1883."

The LNWR would be able to serve Loughborough and brake the Midland railways monopoly of traffic.

Plans were deposited with parliament in November 1880, for extension of time and powers for the LNWR to acquire shares. The Act of 23rd June 1881 authorised -

"Whereas the 1876 authorised 2 short branches and extended the 1874 act, which expired on 17th July 1880 should be revived and extended. Only a small portion of capital authorised by the Act of 1874 has been issued, shares not fully paid up.

1876 Act authorised working by LNWR, after completion it is expedient for that company to hold portion of share capital.

Deviate portion of line at Whitwick beyond limits of deviation.

A railway 1 mile 31 chains 22 links commencing in Township of Hugglescote & Donington in Parish of Ibstock by junction with companies authorised line at a point in the field No.19 on the plans of that authorised line deposited in November 1875 and terminate in Township and Parish of Whitwick by a junction with same authorised line at point in field No.60 of plan deposited in November 1873.

To be completed in 3 years and abandon authorised lines rendered unnecessary by construction of last mentioned railway.

Enpower the LNWR, who may with with threequarters of shareholders, allow the LNWR to subscribe £50,000. Company to work all powers, rights and privileges.

Authorise extension of 1878 act by 3 years."

The finances of the railway company were very poor. They struggled to raise the necessary capital with no builder willing to undertake construction even though the LNWR had agreed to provide extra funds of £50,000. The company board had become so dispirited that on 10th November 1880, that they proposed to abandon the Charnwood Forest Railway. However the company came to an operating agreement with the LNWR on 17th May 1881 and the company withdrew its abandonment two days later.

The company prospectus promoting the railway, said that the LNWR working costs were about £110 per mile, whilst the Charnwood Forest Railway would be about £42 per mile. The districts population was growing and the former coal railway between Leicester and Coalville was giving a return of 5% on shares. It suggested that this railway would give even better returns!

The contract was awarded to Mr Joseph Fairbanks, who agreed to have the line completed and ready for opening within 18 months of the commencement of works. The 'Loughborough Monitor' reported the cutting of the first sod - "The ceremony of cutting the first sod was a brilliant affair. Tea was provided in a big marquee, and everything and everywhere within the vicinity of the appointed place by Derby Road was decorated with bunting and flags. Lady Alice Packe was presented with a silver spade with which to perform the actual cutting of the sod. The following was inscribed upon it - Presented to Lady Alice Packe on the occasion of turning the first sod of the Charnwood Forest Railway on 31st August 1881, at Loughborough, Leicestershire - Chairman, H. Humphreys Esq.;engineer, C.Liddell Esq. C.E.; contractors Messrs. Maddison and Co.: secretary E.F.Tremayne, Esq."

The contractors used a maximum of 700 men on building the line, but it averaged about 500 men. The line had 31 bridges and 20 cuttings."

On the 25th February 1883, the manager of works Mr J.H.Firbank, in the contractors engine 'Suffolk' took some local people over the line. An account was given - "In a few seconds we were dashing past the goods and engine sheds at Loughborough station into the very heart of the forest. At

Sheepshed the engines were changed."

The Charnwood Forest Railway was opened to all traffic on Monday 16th April 1883, and was worked by the LNWR under an agreement signed on 17th May 1881. The LNWR placed an advertisement in the '*Loughborough Herald*' announcing that the Charnwood Forest Railway had opened. The local press did not give much coverage, a few paragraphs under the headings Loughborough, Sheepshed and Whitwick. Under Loughborough - "The actual opening of the Charnwood Forest Railway, it is hoped, make a further impetus to the prosperity of Loughborough on Monday. The event has long waited for but the project has had to pass through numerous vicissitudes before being able to reach its completed stage. Now it has been finished, and that even circumstances has been seized to make it successful. There will be every intention of extending to Nottingham and Ashby de la Zouch."

Under Whitwick - "A considerable number of people and visitors was brought into the place, the approaches to the station was enlivened by a number of flags, during the whole day the place presented a holiday appearance. Announced on Saturday that on Monday morning the commences for passenger, goods and mineral traffic. The station was a centre of attraction.

Whilst under Sheepshed - "Hailed throughout the village with great satisfaction. The first train which reached Sheepshed was witnessed by a large number of persons and not a few has secured tickets to have the first train over the line. The scenery through which this line plys runs exceedingly pretty, especially at Grace Dieu, where the ruins of the ancient abbey are seen close beside the line. Sheepshed station is within easy walking distance of the Cistercian abbey of St. Bernard Longcliffe.

Table 1 gives the first timetable -

proposed railway did not reach the statute book. However with this companies finances, it would never have been built.

In 1885 the directors announced that £45,000 of debenture stock had been authorised, £150,000 of stock had been dealt with. The directors had signed the debentures and were held responsible, one director alone having to find £40,000. The extent of the troubles can be gathered from these figures, and the chairman, dissatisfied with the state of affairs, went to London to find the 'root of the evil' - the secretary manager. As the chairman entered the office and confronted the secretary manager, he muttered "Oh Mr Humphries, I will be back in a minute." He was never seen again. The examination of the company's papers led to the conclusion that forged debentures had been sold. The company losses forced the company into chancery, and a receiver was appointed in November of that year.

Sheepshed stations spelling was altered to Shepshed in May 1888, as some Victorians thought was less vulgar.

The LNWR placed advertisements in the '*Coalville Times*' of 15th June 1906, announcing the introduction of one class Railmotors from Shackerstone to Loughborough on 18th June. This increased the service from three trains on Weekdays and four trains on Saturdays, to seven on Weekdays and nine on Saturdays. The '*Coalville Times*' reported that 400 to 500 people witnessed the first Railmotor at Coalville enroute from Loughborough to Shackerstone on the first trip. Many people joined for their first trip. The railmotor was the LNWR attempt to boost usage as well as to reduce costs.

The railmotors led to the construction of three halts at Thringstone, Grace Dieu and Snell's Nook between Coalville East and Loughborough

Table 1

Weekdays		a.m.	a.m.	p.m.	p.m.	p.m.
Nuneaton	d	7.55	10. 5	1.35	5.45	9. 5
Shackerstone	d	8.22	10.32	2. 2	6.12	9.32
Hugglescote	d	8.34	10.43	2.14	6.23	9.44
Coalville East	d	8.39	10.47	2.19	6.27	9.49
Whitwick	d	8.43	10.50	2.23	6.30	9.53
Sheepshed	d	8.53	10.58	2.32	6.38	10. 2
Loughborough	a	9. 0	11. 5	2.40	6.45	10.10

Weekdays		a.m.	a.m.	a.m.	p.m.	p.m.
Loughborough	d	8. 5	9.10	11.20	3.30	6.55
Sheepshed	d	8.13	9.17	11.28	3.38	7. 2
Whitwick	d	8.22	9.25	11.37	3.47	7.10
Coalville East	d	8.26	9.28	11.41	3.51	7.13
Hugglescote	d	8.32	9.36	11.46	3.56	7.17
Shackerstone	a	8.43	9.48	11.58	4. 8	7.28
Nuneaton	a	9.10	10.10	12.25	4.35	7.55

Omnibus connection -

	a.m.	a.m.	p.m.	p.m.	p.m.
Town d	7.50	8.55	1.10	3.15	6.40
Railway Station d	9.10	11.15	2.45	6.55	

Later in that year the directors of the Charnwood Forest Railway were in a very confident, and sort to extend the companies network. It put forward plans for a railway from Grace Dieu Abbey to Lichfield, joining the LNWR line from Burton to Lichfield just north of Trent Valley station. The line to pass south of Ashby de la Zouch, Haselour, and dive under the MR at Elford, and on to Lichfield. To be 19 miles 75 chains in length. The

Derby Road. And opened to public traffic on 1st April 1907. The halts were of a basic shelter and a low short platform. Approached from the road by a set of stairs. These halts opened without any local press coverage. The service was greatly enhanced between Coalville East and Loughborough, and the new timetable is listed below -:

Table 2

Weekdays		RM a.m.	a.m.	RM a.m.	RM p.m.	p.m.	RM p.m.	RM p.m.	p.m.	SO p.m.
Nuneaton	d		8. 0	9.35		1.30			6.35	
Shacklestone Jn	d		8.32	10. 7	12.10	2. 2	3. 0		7. 1	
Heather & Ibstock	a		8.40	10.14	12.17	2.10	3. 7		7. 9	
Hugglestone	a		8.47	10.29	12.22	2.16	3.12		7.15	
Coalville	a	8.20	8.53	10.34	12.27	2.23	3.17	5.25	7.22	8.30
Whitwick	a	8.24	8.59	10.38	12.31	2.29	3.21	5.29	7.27	8.35
Grace Dieu Halt	a	8.26		10.40	12.33		3.23	5.31		
Thringstone Halt	a	8.30		10.44	12.37		3.27	5.35		
Shepshed	a	8.34	9.10	10.49	12.42	2.40	3.34	5.40	7.36	8.45
Snell's Nook Halt	a	8.39		10.53	12.46		3.38	5.44		
Loughborough	a	8.45	9.20	11. 0	12.52	2.59	3.45	5.50	7.46	8.56

RM Railmotor

Weekdays

		a.m.	RM a.m.	RM a.m.	RM a.m.	SO RM p.m.	RM p.m.	p.m.	RM p.m.	SO p.m.	p.m.
Loughborough	d	7.30	7.50	9. 0	11.15	1. 0	1.50	3.25	4.45	6.00	8.00
Snell's Nook Halt	d		7.56	9. 6	11.21	1. 5	1.56		4.51		
Shepshed	d	7.40	8. 0	9.11	11.25	1. 9	2. 0	3.34	4.55	6.10	8.10
Thringstone Halt	d		8. 5	9.16	11.30	1.14	2. 5		5.00		
Grace Dieu Halt	d		8. 8	9.19	11.33	1.17	2. 8		5.03		
Whitwick	d	7.51	8.11	9.24	11.38	1.20	2.11	3.43	5.08	6.21	8.21
Coalville	d	7.55	8.15	9.28	11.40		2.16	3.48	5.13	6.26	8.25
Hugglestone	d	8. 1		9.37	11.45		2.23	3.56		6.33	
Heather & Ibstock	d	8. 7		9.41	11.52		2.27	4. 2		6.41	
Shacklestone Jn	a	8.15		9.46	12.00		2.35	4. 8		6.47	
Nuneaton	a	8.45		*10.28*	12.31		3.15	4.40		7.18	

RM Railmotor

The LNWR station at Coalville had started its life with the suffix East to distinguish it from the Midland Railway station. The suffix was deleted from 1st May 1905. In May 1910 it became Coalville (LNW).

Charnwood Forest Railway was released from receivership on 1st July 1909 and the company commenced managing its own affairs.

The Whitwick Granite Company opened a quarry at Pedlar Tor between 1904 and 1923, it was connected by a long length of single track mineral railway to join the Charnwood Forest railway at Coalville East. Four sidings were provided for this traffic.

In January 1923, the Charnwood Forest Railway ceased to exist, and the London Midland and Scottish Railway (LMSR), took over all the affairs of the company. The LMSR restored the East suffix to Coalville on 2nd June 1924, but it was not affixed to the station name board.

From 1930 the railway company was allowed to purchase shares in the local bus company. The LMSR took a large share in the local bus company Midland Red which competed with it for local passenger traffic. The bus service ran through the town and village centres, whilst the train served the outskirts of Loughborough, Shepshed and Coalville. By 1930 passenger numbers had slumped to 30 or 40 per day. From 13th April 1931 the LMSR withdrew all passenger services from Loughborough Derby Road, Shackestone to Nuneaton. The last passenger timetable is listed below in Table 3. There being no Sunday service the last trains ran on Saturday 11th April. The 'Coalville Times' gave the news of the withdrawal of passengers in just one short column, whilst the 'Loughborough Monitor' devoted half of page 15, giving a potted history.

War, it is thought the last train was run by the Whitwick Coal Company, from Whitwick to Southsea on 15th August 1939.

Whitwick goods became an unstaffed public siding from 5th July 1954. In 1955 a daily pickup goods (T150) ran from Coalville Mantle Lane to Loughborough Derby Road servicing the branches public and private sidings. It arrived at Charnwood Forest Jn at 8.00 a.m., Coalville East 8. 5 - 8.20 a.m., Shepshed 8.40 - 8.50 a.m., Loughborough Derby Road 9. 5 - 10.35 a.m., Shepshed 10.50 - 11.50 a.m., Whitwick 12. 5 - 12.25 p.m., Coalville East 12.30 - 12.45 p.m. and arriving at Charnwood Forest Jn at 12.50 p.m. The line was closed to al traffic from Charnwwod Granite siding (Shepshed) to Loughborough Derby Road on 31st October 1955. The pickup goods was retimed and continued to run to Charnwood Granite siding.

Although officially closed, the line from Shepshed to Loughborough Derby Road was converted to a siding on 20th March 1958.

Whitwick Colliery to Shepshed (locally known as the Bluebell line) was closed on Monday 11th December 1963. British Railways withdrew public goods from Shepshed, Whitwick and Coalville East depots. Traffic from Charnwood Granite quarry was not sufficient to warrant the lines continued existence. A Coalville 4F manned by Mr V.Jinks (Driver), Mr R.Spencer (Fireman) and Mr A.Overton (Guard) traversed the line to Charnwood Quarry for the last time on 8th December 1963. Loughborough Derby Road station was demolished in November 1965.

The last portion of the Charnwood Forest Railway from Charnwood Forest Jn to Whitwick colliery closed 17th April 1967. The coal traffic was

Table 3

Weekdays

		a.m.	a.m.	a.m.	p.m.	p.m.	p.m.	A p.m.	p.m.	SO p.m.	p.m.
Nuneaton T.V.	d		7.35	9. 8		1.25	3.15			7.30	
Shackerstone	d		8. 1	10. 0	12.13	2. 5	3.51	4.30		8. 8	
Heather & Ibstock	d		8. 8	10. 6	12.19	2.11	3.59	4.36		8.14	
Hugglescote	d		8.13	10.11	12.24	2.16	4. 7	4.41		8.19	
Coalville East	d	7.35	8.18	10.16	12.29	2.21	4.15	4.47	5.55	8.24	9. 0
Whitwick	d	7.38	8.22	10.20	12.32	2.25	4.19	4.51	5.59	8.28	9. 4
Grace Dieu Halt	d	7.40		10.23	12.36	2.28		4.54	6. 1	8.31	
Thringstone Halt	d	7.44		10.27	12.40	2.32		4.58	6. 5	8.35	
Shepshed	d	7.50	8.34	10.33	12.46	2.38	4.30	5. 4	6.15	8.41	9.14
Snell's Hook Halt	d			10.37		2.42		5. 8			
Loughborough Derby Rd.	a	8. 0	8.43	10.45	12.57	2.50	4.40	5.15	6.29	8.53	9.23

Weekdays

		a.m.	a.m.	a.m.	a.m.	p.m.	p.m.	p.m.	p.m.	p.m.	SO p.m.	SO p.m.
Loughborough Derby Rd.	d	6.15	7. 0	8.58	11.10	1. 3	3.20	5.20	6. 5	7.10	8.27	9.30
Snell's Hook Halt	d			9. 3		1. 8	3.25					
Shepshed	d	6.24	7.11	9. 8	11.20	1.15	3.30	5.30	6.15	7.20	8.42	9.39
Thringstone Halt	d			9.15	11.27	1.20	3.37	5.37				
Gracedieu Halt	d			9.18	11.30	1.23	3.40	5.41				
Whitwick	d	6.34	7.22	9.22	11.34	1.27	3.44	5.45	6.26	7.34	8.52	9.49
Coalville East	d	6.39	7.29	9.26	11.38	1.31	3.48	5.50	6.31	7.38	8.54	9.55
Hugglestone	d		7.34	9.32	11.44	1.37	3.54		6.38	7.44		
Heather & Ibstock	d		7.42	9.37	11.49	1.42	4. 0		6.44	7.49		
Shackerstone	a		7.48	9.44	11.58	1.50	4. 7		7. 0	7.56		
Nuneaton T.V.	a		8.26	10.37	12.33	2.30	4.46		7.42			

A From Market Bosworth 4.20 p.m.

Saturdays Excepted.

The LMSR continued to deal with parcel traffic at Whitwick and Shepshed stations. Excursion traffic continued until the Second World diverted onto the ex Midland Railway line. Thus ended branches eighty four years of operations.

Coalville East station on 12th May 1962, looking south towards Nuneaton. The gas lamp is bent over and missing its glass (not bad after being closed for over 31 years), the platform coping edge has been removed. Whilst the station building still retains two wooden signs, and the station masters accommodation is still being occupied. The lines which diverge to the left serve the exchange sidings, just visible with a rake of wagons and a brake van. Two home signals protect the line. *(R.M. Casserley)*

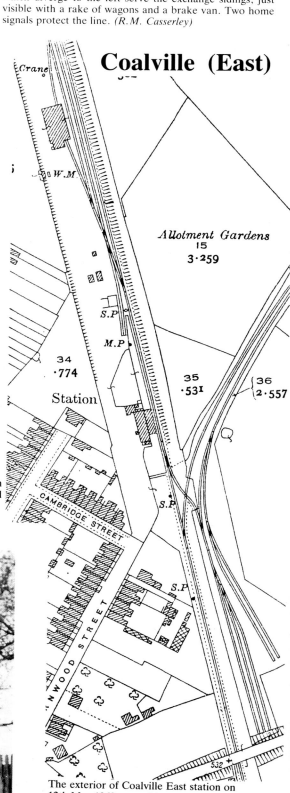

Coalville (East)

(above) A Midland Johnston 0-6-0 3642 (17B) stands at the southern end of Coalville East station on 10th October 1935, whilst working target 51. Although the station is closed to passengers, all the structures are still insitu. Note the gradient profile on the platform. *(H.C. Casserley)*

The exterior of Coalville East station on 12th May 1962, over thirty years after its closure to passengers. The entrance to the booking hall was a simple brick arch. *(R.M. Casserley)*

Whitwick

The REC Charnwood Forester' railtour hauled by ex Midland Railway 4F 43723 stops at Whitwick station for a photograph stop on 14th April 1957. The occupants have got out and are exploring the out of use station. The loop for passing freight has long been lifted and is well grassed over. (R.M. Casserley)

A crowded Whitwick platform sees the arrival of a LNWR Railmotor, from which a Edwardian lady has alighted and is showing her ticket to a member of staff. Two large churns are stood next to the building wall. (Lens of Sutton)

Whitwick station was built on a curve and was one of the few stations to be in a convenient position. This photograph was taken on 3rd August 1952 from rail level looking south. The original Ladies Waiting Room and Gentlemen signs was still in place. The booking hall was at street level, and the platform was approached down a set of steps. Platform buildings are still in place, but some of the windows are boarded up. (Alec Ford)

Thringstone Halt

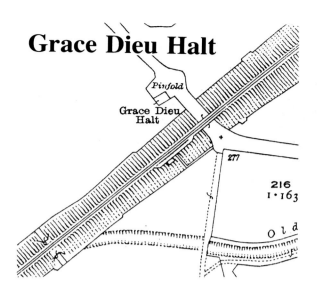

Grace Dieu Halt

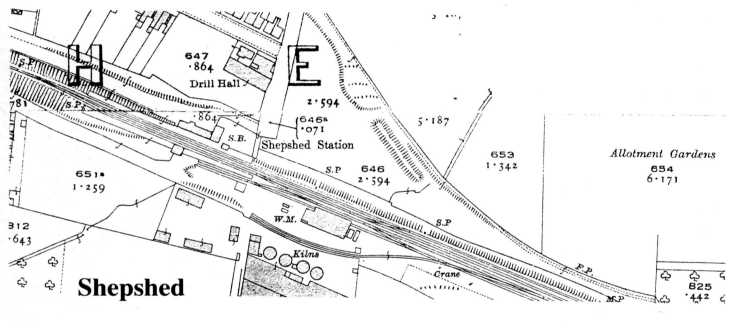

Shepshed

4F 43723 having run round at Shepshed on R 'Charnwood Forester' Railtour on 14th April 1957. *(R. Casserley)*

SHEPSHED. L.N.W.R

*(above left)*Seven passengers stand partly beneath the awning as a push - pull train arrives at Shepshed from Nuneaton and will depart to Loughborough, just before the First World War. Posters adorn the station wall offering passengers the various delights of the LNWR system. *(Lens of Sutton)*

*(above right)*Shepshed station at the turn of the century, with a well kept border. An archway partially protects a seat, occupied by an Edwardian lady. The main station building is of similar design to Coalville East station. An awning covers the platform to the edge. Paraffin lamps stretch along both platforms. A group of passengers are awaiting the arrival of a Loughborough, which has been signalled through the station. The Whitwick bound platform has a small awning and wooden waiting room. *(Lens of Sutton)*

Looking towards Loughborough in June 1951, the loop is still in position and is well used, even after 20 years of closure, most of structures are still in place. The paraffin lamps had been changed to gas, of which four were still there. The station awning has been removed, whilst the waiting shed on the other platform was gently decaying. Shepshed goods shed is clearly visible, with a handful of wooden sided wagons placed on the loop. *(G.S.Lloyd)*

The exterior of Shepshed station is exactly like that at Coalville East. It remained intact along after its closure. *(R.M.Casserley)*

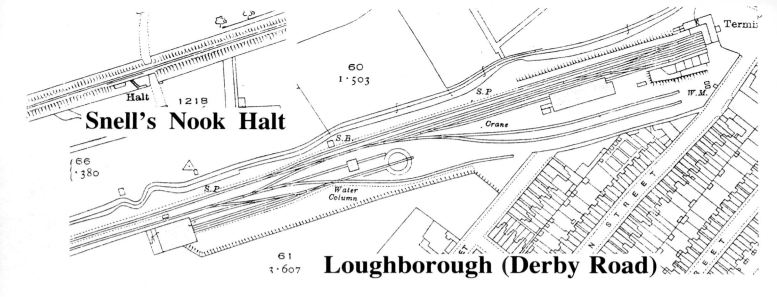

Snell's Nook Halt

Loughborough (Derby Road)

*(right)*The motive power depot at Loughborough was capable of having four roads, plans show it only was fitted with three. It serviced the locomotives that worked the local passenger trains, but with the cessation of passenger train in April 1931, it would have been surplus to requirements. By 3rd may 1952, it was occupied by a wood merchant, but retained they did not alter its appearance. *(T.J.Edgington)*

*(below)*Loughborough Derby Road on a wet 3rd May 1952 is host to the last passenger train to arrive here. The SLS (Midlands Area) special started from Coventry and was made up of 2 two coach push-pull sets and worked by an Ivatt 2-6-2T 41218, although it was hoped to use a LNWR Webb 2-4-2T and a two coach set, but due to demand, the Ivatt was used instead. The over grown platform has a gradient post showing that the line climbs at 1:254 out of Loughborough. *(T.J.Edgington)*

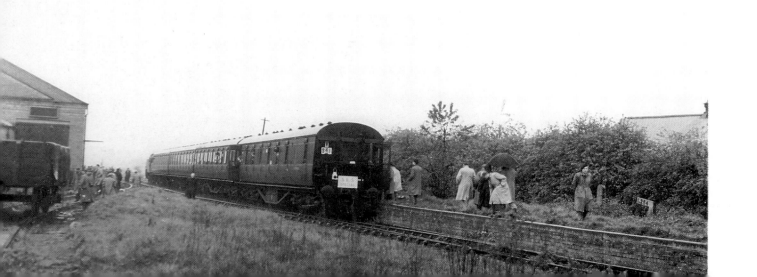

On 15th July 1952, Loughborough (Derby Road) sees a LMS 4F 43291 resting next to the old watertower, having brought the daily tripper from Mantle Lane sidings. A single van has been shunted into the head-shunt. The goods depot doors are open and it looks as though some vans are inside being loaded or emptied. Four coal wagons are positioned around the coal yard which is well stocked. *(Alec Ford)*

Loughborough Derby Road station (complete with a long nameboard) was a single platformed station, with wooden awning covering the entrance hall and round the station building along the platform. A set of six wheeled vans are stabled in a siding on the side of the station. The metal letters on the station seat spelt out just plain - Loughborough. A barrow has been placed on its side, next to the wall. The fencing is covered in enamel advertising signs. LNWR and LMS noticeboards are to be found on any unused station wall space, advertising timetables and fares. *(D.T.Thompson)*

The exterior of Loughborough Derby Road station as viewed on 15th July 1952. It has not changed very much since closure to passengers. The notice boards on the station building are still for cheap tickets. The large board proclaims - LONDON MIDLAND SCOTTISH RAILWAY - COAL AND GOODS DEPOT, and beneath BR have posters advertising London for 22/9 (£1-13p in todays money!). *(Alec Ford)*

2. Nuneaton T.V. - Wigston North Jn

A railway was proposed to connect the two towns of Nuneaton and Hinckley, a railway company was set up and placed its plans before parliament in November 1858. The railway was authorised in the Act of 12th August 1859. This enabled the company to construct the following works -
"A railway from the Trent Valley Railway of the LNWR at Nuneaton to Hinckley.

The following subscribers to be made directors of the company Thomas Edward Bigge; Will Field; Joseph Knight; Richard Banner Oakley; Hon. Standish Prendergast Vereker and Eramus Wilson.

The company to raise £45,000 in 4,500 £10 shares, and powers to borrow upto £14,000.

Works to be completed in 3 years."

Only three months after the Hinckley line was authorised, the railway company placed plans for the line to be extended to Leicester. The extension was sanctioned in the Nuneaton and Hinckley Extension Railway Act of 14th June 1860. This enabled the railway company to extend their railway from Hinckley to the Midland Railway at Wigston Magna. And to alter the company name to South Leicestershire Railway.
"Running powers over Nuneaton and Coventry Railway, use of stations, and over Midland Railway part of Rugby to Leicester line between Wigston Magna and Leicester.

To commence in Field No.99 in Parish of Hinckley to terminate with junction in Parish of Wigston Magna by junction with Midland Railway. Line not to deviate north of plan 42 in Parish of Narborough

Road from southeast of Market Place to terminate at Nuneaton to Hinckley railway in field No.71 road when completed to satisfaction of two justices, deemed as an highway repairable by Parish of Hinckley.

One level crossing No.42 in Parish of Narborough, public road, no more than two lines, not to shunt on level crossing and erect lodge for crossing. May require bridge instead of level crossing.

Appoint watchman/pointsman exclusively to Midland Railway and to be prepaid half yearly to Midland Railway.

The railway to be built within 5 years.

The company to issue £150,000 in new shares

The LNWR to have powers to supply own staff at Midland Railway stations between Wigston and Leicester.

The LNWR to have running powers from Wigston and Leicester. The Midland Railway to having running powers between Wigston Magna to Nuneaton and Nuneaton to Coventry.

Accommodation for Midland Railway at Hinckley; Nuneaton; Coventry and intermediate stations."

LNWR to construct a line from a junction near Nuneaton on Nuneaton - Coventry line to Nuneaton - Hinckley line. To facilitate through running between Coventry and Leicester. Mode and effect of this junction shall be settled by Thomas Elliott Harrison Esq. CE or him failing, by some engineer to be agreed by MR and LNWR; or by an engineer appointed by Board of Trade. The extension to be single line of rails, but if Board of Trade on approval of MR anytime after 3 years require company to lay additional rails".

The South Leicestershire Railway proposed in November 1861 to deviate its Hinckley to Wigston line a small distance to the south of the authorised line through the village of Narborough.

The South Leicestershire railway companies line from Nuneaton to Hinckley opened to all traffic from 1st January 1862 and the 'Leicester Mercury' reported that - "On Wednesday last, the long delayed opening of the line from Hinckley to Nuneaton, became an acknowledged fact. On the previous day time tables had been distributed through the town (Hinckley), in which it announced that the opening for passenger traffic would take place on the 1st of January, 1862. The first train from Nuneaton was set down for 7.10 a.m., and long before that period an unusual stir might have been perceived in the streets, the general tendency of the crowds bring towards what was formerly the rural and pleasant, but not over frequented, Priesthills, but now the more business like railway station. On moving along the new road, we were struck by seeing for the first time, the 'buss' with its living freight, intended to convey passengers 'to and from the railway station'. On a further approach the novelty of the gas lights, together with the crowds assembled at that comparatively early period presented rather an imposing aspect, and one could scarcely fancy oneself in the quietest suburb of the hitherto quiet town of 'old Hinckley'. After the usual preliminaries of bell ringing, etc., and the more than ordinary care on the part of the officials, that none of the navvies assembled should by mistake find themselves under the carriage wheels, the train hove in sight, when on its approach a number of passengers emerged from the carriages. About a quarter of an hour was now occupied in reversing the engine, and getting the train ready for those who had taken 'down tickets.' When the passengers were seated, and the signal have been given, the huge monster whisked away, with the to-him little burden of have a dozen carriages. After a pleasant run of about 10 minutes the station of Nuneaton was approached. Either from the rails being newly laid, or from some better principle being adopted than is usual on the old lines, the annoying rocking and shaking usually felt by rail travellers, had in this case not been experienced. The crowds assembled to view the arrival and departure of subsequent trains, must in the whole have numbered some thousands".

Table 1

Weekdays		a.m.	a.m.	p.m.	p.m.
Nuneaton	d	7. 0	9.55	12.15	6.10
Hinckley	a	7.10	10.05	12.25	6.20
Weekdays		a.m.	a.m.	p.m.	p.m.
Hinckley	d	7.25	10.15	12.45	6.35
Nuneaton	a	7.35	10.25	12.55	6.45

Fares	1st	2nd	3rd
Single	1s.0d	0s.9d	0s.4d
Return	1s.6d	1s.9d	

The deviation of the line at Narborough was approved in the South Leicestershire Railway Additional Powers Act of 7th August 1862.
"A deviation commencing in Parish of Croft, junction with authorised line in field No.31 in Parish of Croft terminating in parish of Narborough in field No.67. Powers upto three years to purchase land and three years to complete deviation.

One level crossing in field 42 in Parish of Narborough.

The company not allowed to shunt train on level crossing or train engine easing or coming to a stand on the level crossing. Railway company to erect lodge at point of crossing. Board of Trade may require railway erect bridge instead of crossing."

Before the South Leicestershire Railway (SLR) opened its extension from Hinckley to Wigston Magna, the SLR made an agreement with the LNWR on 2nd March 1863, that the LNWR shall purchase the SLR undertaking, giving 3 months notice of purchase at par for shares on or before 1st January 1865 at 5% premium on shares, take up deficient dividend upto 4½% it any before opening of respective portion of railway. This agreement was sanctioned as part of the LNWR Additional Powers Act of 28th July 1863.

The line was extended to Wigston, and by using its running powers the LNWR was able to enter Leicester. The line from Hinckley to Wigston was opened on 1st January 1864. The 'Leicester Advertiser' gave the following report on the lines opening - "The remaining section of the (South Leicestershire) line, It was believed that on the opening through to Leicester a more general rejoicing would be made. It was anticipated a grand demonstration would take place on the opening of the line to Leicester. However this was not the case, for although various opinions existed as when it would be opened, nothing was positively known until 31st December, the day previous, public confidence being established by the circulation of a very limited number of timetable, which were so scarce that public establishments were called upon repeatedly to get a sight of the announcement. Having pursued the bills, and ascertained the fare, which many considered a high one for the distance to Leicester, a calm ensued for the evening, there being no time to prepare for rejoicing. Next morning, the number present to witness the first train to Leicester, and have a ride by railway, was not half so many as it was two years previous when the line opened to Nuneaton, the curiosity of the beholders having so far subsided that not a shout or cheer was given for the departure of the first train to Leicester. The line between Nuneaton and Leicester is about 20 miles in length, and is worked by the London and North Western railway Company. The Midland Railway Company have running powers; the two companies together affording great accommodation to the inhabitants of Blaby, Narborough, Elmsthorpe, Hinckley and Nuneaton, giving easy access to Birmingham, Manchester and Liverpool. Since the opening of the Nuneaton section we are told that the traffic is more than was anticipated, and we doubt not but the connecting link to Leicester will fully answer the expectations of the projectors of this line of railway."

Both the LNWR and Midland Railway placed adverts announcing the opening of the line from Hinckley to Leicester, one day after it actually opened. The LNWR advertisement gave both the timetable and local fares from Leicester to Hinckley and Nuneaton, while the Midland advert firstly announced the revision of passenger fares between Leicester and Birmingham (which used the companies route via Coalville and Burton). The fares were reduced to 7s.9d *1st*; 5s.6d *2nd* and 3s.7d *Government* Single and 11s.9d *1st* and 8s.3d *2nd* Day Ticket. This as a direct consequence of the LNWR now being able to offer a Leicester to Birmingham ticket via Nuneaton and Coventry. The second part of the Midland advert gave the companies timetable between Leicester and Nuneaton. Both the LNWR and MR timetables have been condensed into Table 2

1st September, the Midland Railway diverted all its passenger trains onto the Wigston Central Jn North to Wigston Central Jn West line. The Midland ceased using the LNWR line between Wigston North Jn and Glen Parva Jn.

The LNWR curve from Midland Jn to Chilvers Coton Jn near to Anker Siding was built and was approved on 26th July 1873, but the facing points were not connected and the line was not opened as a through route. The maps show it as a two line siding skirting the back of Nuneaton shed.

Croft station opened without any acknowledgement in the local press. It suddenly appeared in Bradshaws December 1877 edition and then in the local timetables printed in a mid-January edition of the 'Hinckley News'. Trains departed to Nuneaton at 6.53 a.m.(MO), 8.51 a.m., 11.58 a.m., 3.17 p.m.(SO), 5. 0 p.m. and 8.10 p.m. To Leicester at 8.21x a.m., 9.34 a.m., 11. 9 a.m.(SO) , 1.34 p.m., 8.16 p.m. and 9.28 p.m. (x Calls to pickup on request). Sunday trains did not call at the beginning. Fares did not appear until the March 1878 edition, and said it would cost 1s.7d *1st*, 1s.2d *2nd*, and 9d *3rd Class* from Leicester to Croft and 1s.6d *1st*, 1s.1d *2nd*, 9½d *3rd Class* from Nuneaton to Croft.

Glen Parva was the last station to be opened by the LNWR on this line. The company took out an advertisement in the 'Leicester Mercury' announcing that Glen Parva station would open for passenger and parcel traffic from 1st April 1884 and to be served by six trains, departing to Leicester at 8.30 a.m., 1.53 p.m. and 6.30 p.m. and Nuneaton at 8.33 a.m., 11.38 a.m. and 6.28 p.m. and taking 8 minutes to Leicester and 30 minutes from Nuneaton.

Table 2

Weekdays

		a.m.	a.m.	a.m. MR	a.m.	p.m.	p.m. MR	p.m.	p.m. MR	p.m. MR	Sunday a.m.	p.m.
Nuneaton	d	7. 0	7.50	8.30	10.35	12.30	12.55	3.30	6.20	6.50	10.15	4.15
Hinckley	d	7.10	8. 0	8.40	10.45	12.40	1. 5	3.40	6.30	7.00	10.25	4.25
Elmesthorpe	d		8. 8		10.53		1.13		6.38		10.33	4.33
Narborough	d		8.18		11. 3		1.23		6.48		10.43	4.43
Blaby	d		8.24		11. 9		1.29		6.54		10.49	4.49
Leicester	a		8.40	9.20	11.25	1.20	1.45	4.20	7.10	7.40	11. 5	5. 5

Weekdays

		a.m.	a.m. MR	a.m.	a.m. MR	a.m.	p.m.	p.m. MR	p.m.	p.m.	Sunday a.m.	p.m.	Single 1st	2nd	Gov	Return 1st	2nd
Leicester	d		7.20	9.30	11.25	11.40	2.10	4.40	5.20	7.30	11.40	5.35					
Blaby	d			9.42		11.52		4.52		7.42	11.52	5.47	0s.9d	0s.6d	0s.4½d	1s.3d	0s.9d
Narborough	d			9.47		11.57		4.57		7.47	11.57	5.52	1s.3d	0s.11d	0s.6½d	2s.0d	1s.6d
Elmesthorpe	d			9.58		12. 8		5. 8		7.58	12. 8	6. 3	2s.0d	1s.6d	0s.11d	3s.0d	2s.0d
Hinckley	d	7.25	8. 0	10. 7	12. 2	12.17	2.47	5.17	5.57	8. 7	12.17	6.12	2s.6d	2s.0d	1s.2½d	3s.9d	3s.0d
Nuneaton	a	7.35	8.10	10.20	12.15	12.30	3. 0	5.30	6.10	8.20	12.30	6.25	3s.3d	2s.6d	1s.6½d	5s.0d	3s.0d

Fares from Leicester

On the 1st November 1864, the Midland Railway opened its line from Whitacre Jn to Midland Jn (Nuneaton) to passenger traffic, it immediately ceased using the LNWR station at Nuneaton. Through freight traffic started in 1st December 1864. The Midland now competed for through traffic from Leicester and Hinckley to Birmingham.

The Midland Railway in November 1865 submitted plans to three railways, two linking Ashby de la Zouch, Ibstock and the LNWRs South Leicestershire Railway to the west of Hinckley. The junctions at Hinckley to face both ways. These railways were sanctioned by parliament in the Midland Railway Act of 6th August 1866. A year later the Midland Railway sort the inclusion of the LNWR into the Ashby and Nuneaton lines. The LNWRs involvement into a joint company was approved in the LNWR Act of 17th June 1867.

On the 15th July 1867 the LNWR Additional Powers Act approved the dissolution of the South Leicestershire Railway company.

Both the Midland and LNWR as joint operators of the Ashby and Nuneaton lines sort to change the 1866 Act. They wanted to build two new lines to leave the original line at Weddington and join the LNWR mainline north of Trent Valley station and the Midland Railway to have a spur into there station at Abbey Street. They also proposed to abandon the west to north curve at Hinckley. This work was approved in the Midland & LNWR Act of 25th June 1868.

At Wigston, the Midland Railway had constructed a curve from Wigston South Jn to join the LNWR at Glen Parva Jn. The Midland Railway commenced using the line for goods traffic from 1st January 1871. Later that year a short north to west spur was laid off the Rugby line at Wigston. On

renamed Wigston Glen Parva.

In November 1889, the Midland Railway submitted proposals to a branch from the LNWR line at Narborough to Enderby Quarry of 2 miles and 56 chains and a reverse branch off the Enderby line to Huncote of 1 mile and 12 chains. The Enderby branch was approved as part of the Midland Railway (Additional Powers) Act of 25th July 1890. Three years later the Enderby branch was passed into Midland & LNWR Joint control as part of the LNWR Act of 27th July 1893. The Enderby branch opened that day to goods and mineral traffic, it was single line worked by train staff without tickets. Each company operated the line in yearly turns.

A branch siding appeared on the eastern side of the Enderby branch, this came into use by 19th October 1904 and served the Enderby & Stoney Stanton Granite Company. Within four years the Midland Railway ceased to use the Enderby branch. The Enderby line was extended by 13 chains to serve another granite quarry. It came into use on 1st January 1912.

By 1905 most of the goods sidings were in place. Granite was the main source of outward traffic from this line, originating from quarries at Enderby, Croft and Stoney Stanton and a brickworks at Wigston Glen Parva, which was located beside the goods depot. A public goods depot was attached to each station. The majority of incoming goods was coal, with Hinckley having the largest depot. The LNWR had its own goods depot in Leicester and was located to at Humberstone Road next to the Midland Railways depot.

On 1st January 1923, the LNWR and Midland Railways were two of companies merged to form part of the London Midland and Scottish Railway (LMSR).

The groundframe and connection to the Asylum Siding was removed on

11th October 1942.

British Railways London Midland Region took over from the LMSR on 1st January 1948.

In the 1956 RCH Handbook listed private sidings belonging to Constone's Siding (next to Glen Parva goods depot), Enderby & Stoney Stanton Granite Co. had sidings at Narborough and Enderby quarries. Whilst at Croft the quarry siding was owned Croft Granite, Brick and Concrete Co. Stoney Stanton siding (between Croft and Elmesthorpe) served the granite quarries on the southside of the line.

Cravens three car diesel multiple units (e.g. M50754-M59309-M50787) took over the Leicester (London Road) - Birmingham (New Street) local services on 14th April 1958, the units showed B7 on the indicator box. The units were allocated to Derby Etches Park and operated from Leicester or Nottingham depots, one set was stabled overnight at Saltley carriage sheds. When a three car Cravens failed, a two car set appeared and this resulted in severe overcrowding. Steam locomotives continued to haul the Nuneaton (Trent Valley) - Leicester (London Road) locals. Nuneaton shed provided a Class 4 2-6-0, however 2-6-2T's and Class 5's did appear.

The last steam hauled locals ended in 2nd January 1961 when Derby Lightweight, Metropolitian Cammell and BRCW diesel multiple units took over. The last steam workings was 42331 (15C) on four coach trains. The new improved diesel service involved a total recasting of services. A train left Birmingham at 15 minutes past each hour all stations to Hinckley and then non stop to Leicester. An hourly all stations local service from Nuneaton Trent Valley to Leicester following the fast, connecting at Hinckley for local passengers from Birmingham to Wigston Glen Parva. This service also meant that there would be good connections onto the Coventry and Leamington trains.

As wagon load goods traffic was moved to road haulage, the Goods depots were axed. Croft and Elmesthorpe closed on 6th April 1964, followed in 1966 by Wigston Glen Parva on 4th July and Narborough on 1st August.

The main trunk route from Birmingham - East Anglia ran through Rugby, Oundle and Peterborough East. However this line was closed to passenger and through freight traffic from 6th June 1966. All traffic was diverted through Nuneaton and Leicester. This line was suddenly upgraded from a minor line to the main Midlands - East Anglia trunk route, and most cross country expresses called only at Nuneaton Trent Valley and Hinckley.

Sunday services were withdrawn from Wigston Glen Parva and Narborough stations on 5th March 1967, leaving only Croft and Hinckley.

Local services from Leicester (London Road) to Nuneaton and Birmingham withdrawn from 4th March 1968 were replaced by trains only calling at Hinckley and Nuneaton (Trent Valley), and the following stations were closed to passengers - Wigston (Glen Parva), Blaby, Narborough, Croft, and Elmesthorpe. The last year of local service is listed below in Table 3.

Table 3

Weekdays			B	B	NB	B	CB	B	B		YB	B	B	B
										SO		SX	SO	
Leicester London Rd.	d	06 25	06 45	07 20	08 20	08 55	09 44	10 10	10 55	11 25	11 50	12 10	12 10	12 52
Wigston Glen Parva	d	06 32	06 52	07 27	08 27	09 02			11 02	11 32		12 17		12 59
Blaby	d	06 35	06 55	07 30	08 30	09 05			11 05	11 35				13 02
Narborough	d	06 39	06 58	07 33	08 33	09 08			11 08	11 39		12 22		13 05
Croft	d	06 44	07 02	07 37	08 37	09 12			11 12	11 44		12 26		13 09
Elmesthorpe	d	06 50	07 08		08 43				11 18	11 50				13 15
Hinckley	d	06 56	07 16	07 46	08 49	09 21	10 04		11 25	11 58	12 09	12 35	12 33	13 21
Nuneaton Trent Valley	a	07 05					10 12	10 30		12 05	12 17			
Nuneaton Abbey St.	a		07 27	07 58	08 58	09 30			11 34			12 46	12 46	13 32

Weekdays		NB	B	CB	B		B		NB	EB	B	B		
						SX							SX	
Leicester London Rd.	d	14 04	14 55	15 44	16 05	16 12	17 00	17 25	18 10	19 05	20 05	21 00	21 26	
Wigston Glen Parva	d		15 02		16 12	16 20	17 08	17 32	18 18	19 13	20 11	21 07		
Blaby	d		15 05		16 15	16 23	17 11	17 35	18 21	19 16	20 15	21 10		
Narborough	d		15 08		16 18	16 27		17 39	18 24	19 19	20 18	21 14	21 38	
Croft	d		15 12		16 22	16 32		17 44	18 28	19 23	20 22	21 19		
Elmesthorpe	d		15 18		16 28	16 38		17 50	18 34	19 29	20 27	21 25		
Hinckley	d	14 23	15 25	16 04	16 34	16 46	17 23	17 58	18 40	19 38	20 34	21 32	21 49	
Nuneaton Trent Valley	a			16 13		16 54		18 06		19 47			21 59	
Nuneaton Abbey St.	a	14 34	15 34		16 43		17 32		18 49	19 56	20 43	21 41		

Sunday		B	B	B	B	B	NB	B	PB		B
Leicester London Rd.	d	07 40	09 50	12 00	14 00	15 10	17 00	19 00	20 10	21 15	21 55
Croft	d							19 13	20 25	21 29	22 07
Hinckley	d	07 59	10 09	12 21	14 19	15 32	17 18	19 25	20 36	21 39	22 16
Nuneaton Trent Valley	a	08 06	10 16	12 29	14 26	15 43	17 26	19 36	20 46	21 49	22 26

B   To Birmingham New Street

EB   Ely to Birmingham New Street

PB   Perborough North to Birmingham New Street

CB   Cambridge to Birmingham New Street

NB   Nottingham Midland to Birmingham New Street

YB   Yarmouth Vauxhall to Birmingham New Street

Weekdays				B	B	BN		BC	B	B	BN	B	B	
									SX	SO	SO	SX		SO
Nuneaton Abbey St.	d			07 57	08 30	08 53	09 27		10 26	10 26	11 26	11 26	12 24	
Nuneaton Trent Valley	d	06 17	07 33					09 45					12 30	12 47
Hinckley	d	06 29	07 43	08 06	08 40	09 02	09 36	09 56	10 36	10 36	11 36	11 36	12 40	12 56
Elmesthorpe	d	06 34	07 48		08 45	09 07				10 41			12 45	13 01
Croft	d	06 40	07 53	08 13	08 51	09 12			10 47	10 47	11 43	11 43	12 50	13 06
Narborough	d	06 44	07 57		08 55	09 16	09 45		10 51	10 51	11 47	11 47	12 54	13 11
Blaby	d	06 48	08 01		08 59	09 20			10 55	10 55	11 51	11 51	12 58	13 15
Wigston Glen Parva	d	06 52	08 04	08 21	09 03	09 23			10 58	10 58			13 01	13 18
Leicester London Rd.	a	07 00	08 13	08 26	09 12	09 32	09 57	10 13	11 05	11 05	12 00	12 00	13 09	13 27

14

Weekdays		B	B	B	BY	B	SX	B	BN	B		BN	BN	B	B
Nuneaton Abbey St.	d	13 26	14 26	15 28		16 25		17 36	17 52	18 26		19 16	20 32	21 15	22 19
Nuneaton Trent Valley	d				16 02		17 00		17 58		18 50				
Hinckley	d	13 35	14 35	15 39	16 16	16 34	17 11	17 46	18 13	18 36	19 01	19 26	20 42	21 25	22 29
Elmesthorpe	d		14 40			16 39	17 16						20 47		
Croft	d	13 43	14 45	15 47		16 44	17 21		18 20	18 43	19 12		20 52		
Narborough	d	13 47	14 49	15 50		16 48	17 25			18 47	19 17		20 56		
Blaby	d	13 51	14 53	15 54		16 52	17 29		18 26		19 21		21 00		
Wigston Glen Parva	d	13 54	14 56	15 57		16 55	17 32		18 29	18 52	19 24		21 03		
Leicester London Rd.	a	14 01	15 03	16 05	16 41	17 03	17 41	18 03	18 37	19 00	19 31	19 43	21 10	21 44	22 46

Sunday		B	B	B	B	B	B	B	B	BP	B	B
Nuneaton Trent Valley	d	08 07	10 54	12 19	13 40	15 07	16 22	17 53	19 47	20 57	22 12	22 53
Hinckley	d	08 17	11 03	12 29	13 51	15 17	16 32	18 03	19 57	21 07	22 22	23 03
Croft	d				13 56		16 39	18 10	20 04	21 14	22 29	
Leicester London Rd.	a	08 34	11 20	12 48	14 10	15 34	16 51	18 22	20 16	21 26	22 41	23 21

B   From Birmingham New Street
BY Birmingham New Street to Yarmouth Vauxhall
BN Birmingham New Street to Nottingham
BC Birmingham New Street to Cambridge
BP Birmingham New Street to Peterborough North

In the week following closure of the intermediate stations, the 'Leicester Mercury'sof 5th March 1968 reported - "That Blaby Councillor Mr D. Williams had formed Friends of Narborough Station whose aim was to press British Rail to reopen Narborough station at peak hours". Whilst at a meeting of Hinckley Council the councillors stood for one minute silence to mark the closure of Elmesthorpe and Croft stations. The Councillor for Elmesthorpe commented that the train service was regular yet the bus service was non existent, and it had dire consequences for the district.

Demolition of all closed station buildings commenced in January 1969, Narborough was retained, while Blaby Rural Council sought to reopen it.

After a long battle Blaby Rural Council persuaded British Rail to reopen Narborough station, for an experimental three year period. The Council to pay £15,000 in the first year and approximately £16,000 for the following two years. The passenger service commenced on 4th January 1970 with four trains each way. Passenger traffic had grown so much that by January 1973, no council subsidy was required.

Other than Summer Saturday trains, all cross country trains between Birmingham and Cambridge or Norwich were a mixture of diesel multiple units, Swindon Cross Country (Class 120), BRCW (Class 104), Cravens (Class 105), Metropolitian-Cammells (Class 101) or even a Derby Suburban with no toilets (Class 116).

In 1974 the Summer Saturdays only 1050 Poole - Sheffield does not call at Nuneaton and uses the Nuneaton avoider. The first regular train to do so since 1968.

The Birmingham to East Anglia services reverted to locomotive hauled stock from .2nd May 1977. Six or seven trains were hauled by Class 31 diesels based at March (MR), and 25's, 37's and 47's appearing in place of the normal power. This innovation cut journey times, increased passenger comfort brought a steady increase in customers. An invitation in this timetable was the 1316 Norwich to Birmingham New Street ran non stop from Leicester to Birmingham and ran over the Nuneaton avoider.

Regular freight ceased from Enderby quarry in May 1976, and by March 1977 it was listed as out of use due to condition of track. The last public goods depot at Hinckley closed on 29th July 1979, however private siding traffic to the coal merchants continued into the 1980's. The Enderby branch was used for a time to store condemned steel tube wagons. The connection onto the branch at Narborough was taken out of use on 30th April, the pointwork was severed on 25th May 1980.

The 1316 Norwich to Birmingham New Street started to call at Nuneaton from 1st June 1981, and this ended a regular passenger train over the Nuneaton avoider line. It was then used by diverted North East - South West trains as required.

In 1985, Leicestershire County Council sort to ease congestion in Leicester City Centre. The scheme was to transfer car and bus passengers onto an under utilised local railways, by opening stations around the fringe of Leicester. The first station was to be at Wigston, and the County Council paid British Rail £135,000 to construct the station. Work commenced in January 1986. The new station to be named South Wigston and to be built where the Kenilworth Road footbridge crosses the line. Just to the east of the old Wigston Glen Parva station. The South Wigston station was a modern concrete platform with a bus type shelter on each platform. Linked by a ramp to the footbridge. The station was opened on Saturday 10th May 1986 by County Councillor Peter Hill, Chairman of Leicestershire County Council.

South Wigston was initially served by Leicester to Birmingham locals, and was an immediate success causing overcrowding with upto 400 people using the station daily. Additional trains were run between Leicester and Hinckley in the peak periods. The paytrain guard was unable to collect all fares between South Wigston and Leicester and to solve this problem a small cabin was provided and staffed during peak periods to sell tickets.

Regular locomotive hauled Cross-Country trains ran for the last Sunday 15th May 1988, they were replaced the next day by Metrocammell Class 156 Sprinter diesel units. The timetable was overhauled and relaunched with an hourly East Anglia - Birmingham service, from Leicester calling at Hinckley (alternate hours) and Nuneaton. Local stations were served by Class 150 sprinters on an hourly Coventry - Nottingham service. As a result South Wigston and Narborough service to and from Birmingham was reduced to peak hours only, whilst Hinckley's was reduced by half. The Summer Saturday's Birmingham to East Anglia remained locomotive hauled, although the number has been gradually reduced.

The number of passengers rose as the train service was improved and overcrowding was experienced on certain peak trains. Instead of increasing capacity peak fares were hiked up and some local fares doubled, to choke off and in some cases kill demand. The usage of South Wigston fell as it was much cheaper on the bus into Leicester.

Nuneaton Midland Jn to Abbey Jn closed to all traffic, when Nuneaton Midland Jn signal box was taken out of use on Sunday 8th March 1992 and Hinckley Signal box became the boundary box to Nuneaton power box. The withdrawal of passenger trains over the Nuneaton avoider has not been authorised as required in the 1962 Transport Act, is this another example of an illegal closure.

Leicestershire County Council have produced plans for the reopening of some intermediate stations at Blaby, Croft and Elmesthorpe in the future. This all depends on local authority funds, which will remain tight for the foreseeable future.

Freight had been reduced to a handful of trains when most of the surviving East Anglia to West Midlands freight was diverted via Loughborough. Croft Quarry is the only source of freight along this line, sending block trains to Bow Marshgate and Bishop's Stortford. The former London Midland Region Civil engineers have ballast trains to Crewe, Bescot and Washwood Heath. One coal train is booked from Toton to Three Spires Jn for Coventry Homefire plant, but can run as required. The Lindsey Oil Refinery to Bedworth LPG (Liquid Petroleum Gas) can run every day but Sunday.

Nuneaton
(Trent Valley)

A well filled three car BRCW diesel multiple unit (Norwich Set 82) is seen leaving Nuneaton Trent Valley station with the late running 13.15 Birmingham New Street to Norwich cross country service on 21st August 1976, the last year of passenger discomfort on this service. Meanwhile on Platform 5 the 09.15 Paignton to Nottingham holidaymaker train hauled by 47254 will follow the unit to Leicester. *(Michael Mensing)*

A two car Derby lightweight diesel multiple unit arrives on Platform 5 of Nuneaton (Trent Valley) station with the 4.10 p.m. local from Leicester (London Road) on 11th March 1961. *(Michael Mensing)*

Nuneaton Midland Junction signal box until recently acted as a boundary box to Nuneaton panel. The brick structure held all the electrical equipment. The junction marked the eastern end of the former Midland Railway branch from Whitacre Jn. *(N.D.Mundy)*

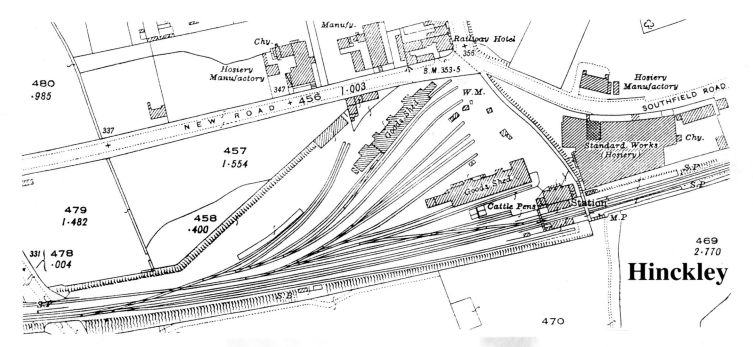

Hinckley

Ex Midland Railway 4F 43858 approaches Hinckley through driving sleet with a mixed goods train from the Nuneaton direction on 22nd February 1958. An Ivatt (beetlecrusher) 2-6-0 is shunting in the goods yard. A ex SR PMV parcels van is stabled in the parcels bay. *(Michael Mitchell)*

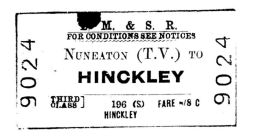

A two car Cravens dmu, with M50390 leading enters Hinckley on 3.10 p.m. Nuneaton (Trent Valley) - Leicester (London Road) local on 3rd June 1961. The headcode B5 is used for this service. The goods depot is well used and is full of vans and 16 ton coal wagons. Hinckley sttation signal box is on the left in the distance. *(Michael Mensing)*

Wet dull day Stanier 2-6-2T 40207 comes to a halt at Hinckley having just arrived with the 11.37 a.m. from Leicester (London Road) - Birmingham (New Street) on 16th April 1959. The train is formed of 7 coaches of various origins, the steam seeping from beneath the stock. LMR enamel signs have now replaced those of pre grouping origin. A station trolley is piled high with parcels waiting to be despatched all over the country. *H.B.Priestley/Geoff Hurst Collection)*

Fairburn Class 4 2-6-4T 42187 (15C) arrives at Hinckley with the 6.30 p.m. Leicester (London Road) - Birmingham (New Street) local on Sunday 14th April 1957. In the evening sun two passengers await to board this train. The LNWR wooden signs 'CROSS THE LINE BY THE BRIDGE' are still in place and have not been replaced by LMR maroon enamel plates. The 'down' platform still has its round corrugated iron roof. *(Michael Mensing)*

A three car Cravens dmu stands in Hinckley station on a Birmingham (New Street) - Leicester (London Road) - Nottingham (Midland) train on 21st March 1961, this service has been allocated B5 as its headcode. A wooden waiting shed has been provided to the east of the bridge carrying the public footpath over the railway. Wooden station seats have been placed along the platform, each with the station picked in metal letters. The platforms are still light by gas lamps, to which maroon enamel totems have been attached. *(D.T.Thompson)*

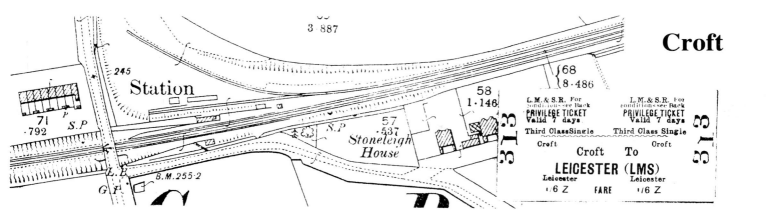

Croft

PRIVILEGE TICKET Valid 7 days | **PRIVILEGE TICKET** Valid 7 days
Third Class Single | Third Class Single
Croft | Croft
Croft To |
LEICESTER (LMS) |
Leicester 1/6 Z | FARE | Leicester 1/6 Z

*(right)*Croft station on 22nd August 1959 looking east towards Croft signal box, the station was a simple affair with the booking hall and waiting room located on the Leicester bound platform and heated by coal fires. Whilst on the Hinckley bound platform the LNWR provided an open waiting shed. It was light by gas lamps, but had disappeared by now. The LMR maroon totems are attached to the gas lamp standards. The goods depot was located behind the main station building, and only had a very small wooden shed. In the a line of coal wagons are positioned opposite the signal box. *(H.B. Priestley/G. Hurst Collection)*

*(below)*An occasional runner on a Sunday is the 1657 Croft to Bow Depot (London) train, seen here leaving Croft ECC behind 60010 'Pumlumon Plynlimon'belonging to FAXN - Construction. TO based at Leicester. On the right is the ECC shunter, and on the left is Croft Signal box, now only one of three mechanical boxes left on this line. *(Steve Turner)*

Elmesthorpe

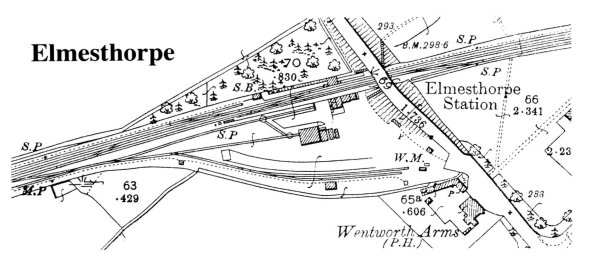

(below)Elmesthorpe station six years later looks a totally different picture, the remaining LNWR signs have been totally replaced by BR enamel, although the steps remain for the low platform. Its signal box, now only controls the mainline, having now lost the goods yard, loop siding and connection into Stoney Stanton sidings. (H.B.Priestley/G.Hurst Collection)

(above) In May 1959, Elmesthorpe station has not changed much in its appearance. Most of LNWR signs are still in place, although the nameboard has become LMR maroon enamel, and totems have been added. The sign states this station also serves the villages of Barwell and Earls Shilton. A member of the station staff stands on the Leicester bound platform, and which also has a station trolley as well as a set of steps for use with the low platform. Note the unusual water tower at the end of the Hinckley bound platform. Note the signal post in the distance, the tall signal is for the mainline and the other is for access into Stoney Stanton sidings. (D.T.Thompson)

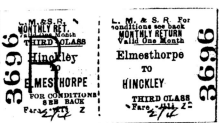

(left)The Leicester Railway Circle as part of its 21st Anniversary, it arranged a railtour on Saturday 27th May 1961, hauled by Ivatt 2-6-2T 41321 (15F) comes to a halt beneath a minor road bridge, on the Enderby branch. It was the first passenger train to travel over the branch. (Horace A.Gamble)

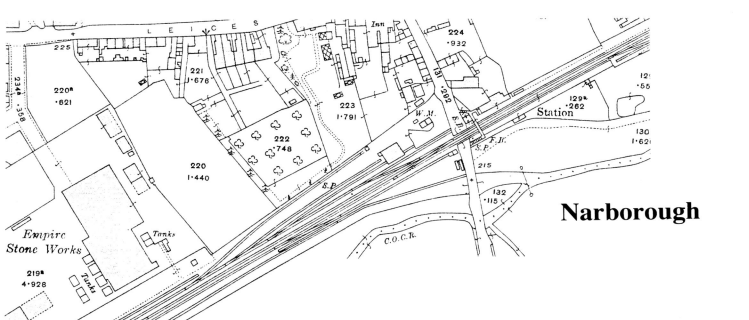

Narborough

The coal depot at Narborough was on the up side west of the station. On 14th June 1963 it had one loaded and one empty coal wagon. 8F 48619 is about to pass under the footbridge with an eastbound empty coal. Teddy Boston's Aveling & Porter steam roller is waiting at the level crossing gates, enroute from Blaby to Hinckley Hospitals fete. Today a coal merchant still occupies the site but is no longer rail connected. *(R.C.Riley)*

2nd - SINGLE	SINGLE - 2nd
Narborough (Leicester) to	
Narborough (Leicester) Blaby	Narborough (Leicester) Blaby
BLABY	
(M) 0/4	Fare 0/4 (M)
conditions see over	For conditions see over

1463   1463

In the 1950's, Narborough station had remained unaltered for a long time. The LMS added a target sign between the way out and the signal box. A wooden waiting shed had been provided on the down platform. Today only a bus shelter can be found on this platform. Surprisingly the iron footbridge is still in place and hardly altered. *(D.T. Thompson)*

The main station buildings of Narborough station as seen on 31st July 1963, were located on the Leicester (up) platform, and was built of local brick, it housed the booking hall (situated just behind the lady), a Ladies waiting room and a Gentlemens toilet. The general waiting room was a typical LNWR wooden structure (this is longer there). Narborough signal box remains and now acts as a boundary box to Leicester Panel. The fine metal footbridge still survives. The mains goods shed (now used by builders merchant) is located on the opposite side of the level crossing, and is well used, holding a couple of scrap wagons, as well as some coal wagons and a ballast wagon. G.Biddle)

(centre)The 1335 Norwich - Birmingham (New Street) 1M68 pulled by 31200 (MR) on 8 Mark 1 coaches, approaches the B582 roadbridge between Blaby and Narborough on Late Summer Bank Holiday 26th August 1974. In the background, the former GC mainline is carried over the LNWR. (Michael Mensing)

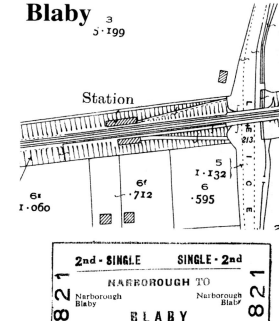

Blaby station was the only one along this line to be built on top of the railway embankment, and was approached by separate ramps from the A426. The platform was built of wood on concrete foundations. the first station buildings were of a typical pine box construction, but was burnt beyond repair by the Suffregettes on 12th July 1914. A larger wooden building was built in its place. Each platform had a booking office and waiting room, but the Leicester bound platform was much larger and was provided with toilets. Today the only remains are a line of fir trees on the southside of the line.(H.B.Priestley/ Geoff Hurst Collection)

Wigston (Glen Parva)

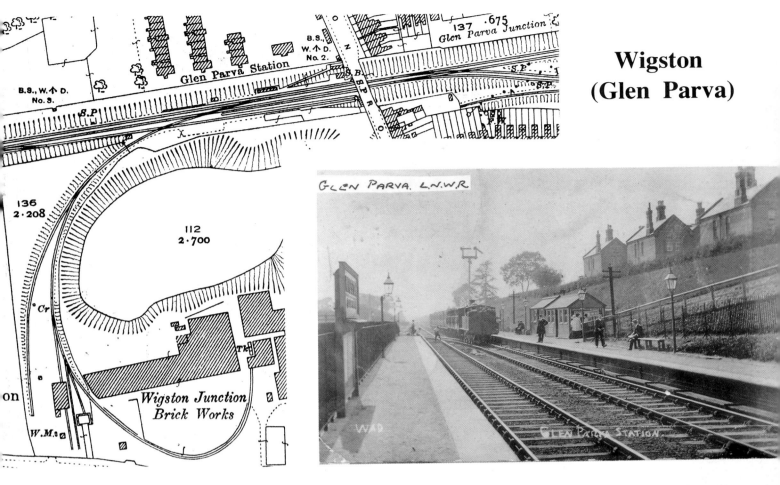

(above) The tall drop semaphore signal gives the road to the Webb 2-4-2T, hauling a Nuneaton (Trent Valley) - Leicester stopper into Wigston Glen Parva station, at the turn of the century. The train is formed of three vans and six non bogied passenger coaches. Several passengers await to join this service. A porter and the stationmaster place themselves into the correct position to carry out their station duties. At the Blaby end of the station, four members of the permanent way gang stand aside to allow the train to pass. The crossover leads into the goods depot. *(Lens of Sutton)*

(right) Stanier 2 cylinder 2-6-4T 42588 (15A) enters Wigston (Glen Parva) station with 7.40 a.m. Birmingham (New Street) - Nottingham (Midland) service on 3rd November 1962, this was in place of the usual dmu. A 4F is waiting to depart from Glen Parva Wharf goods depot with a train load of vans. *(Michael Mitchell)*

Wigston (Glen Parva) station as viewed east from the 'up' platform in October 1961. Little has changed since it opened, gas lamps light the platforms. The only thing seems to have changed is the signals, which have changed from LNWR drop semaphores to enamel semaphores. A trackman stands on the wooden crossing between the two platforms. Four passengers are awaiting the next westbound departure, the 'down' side had a simple wooden shed for use as a waiting room, with a ticket collectors hut at the bottom of the steps. *(Michael Mitchell)*

2nd - SINGLE   SINGLE 2nd

7799   7799

Wigston (Glen Parva) to

Wigston (Glen Parva)   Wigston (Glen Parva)
Leicester   Leicester
(London Road)   (London Road)

LEICESTER
(LONDON ROAD)

(M)   1/0   ▲ Fare   1/0   (M)
For conditions see over   For conditions see over

8F 48053 is throwing out exhaust as the engine works hard to pull its train of loaded coal wagons west through Wigston (Glen Parva) station on 27th June 1959. Wigston (Glen Parva)s booking hall is located next to the roadbridge, it was a small prefabricated wooden structure. A member of staff has 'green fingers' as can be seen by the garden that clothes the bankside next to the ramp. Glen Parva Junction signal box controls the junction the curve to Wigston South Junction. *(H.B. Priestley/G. Hurst Collection)*

On 26th June 1965, 8F 48699 (15E) has just passed a modern co-actor signal as it approaches Glen Parva Junction, with its trainload of coal, probably on its way to Ham Halls Power station. *(Michael Mitchell)*

South Wigston

The Leicester platform at South Wigston as seen from the Narborough platform, through the arch of the footpath. This platform is straight and is connected by a sloping ramp. Just beyond the next bridge is the site of Wigston Glen Parva station. *(Geoff Hurst)*

A pair of Class 150/1 sprinters stand on the westbound platform at the newly opened South Wigston station on Gala day 10th May 1986. There is long curving concrete platform, with a basic waiting shelter, a gently sloping ramp connects the platform with the public footpath and the overbridge. Station lighting had not yet been fitted. Repeaters have been placed at the Leicester end of the platform, showing that this curve has a signalling blind spot. *(Fastline Promotions Ltd)*

(below) A hybrid dmu formed of a Cravens driving motor brake a BRCW trailer and driving motor passes Blaby Sidings as it rounds the curve at Wigston on the 4.30 p.m. Ely - Birmingham (New Street) on 12th June 1967. In the middle background is Wigston Central signal box, which closed in November 1967. This box controlled the ex Midland Railway flat crossing to Rugby and the spur onto Wigston South curve. *(Michael Mitchell)*

(above) Wigston North Junction marks the start of the LNWR South Leicestershire line, the signal box is ex Midland Railway. Fowler side window cabbed 42415 hauls the 9.18 p.m. Leicester (London Road) - Nuneaton (Trent Valley) stopper on 22nd June 1961, formed of 1 BG and 4 ex LMS coaches. The BG was the last LMS type of coach to survive. *(Michael Mitchell)*

Leicester (London Road)

Steam rises from Class 4 Fairburn 2-6-4T 42087 (15A) as it rests in Platform 1 of Leicester (London Road) station, having hauled the 1.20 p.m.(SO) 4 coach local from Nuneaton (Trent Valley) on a misty 7th December 1963. A large number of passengers have detrained and disappear into town for the Christmas shopping. *(Michael Mitchell)*

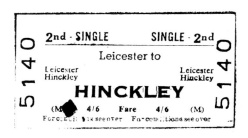

The high overall roof of Leicester (London Road) station is host to a Stanier Class 3 2-6-2T 40087 (2E) as it sits on Platform 3 and awaits to depart with the 4.10 p.m. four coach stopper to Nuneaton (Trent Valley) on 10th October 1960. *(Michael Mitchell)*

3. Nuneaton T.V. - Coventry

In November 1845 the London and Birmingham Railway (L&B) proposed to construct a branch line from Coventry to join the Trent Valley Railway near Nuneaton by a triangular junction. At the same time the Oxford, Coventry and Burton on Trent Railway company proposed to construct a cross country line, part of which would compete with the Coventry and Nuneaton railway. The L&B came to an agreement with the Oxford, Coventry and Burton company to withdraw their plan in favour of the L&B's.

The Coventry and Nuneaton railway was sanctioned by parliament on 3rd August 1846. It enabled the London and Birmingham railway to construct the following -
"London and Birmingham Railway (L&B) to make a branch from the L&B near Coventry to join Trent Valley Railway in Parish of Nuneaton. Commencing in Parish of St Michael and John the Baptist, Coventry. Pass through the parishes through Foleshill; Exhall; Bedworth; Chilvers Coton and Nuneaton. Divert tramway. The railway to cross the following roads listed on the plans in the - Parishes of St John Baptist No.62, and 66; Holy Trinity, Coventry No.1, 2, 42; Foleshill No.11, 49, 116 and Exhall No.12. Construct within 3 years.
Not possible to build or use branch A-B (Bulkington curve) on the plans."

The L&B joined forces with the Grand Junction Railway and the Manchester & Birmingham railway to form the London and North Western Railway Company in 1847. The new company was empowered under the Act of 2nd July 1847, to purchase shares Oxford, Coventry and Burton on Trent Railway company valued at £275,000, made up 20,000 shares at £13 10s each. The LNWR to provide locomotives and stock. Profits of undertaking £5 per annum with additional 2½% for depreciation of stock. Coventry and Nuneaton railway to have separate accounts. Three fifths of proprietors for LNWR to purchase.

During November 1847, the LNWR placed plans before parliament for two branch lines to tap the lucrative coal traffic of the South Warwickshire coalfield. Diverging off the as of yet unbuilt Coventry and Nuneaton railway. Parliament authorised its construction in the LNWR Act of 14th August 1848 -:
"A branch diverges off branch line of Coventry - Nuneaton railway in Parish of Exhall and terminate at or near certain colliery in Parish of Wyken, called Craven Colliery.
Authorise branch leaving Coventry - Nuneaton railway in Parish of Bedworth, near township of Bedworth and terminate in Parish of Bedworth at or near certain colliery called Mount Pleasant Colliery.
Level crossings on Craven Colliery branch in Parish of Foleshill Road No.6, in Parish of Sowe Turnpike No.1; Parish of Stove Road No.31; and Parish of Wyken Road No.5 on the plans. On branch to Mount Pleasant Colliery in Parish of Bedworth the Road No.8 on the plans and provide lodges where road crosses railway on the level.
Seven years to complete works. Company authorised to raise £34,000.
The Wyken branch pass over Coventry Canal and not to interfere with canal and to build bridge over Oxford Canal."

The opening of the Coventry and Nuneaton Railway was eagerly awaited by the local population. During the middle of 1850, the Coventry Herald received many letters enquiring when the line would open. The LNWR placed an advertisement in the 'Coventry Herald' on 23rd August announcing that the Coventry and Nuneaton railway would open on 2nd September. The advert listed the timetable and some fares, and it is reproduced in Table 1.

Table 1

Weekdays

		a.m.	a.m.	p.m.	p.m.	p.m.
Nuneaton	d	8. 0	10.30	1.15	3. 0	5. 0
Chilvers Coton	d	8. 8	10.38	1.20	3. 5	5. 5
Bedworth	d	8.14	10.44	1.25	3.10	5.10
Hawkesbury Lane	d	8.19	10.49	1.30	3.15	5.15
Longford & Exhall	d	8.22	10.52	1.33	3.18	5.18
Foleshill	d	8.25	10.58	1.35	3.20	5.20
Counden Road	d	8.35	11. 5	1.42	3.27	5.27
Coventry	a	8.45	11.15	1.50	3.35	5.35

Weekdays

		a.m.	a.m.	p.m.	p.m.	p.m.
Coventry	d	9. 0	11.35	2. 0	3.45	6.35
Counden Road	d	9. 5	11.40	2. 5	3.50	6.40
Foleshill	d	9.15	11.50	2.15	4. 0	6.50
Longford & Exhall	d	9.18	11.53	2.18	4. 3	6.53
Hawkesbury Lane	d	9.22	12. 2	2.22	4. 7	7. 2
Bedworth	d	9.26	12. 6	2.26	4.11	7. 6
Chilvers Coton	d	9.33	12.13	2.33	4.18	7.13
Nuneaton	a	9.45	12.25	2.45	4.30	7.25

No mention of the opening appeared in the local press, it must be assumed that no official ceremony took place. However within ten days of its opening the 'Coventry Herald' carried a letter complaining that -
1) There is no Sunday trains at all.
2) There are no day tickets, very disproportionate fares that are charged people from Foleshill are charged the same as Bedworth, either too little from Bedworth, which is three times as far, if fares were reasonable, three times the people would be found to use Foleshill to Coventry.

Passenger services were increased to meet demand, however disaster struck on 26th January 1857 when Spon end viaduct collapsed. The 'Coventry Herald' of that week reported that - "Early on Monday morning the neighbourhood around Spon-end became the scene of one of the most extensive pieces of spontaneous demolition ever witnessed, namely the very deliberate tumbling down of 23 out of the 28 immense arches forming the viaduct on the Nuneaton branch of the LNWR. This branch commenced in 1847, completed in early 1850. the viaduct in question extended to curve for a little south out of Spon-end to low meadows adjoining Windmill field, and was nearly a quarter of a mile in length, the construction of the line each way from viaduct, being an embankment of considerable height. The arches each 40 feet span built with red bricks; the pillars and outwall being stone, and this part of the undertaking was believed erected by contractor named Hayton, since dead. For the last year or two, the stretch of viaduct has been doubted be good judges. Soon after midnight on Sunday the first part of down fall commenced with the first arch and was followed by at short intervals until 6 a.m. on Sunday morning. No human life was sacrificed. The passing time for a coal train was within half an hour, but escaped danger. Traffic must now use the out of the way place Counden Road station."

A survey of the Warwickshire Coalfield of 1859 showed that the following collieries were in operation - Craven, Wyken, Hawkesbury, Bedworth and Griff. Exhall colliery had just commenced the sinking of the first shaft. The Nuneaton to Coventry line followed the outcrop of four coal seams from Griff to Chilvers Coton.

Four years elapsed before Spon end viaduct was completely rebuilt. On 1st October 1860 the LNWR reopened Coventry to Counden Road line to passenger and goods trains.

As part of the South Leicestershire Act 1860, the Midland Railway (MR) obtained running powers over the LNWR Nuneaton - Coventry branch. The MR did not exercise its powers until 1st September 1865 and served most sidings along the line.

The LNWR proposed in November 1876, to build a short branch to serve the collieries to the southwest of Nuneaton around Griff. The branch railway was authorised in the LNWR New Lines Act of 28th June 1877.
"It enabled the company to construct a railway of 1 mile 1 chain and 50 links, from the Coventry to Nuneaton railway, commencing by a junction in the Parish of Chilvers Coton and terminating in the Parish of Nuneaton, at a point 266 yards south east of Nuneaton Colliery at Blacktree Gate and 640 yards south east of a farmhouse known as Haunchwood House. Five years to complete all works."

This branch opened for goods and mineral traffic on 22nd June 1881. By 1904 this short branch boasted two coal mines, an ironstone mine and at least three brick, pipe and terracota works, which used fireclay extracted from the base of the coal seam.

In 1883, Coventry Corporation Tramways extended its line onto Bedworth and entered into competition with the LNWR for the local traffic from Bedworth to Coventry. The LNWR opened a goods depot at Hawkesbury Lane on 21st May 1889. Counden Road station name was altered to the present spelling on 1st November 1894.

The LNWR and MR entered into a reciprocal agreement on 11th September 1899 over the access to the Griff and Stockingford branch lines. The MR could serve the Griff branch, and in return the LNWR would gain aceess to the MR's Stockingford branch.

Work commenced in September 1899 on building a short line to the east of Foleshill. This was a privately run railway and ran to Websters Brickworks, and followed the twisting Coventry Canal for most of its way. Traffic commenced in 1901. The exchange sidings signalbox was called Webster's Sidings. This private railway became the Foleshill Railway in 1904. Another siding was added to the line in 1905 when Lustre Fibres Ltd opened, this factory was a very lucrative source of traffic.

By the early 1900's the LNWR had decided that a solution to the bottleneck around Coventry station was needed. The company then submitted plans in November 1906, for a Coventry avoiding line. It would pass round the north and eastern outskirts of the city. The Coventry Extension railway was approved in the LNWR Act of 26th July 1907. It sanctioned the building of -

"A railway at Coventry 3 miles 43 chains 80 links. Commencing in the Parish of St. Michael without Coventry in the Rural District of Coventry by junction with the London and Birmingham Railway and terminating in the Parish and County Borough of Coventry by junction with Coventry and Nuneaton Railway.

Divert roads and footpaths No.9 and 10 in the Borough of Coventry, No.s 19 ,20 ,22 in the Parish of Foleshill. Stopup one footpath in Parish of St Michaels without Coventry. Acquire common lands known as Gosford Green of 2 acres 1 rod and 26½ perch and Stoke Heath of 3 acres 2 rods and 20 perch.

Midland Railway to have powers to the Coventry extension, by an agreement of 1st July 1892.

The company shall plant the embankment facing Gosford Green between Binley Road and Walsgreave Road with laurels or similar shrubs to the reasonable satisfaction of Coventry Corporation."

Work progressed very slowly on the new line. Pinley Junction signal box opening on 4th May 1913 and was later renamed Humber Road Junction on 26th July 1914. Three Spires Junction Signal box came into use on 28th June 1914 and the Coventry avoider opened on 10th August, six days after the outbreak of the First World War. Goods depots were opened at Bell Gosford Green and Bell Green. The later was used by the Coventry Corporation 3 feet 6 inches tramway to collect ballast and other materials. Ordnance Sidings Signalbox opened on 14th July 1916 and served the Admiralties Burlington Road depot as well as providing an eastern outlet from the Coventry Ordnance Factory on the Foleshill Railway.

The First World War gave rise to a significant growth of engineering works in the north western area of Coventry. In 1916 the LNWR decided to build a workmans platform between Coundon Road and Foleshill stations to serve these factories. The unadvertised halt opened on 12th March 1917 and was named Daimler Halt after the nearby works. It had two long platforms and each had a rudimentary shelter.

Wyken (Alexandria) colliery produced no coal in 1916 and was listed as abandoned in 1917. It was connected to the LNWR by a colliery line to Craven Colliery. At about the same time the Warwickshire Coal Company began to sink the last mine in the area at Keresley. Coventry (Keresley) Colliery commenced limited production in 1918 and reached full production in 1926. The Foleshill Railway became a subsidiary of Courtaulds in 1922.

The LNWR was absorbed with into the London Midland and Scottish Railway (LMSR) on 1st January 1923. Stanley Bros. Bedworth Charity colliery closed in October 1924 and followed by the abandonment of Craven colliery in October 1927. At the same time Longford Power Station was being constructed, and was officially opened on 31st October 1928, by the Mayor of Coventry - Alfred Joseph Makepiece.

The LMSR introduced its first new engine in 1928, their version of successful MR 2P 4-4-0 Compound and was soon followed two years later by the Fowler 2-6-2T. These new steam engines appeared on local passenger services. By the middle 1930's, Coventry based Armstrong Whitworth and Michelin had produced pneumatic tyred railcars and the LMSR ran trials on the Nuneaton, Coventry, Leamington and Rugby lines. It was said that these railcars were so silent, that you could not hear them approaching, and some people said it was because of this, they were too dangerous.

Exhall colliery was abandoned in October 1938, reducing the number of pits on this line to just four. The intensive German bombing of the City of Coventry in December 1940 destroyed so much of Coventry Tramways, that it was decided to close them down. The LMSR lost a major competitor for local passenger traffic from Bedworth to Coventry. Foleshill, Daimler Halt and Coundon Road stations served a host of war related factories and the LMSR undertook vital wartime work, bringing workers and materials to and from the factories.

The LMSR passed into the hands of British Railways (BR) London Midland Region on 1st January 1948. The new Railway Executive decided that Longford and Exhall would close to all traffic from 23rd May 1949. This station never had a public goods depot. Courtaulds at Foleshill hired ex L&Y 'Pug' 51204 five weeks from 12th December 1949.

Griff Clara pit ceased production in May 1955, but still appeared in RCH handbook of 1956.

The RCH handbook of 1956 listed four private sidings between the junction at Coventry and Coundon Road station ranging from cattle sidings, an abattoir to engineering works. Webster's Siding was used for exchanging traffic with the Foleshill Railway. Whilst at Foleshill, Whitmore Park Estate Co. had an extensive internal railway serving Dunlop Rim & Wheel Co., as well as Dunlop Rubber. West Midlands Gas Board had another siding between Foleshill and Hawkesbury Lane. The Griff branch served Griff No.4 pit, plus three sidings belonging to Stanley Bros. Brick & Tile Works, and Haunchwood Brick Tile Co.s sidings at Griff Brick Yard and Heath End. Griff Quarry still produced granite. Griffiths and Co and Anker Mills were still rail connected between Bedworth and Nuneaton. The line between Three Spires Jn and Humber Road Jn still retained its two public goods depots at Bell Green and Gosford Green, with private sidings of Fyffes bananas, Morris Motors and the Admiralty at Bell Green and Smiths Stamping works at Gosford Green.

The Foleshill railway served nine private sidings in 1956, such as Courtaulds, Coventry Cooperative Retail Society, English Electric Co.'s Coventry Ordnance Factory, Shell-Mex & BP, Webster Hemming (Brickworks), W.H.Jones, J.Morton and Redline-Gilco. Courtaulds Ltd hired ex L&Y 'Pug' 51218 (5B) during April 1956 to replace its own failed locomotive.

Daimler Halt appeared for the first time in British Railways Public timetables at the beginning of the Summer timetable on 12th June 1956.

From 2nd July 1956, the basic passenger service between Nuneaton - Coventry and Leamington was taken over by two coach push-pull sets hauled or propelled by Ivatt 2-6-2T locomotives - 41227/8/85, 41321 (Warwick) and 41226, 41322/3 (Nuneaton). They lasted until Sunday 16th November 1958, when Warwick shed provided 41285 for the last day.

The next day saw the introduction of Monument Lane and Ryecroft (Walsall) based diesel multiple units. One benefit of dieselisation was the introduction of a regular hourly interval service on weekdays and 2 hourly on Sundays. The former Midland Railway shed at Coventry (disused since 1904) was demolished on 22nd September 1959.

Griff No.4 pit closed in July 1960, the only source of traffic was from the brick and tile works. However this succumbed and the line from Griff Jn to Stanley Bros. (Heath End) siding closed to all traffic from 31st May 1961.

In March 1962, Nuneaton shed received six Class 4 Moguls and these locomotives soon replaced Ivatt 2-6-2T's on the morning and evening workman trains to Coventry. On 1st May 1962 the new light and airy Coventry station was formally opened.

By 1963, regular goods traffic over the Coventry avoider had been reduced to just two pick goods from Rugby to Nuneaton, and the 5.50 a.m. SX (6.35 a.m. SO) Willesden to Nuneaton empties. The impending electrification of the Euston to Wolverhampton line, decided its fate. The line was to close between Humber Road Junction to Gosford Green Goods on 7th October 1963, and Humber Road junction was to be taken out of use on Sunday 13th October, however this had been delayed and this proved very fortunate. The next day saw a Carlisle - Willesden goods derail at Shelton and block the West Coast mainline. All trains were diverted through Coventry, some goods trains traversed the 'closed' section of track. The following weekend saw the commissioning of the second stage of the Nuneaton Power box and Nuneaton No.1 signal box was closed. Mainline trains were diverted via Stechford and Coventry. The down connection at Humber Road Junction was severed on 10th November, followed two weeks later by the up connection. Stopblocks were erected 300 yards down the branch.

Gosford Green yard was host to some unusual locomotives a N.B. Type 2 D6123 (65A) was noted on a Linwood train, followed by a pair of Polmadie Type 1's.

The London Midland Region posted notices saying that it intended to withdraw passenger services between Nuneaton, Coventry and Leamington Spa Avenue from 2nd March 1964, the announcement was met with a storm of protest and the closure was deferred pending consultations. The public meeting was held on 20th March in Coventry. Seventy eight objections were received including most of the local authorities, as well as several works on the Nuneaton - Coventry section. Nuneaton Council stated that over 550 people used the service daily to and from their work, and during the week 14,000 passengers travelled on the line. It was stated that if 10,000 passengers used the line, it would be economic. The TUCC found that hardship would be endured for passengers between Nuneaton and Coventry. and recommended that this section be retained.

The Minister of Transport ignored the TUCC recommendation for Nuneaton - Coventry and approved the withdrawal of passenger services between Nuneaton - Leamington. However the Minister inserted a proviso that - 'If hardship could be proved they would reinstate the passenger service between Nuneaton and Coventry'

Posters appeared on all the stations between Nuneaton Trent Valley and Leamington Spa Avenue stating that all passenger services would be withdrawn from 16th November 1964. However at the last minute, objections were received about the proposed substitute bus service, and closure was postponed. The 17.08 Coventry to Nuneaton was the last regular steam hauled train on this line and was converted from a Nuneaton Class 5 to a Rugby Type 2 diesel on 16th November 1964. Two weeks later, Coundon Road goods depot was converted to a coal depot.

Local public goods depots at Foleshill, Hawkesbury Lane, and Bedworth were closed on 4th January 1965. The rundown of freight over the Great Central mainline in 1965 resulted in steeltrains from the Northeast being diverted through Burton, Nuneaton, Leamington to Banbury. Polmadie Type 1's had now become rare on the Rootes trains, the engines now being Rugby Type 2's and Willesden Type 1's.

Passenger services were withdrawn from Monday 18th January 1965. On the last day of service (Saturday), two car diesel multiple units plied between Nuneaton, Coventry and Leamington. Foleshill was still issuing LNWR privilege on the last day. The trains were only half full and mainly manned enthusiasts making a last trip. The 19.10 left Nuneaton Trent Valley with

fuel works next to Coventry colliery in 1965. A seperate single line was laid from Three Spires Jn to the works, and production was expected to start in late 1965.

From January 1966 the site of Bell Green goods was used to dump engineers spoil trains from Birmingham New Street hauled by Bescot 8F's or Midland Line diesels. Standard Class 5's were replaced by Bescot Brush 4's on the Coventry Colliery - Ham Halls PS trains during February. Nuneaton shed closed on 6th June and was the last depot operating with steam in the area, and its duties included the Stafford - Kilburn Parcels. The last steam workings were on Saturday 4th June, with Class 4 75018 on the Nuneaton - Coventry Parcels, and 8F 48320 on Nuneaton - Coundon Road pickup. BR/Sulzer Type 2's and English Electric Type 4's took over their duties.

The Gosford Green branch was reduced to being operated as a siding from 6th March 1967. All signalling and signal arms had been disconnected and removed. In July 1967, the Fyffes banana train commenced running from Barry Docks to the old stamping works siding at Burlington Road, next to the Coventry market. Murco opened an oil depot at Bedworth during November 1967, the terminal was located between Hawkesbury Lane and Bedworth on the westside of the line. It was served by three oil refineries at Thames Haven, Ellesmere Port and Lindsey.

As part of the closure, the Minister made a condition that if hardship could be proved, the Minister would consider the reinstatement of passenger services between Nuneaton and Leamington. Notices appeared in the local press in December 1967 asking for evidence to be passed to Warwickshire

Table 3

Weekdays			2 SX	SX				SO	SO			FSX	FO			
		a.m.	a.m.	a.m.	a.m.	a.m.	a.m.	a.m.	p.m.	p.m.	p.m.	p.m.	p.m.	p.m.	p.m.	p.m.
Nuneaton Trent Valley	d	6.37	6.55	7.20	7.40	8.10	9.20	11.10	12.36	1.10	2.30	3.10	4.20	5. 0	5.10	5.20	6.10	7.10
Chilvers Coton	d	6.41	6.59	7.24	7.44	8.14	9.24	11.14	12.40	1.14	2.34	3.14	4.24	5. 4	5.14	5.24	6.14	7.14
Bedworth	d	6.46	7. 6	7.29	7.51	8.19	9.29	11.19	12.45	1.19	2.39	3.19	4.29	5. 9	5.19	5.29	6.19	7.19
Hawkesbury Lane	d	6.50		7.33	7.55	8.23	9.33	11.23	12.49	1.23	2.43	3.23	4.33	5.13	5.23	5.33	6.23	
Foleshill	d	6.55	7.15	7.38	8. 1	8.28	9.38	11.28	12.54	1.28	2.48	3.28	4.38	5.19	5.28	5.38	6.28	7.28
Daimler Halt	d	6.59	7.19	7.41	8. 4	8.31							4.41	5.23	5.31	5x41	6x31	
Coundon Road	d	7. 1	7.23	7.43	8. 8	8.33	9.42	11.32	12.58	1.32	2.52	3.32	4.43	5.26	5.33	5.43	6.34	7.33
Coventry	a	7. 5	7.28	7.47	8.12	8.37	9.46	11.36	1. 2	1.36	2.56	3.36	4.47	5.30	5.37	5.47	6.36	7.37
Leamington Spa Avenue	a	7.25		8. 6	8.32	8.56	10. 5	11.55	1.21	1.55		3.56	5. 7	5. 0	5.56	6.13	6.57	7.56

Weekdays		SX	SO	SX	SX				FO	FSX		FO	FSX	SX		
		a.m.	a.m.	a.m.	a.m.	a.m.	a.m.	p.m.	p.m.	p.m.	p.m.	p.m.	p.m.	p.m.	p.m.	p.m.
Leamington Spa Avenue	d	6.40		7.45	7.45	8.10	10.15	12.15	1.35	2.15		4.15				
Coventry	d	7. 3	7.26	8. 7	8. 7	8.36	10.38	12.36	1.56	2.36	4. 5	4.15	4.36	5. 5	5. 5	5.28
Coundon Road	d	7. 6	7.29	8.10	8.10	8.39	10.41	12.39	1.59	2.39	4. 8	4.18	4.41	5. 8	5.13	5.31
Daimler Halt	d	7. 8	7.31		8.12			12o41			4.12	4.22	4x43	5.10	5.17	5.33
Foleshill	d	7.11	7.34	8.14	8.15	8.44	10.45	12.45	2. 3	2.43	4.16	4.26	4.49	5.13	5.24	5.37
Hawkesbury Lane	d	7.16	7.39	8.18	8.20	8.49	10.49	12.49	2. 8	2.48	4.21	4.30	4.54	5.18	5.30	5.41
Bedworth	d	7.19	7.42	8.22	8.23	8.52	10.53	12.53	2.11	2.51	4.26	4.34	4.57	5.21	5.36	5.45
Chilvers Coton	d	7.24	7.47	8.27	8.28	8.57	10.58	12.58	2.16	2.56	4.32	4.39	5. 2	5.26	5.43	5.50
Nuneaton Trent Valley	a	7.29	7.52	8.31	8.33	9. 2	11. 2	1. 2	2.21	3. 1	4.36	4.43	5. 7	5.32	5.47	5.55

Weekdays		FX	FO	SX	SO
		p.m.	p.m.	p.m.	p.m.
Leamington Spa Avenue	d	5.28	5.33	7.15	7.15
Coventry	d	5.55	5.55	7.36	7.41
Coundon Road	d	5.58	5.58	7.39	7.44
Daimler Halt	d	6x 0	6. 0		
Foleshill	d	6. 5	6. 5	7.43	7.48
Hawkesbury Lane	d	6.10	6.10		
Bedworth	d	6.13	6.13	7.51	7.56
Chilvers Coton	d	6.18	6.18	7.56	8. 1
Nuneaton Trent Valley	a	6.23	6.23	8. 1	8. 5

o Saturday excepted
x Saturdays only

few passengers and hardly anybody joined enroute, and this ended 114 years of passenger service. Diverted passenger trains still continued to use the line. Bell Green goods depot was closed to all traffic from 5th July 1965.

Parcels continued to operate thrice daily from Nuneaton to Leamington operated by Ivatt Class 4's, but by October 1965 it had become Class 2-6-0's. Freight facilities were withdrawn from Bell Green Goods on 5th February 1965. The National Coal Board started to construct a smokeless

County Council.

Rootes signed a contract with British Rail in May 1968, for the transport of car bodies to Linwood until the end of 1969. The trains to be made up of 22 sixty foot wagons. Two sidings at Gosford Green were to be extended to accommodate this traffic.

To facilitate improvements for the Rootes car traffic, the woodworking firm occupying the goods warehouse at Gosford Green were told to vacate the site by April 1968. A new source of traffic commenced on 6th September when car bodies as well as cars being delivered by rail from Linwood. The track layout had been altered and reballasted for this traffic. Redundant lighting towers from Water Orton Yard were erected in the yard to enable night unloading to start.

By October 1968, Bedworth station had been reduced to a bare platform, the signal box and sidings were all gone. The up platform at Coundon Road had been removed by January 1969. At the same time BR is said to have told the local councils, that they would run the service if they paid for it.

The remains of the Wyken Colliery branch serving Alderman's Green (Longford) power station together with the sidings serving it, were being lifted during May and June 1969. Traffic having ceased much earlier.

By early 1969 the goods traffic over the Gosford Green branch had dwindled to a daily Coventry to Gosford Green trip. Normally it was formed of an engine and van, and occasionally bananas were brought in for Coventry Market, as well as loads of timber. This would soon alter as work commenced that year on extensive alterations to Gosford Green goods depot. Four new roads were laid and concrete bases were in place by late summer. Rootes commenced using Gosford Green on 19th December to bring in car bodies from Linwood. Initially the new travelling crane was not in use. The terminal was officially opened on 11th February 1970 with the first train arriving from Linwood hauled by Class 47 1835. The initial traffic to be nine 650 ton trains per week. The old warehouse and the cast iron yard were demolished during April 1970. Massey Ferguson used Coundon Road Goods to despatch its tractors, but by 1970 it had reached such a high level that some traffic was transferred to Gosford Green.

Nuneaton to Coventry was used by cross country coal trains from Burton to Banbury, however this traffic was diverted through Saltley and Tyseley to Banbury on 19th July 1971 and greatly reduced through goods traffic. During December, Rootes started using the new car terminal at Bell Green, even though it was not completed. As there was no crossovers here trains had to travel to Gosford Green to run round.

The last source of traffic on the Foleshill Railway was the delivery of coal to fire the boilers at Courtaulds. This traffic ended on 29th February 1972, when the boilers were converted to gas fired. The coal strike meant that the traffic ended earlier.

In November 1974, NCB hired 08 3426 (DY) to cover for its out of action diesel. At the same time, the NCB loaned a BR brake van for the relaying NCB track from Three Spires Jn to Coventry Colliery.

Chrysler car traffic from Gosford Green ended on 1st July 1976, when the Avenger car production at the Ryton works ceased. Some of the plant was transported by rail to Linwood, leaving Gosford Green on 3rd July hauled by 47157 (LE). In the following year on 19th August a new notice appeared saying that Gosford Green was now - 'Freightliners Coventry Depot'.

Freightliners Ltd started running a nightly Gosford Green - Linwood train for the Chrysler traffic. The new daily service was officially inaugurated by the Mayor of Coventry on 7th December 1977, and was hauled by 25317 (BS). Some Linwood traffic started to arrive at Bell Green from January 1978. Both Gosford Green and Bell Green trains ran as one train to Nuneaton, here they split into two portions. During September 1978, Class 56 diesels commenced working test trains from Three Spires to Didcot. Gosford Green freightliner terminal was subject to vandalism and combat this, a close circuit t.v. came into use on 25th May 1979.

Toton 56's continued on MGR's until March 1980, when they reverted to 47's. Class 44's continued working Toton - Three Spires coal train until their withdrawal. Public traffic had ceased in August from Gosford Green Freightliner terminal, a limited amount of freightliner traffic continued into September 1981. The point work at Three Spires Jn was padlocked out of use. In its short life no booked passenger service used Three Spires Jn to Humber Road Jn, but was visited by three railtours RCTS 1957, SLS 1962 and RCTS in 1967.

Regular rail traffic from Newdigate colliery ceased on 26th June 1981 (the

track connection were removed in the following November) the colliery did not close until February 1982. Leaving Coventry as the last colliery on the line. Track lifting trains appeared on the Gosford Green branch 21st February, but the majority was not lifted until August 1982 and removed to Northampton for reuse.

The 1986 Speller Act enabled British Rail to reopen freight lines to passenger trains for an experimental period, and could withdraw the service without going through the statutory procedures of the 1962 Transport Act. Provincial railways used the Speller Act from 11th May 1987 to divert three trains from its Stafford - Rugby service, from Nuneaton to terminate at Coventry. Instead of a dmu appearing on the Stafford - Coventry service a 304/310's emu would appear. The train would have to be diverted via Rugby for operating reasons or the 1712 departure was occasionally dragged from Coventry to Nuneaton. Local passenger traffic increased and encouraged both Warwickshire County Council and Nuneaton & Bedworth Borough Council to contribute 50% of the cost of building Bedworth station. The station cost £200,000.

The new station at Bedworth was built on the site of the original station, and can hold a three car diesel multiple unit. The station has two concrete platforms, each with a waiting shelter (with tip up plastic seats), and is not staffed, tickets to be bought on the train. A car park is provided on a piece of rough ground.

On Tuesday 10th May 1988 a special train formed of Super-sprinter 155329 arrived at Bedworth at 11.22 and was met by a exploding detonators. The unit cut through a banner declaring 'Bedworth joins Midline'. Cllr. Harold De'Ath, Chairman of Warwickshire County Council and Cllr. Bill Olner, Mayor of Nuneaton and Bedworth unveiled a plaque on the station. They joined a local schoolchildren for a trip to Nuneaton. On the following Saturday MIDLINE held a gala day for local people to sample a 50p return to either Coventry or Nuneaton. Normal services commenced on 16th May, with the hourly Coventry to Nottingham and Coventry to Stafford locals calling at Bedworth. The station was later landscaped and some extra open air seating was provided.

Provincial railways revamped the Birmingham - East Anglia cross-country services from 16th May 1988, and introduced an hourly Nottingham - Coventry local service, worked by Class 150 sprinters.

British Coal announced in October 1991, that production would cease at Coventry colliery by the end of the month. This mine was the last to produce coal in this part of the Warwickshire coalfield. Coal was normally sent to Didcot power station. This was the last regular traffic to be despatched south through Coventry. A stockpile remained at the mine and was despatched after closure to Ironbridge Power Station. Homefire smokeless fuel plant next to Coventry colliery continued to operate.

West Midlands PTE was reported to have undertaken a feasibility study into the reopening of stations at Foleshill and Coundon Road.

Freight traffic over the line has dwindled to Lindsey Oil Refinery (LPG) to Bedworth and Toton - Three Spires Jn (for Homefire) originating from Clipstone and Calverton on Tuesday and Thursday, and Toton on other days. From Autumn 1992 a Three Spires Jn to Blackburn domestic coal started running, taking over from the now closed Wingerworth Coke Works near Chesterfield. Both collieries were to be closed at the end of October 1992, however closure was delayed until March 1993, when Calverton was reprieved for two years and Clipstone was mothballed. Where will the coal come from when these collieries cease production.

First generation diesel multiple units were to be found on the the Stafford to Coventry service and the odd Coventry to Nottingham or Lincoln service, until May 1993. These are due to be replaced by Class 153 units. Due to the closure of Arley tunnel, trains to Birmingham have diverted to terminate in Coventry, thus Nuneaton to Coventry has joined Regional Railways Express service for six months, but during this period of diversion, the Coventry - Lincoln service has been temporarily terminated at Narborough.

Nuneaton
(Trent Valley)

A two car Met-cam dmu enters Platform 1 at Nuneaton (Trent Valley) with the 4.15 p.m. local from Leamington Spa (Avenue) on 11th March 1961. *(Michael Mensing)*

(centre) Ivatt 2-6-0 46512 (5E) stands on Platform 1 of Nuneaton (Trent Valley) station with a single ex ENER 6 wheeled BG, on a parcels train to Leamington Spa on Tuesday 26th April 1966. *(Horace A. Gamble)*

London & North Western Ry.
Issued subject to the conditions & regulations in the Cos Time Tables Books Bills & Notices.

BEDWORTH TO
NUNEATON (L.&N.W.)
(B)

THIRD CLASS   125 (S.) NUNEATON   [Parly FARE -/3½

7153

18AU 9

(below) Looking down from Hinkley Road bridge on 5th September 1957, you would have seen Ivatt Class 4 2-6-0 43023 (2B) arriving into Platform 2 with a single brake from off the Coventry line. A diesel shunter is stood on the mini hump with an oil wagon. The stations tall lift tower has Trent Valley emblasoned on it. *(H.B. Priestley/G. Hurst Collection)*

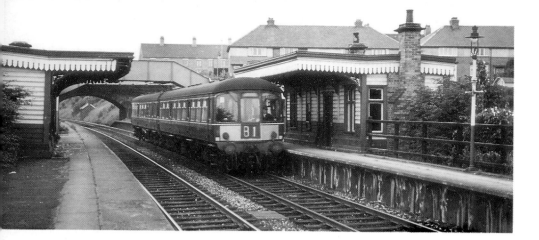

Chilvers Coton

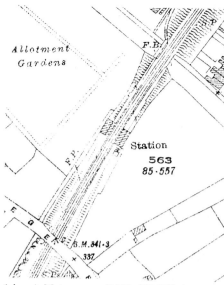

(above) Met-cam m 51178 (DMBS) is seen leaving Chilvers Coton Station with 6.10 p.m. Nuneaton (Trent Valley) - Leamington Spa (Avenue) on 12th May 1964. This station was light by gas lamps. *(Michael Mensing)*

(centre) A Park Royal dmu passes through the now closed Chilvers Coton Station with an ecs to Nuneaton from Coventry, to form a return engineering shuttle on Sunday 12th September 1965. Only the enamel totems have been removed since closure. *(Michael Mensing)*

(left) Hybrid dmu T043 (53171 53826) passes the site of Griff Jn with 1351 Coventry - Stafford local on 2nd June 1990. *(Steve Turner)*

(below) Griff Jn signal box on 13th June 1966. The brick building houses the electronics to interface with signalling of Nuneaton Power box. *(N.D. Mundy)*

(right)The original Bedworth station as pictured about 1900. Its a small wooden building, covered in advertisements. The entrance onto the platform is by a gate, next to northern side of the building. A handful of gas lamps (with Bedworth painted at the top of the glass) illuminated the platforms. A gentlemens toilet was built of brick and added onto the south end of the building. The platform has one simple seat set back to some shrubbery. A chest is waiting to be put on a train. A churn is placed next to the way out. The Goods depot is built of wood and is full of wagons. A horse drawn wagon is stood by itself in the yard. (Lens of Sutton)

(centre)The second station at Bedworth was a more substantial brick building, this view taken in June 1951, shows that the entrance to the booking hall was covered by a canopy. Only two notice boards are attached to the exterior of the building, and one of them is a bus timetable. The vents in the roof show where the gentlemens toilets were located. (R.E.G.Read/Courtesy G.Biddle)

(below) The second station at Bedworth was built on a slight curve, and the station staff have created a well tended garden. The signal box can be seen at the Nuneaton end of the platform. A couple of wooden wagons stand in the goods depot siding. (R.E.G. Read/Courtesy of G. Biddle)

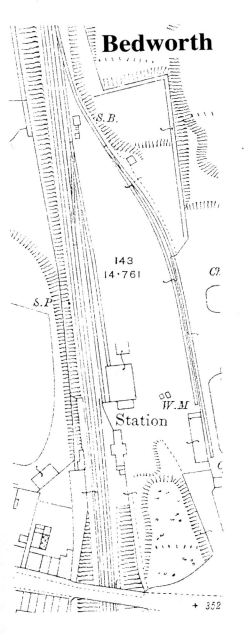

Bedworth

S.B.

143
14.761

S.P.

W.M

Station

+ 352

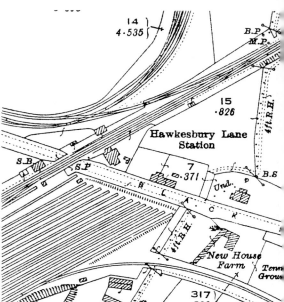

Hawkesbury Lane

(above)Bletchley based 8F 48656 hauls its coal train north through Hawkesbury Lane station on 10th October 1964. Note that the top lamp bracket has been removed and placed to one side of the smoke box, this alteration was aimed at stopping arcing of electricity from overhead lines and protecting the driver and fireman from electrocution. Note the line diverging to the right was used to gain access to Bedworth Charity colliery and is at present in use stabling small oil tanks. The gentlemens toilet was a small brick building just before 'down' signal. (Michael Mensing)

(centre)Hawkesbury Lane station sees the arrival of 2-6-4T 41214 on a Coventry bound push-pull train in September 1958. This shot shows the low platforms on either track. The station booking office is on located just behind the second passenger. A barrow sits outside the office. On the Nuneaton platform a wooden waiting shed has been provided, and a set of steps rests next to it. The station was light by gas lamps and paraffin lamps. (R.E.G.Read/ Courtesy G.Biddle)

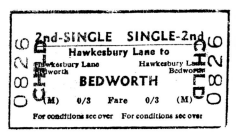

A Park Royal dmu (M56156 Leading) comes to a rest in Hawkesbury Lane station with the 1.10 p.m. Nuneaton (Trent Valley) - Leamington Spa (Avenue) stopper, on 10th October 1964. A closure notice has been posted by the booking hall door, ironically the local bus timetable is affixed next to it! (Michael Mensing)

Ivatt 2-6-2T 41320 stands in Bedworth station on 5th September 1957 on an afternoon two coach from Nuneaton (Trent Valley) to Leamington Spa (Avenue) local. The station was well constructed in brick and both platforms were provided with booking halls. This was probably because this station had no footbridge and the walk between the main booking hall and the Nuneaton platform would take at least 5 minutes quick walk. The fireman looks out of his cab as he takes a short breather before they depart. The goods shed looms behind the main station building and has been built of wood, its goods yard is full of 16 ton wagons, both newer metal and older wood builds. *(H.B.Priestley/G.Hurst Collection)*

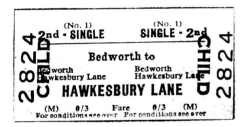

The first train to call at the rebuilt and reopened Bedworth station was the Nuneaton Railway Circle charter called 'Bedworth Boomerang' which ran early on Saturday 14th May 1988, formed of Tyseley set Class 117 T305 Pressed Steel three car suburban painted in non standard GWR chocolate and cream livery, it started at Nuneaton, called at Bedworth and ran out to Rugby via Coventry and direct to Nuneaton. The gala opening day started a bit later in the day with the Midline 'Monty the Hare' making an appearance. *(Fastline Promotions Ltd.)*

Stanier 2-6-0 Class 5 42981 approaches Newdigate Sidings from the south with an empty permanent way train composed entirely of Catfish Wagons, on 12th May 1964. The driver is just visible hanging out of the cab. This locomotive has had its top lamp bracket removed to the side of the smokebox to be able to work safely underneath the wires. On the horizon, the six cooling towers and three chimneys of Aldermans Green power station loom large over the area. *(Michael Mensing)*

(above)On 1st November 1990, a newly painted Hawkesbury Lane signalbox is slowly passed by 31233 and 31126 as they haul their empty tanks from Bedworth Liquid Petroleum Gas into the sidings to run round and proceed north to Lindsey Oil Refinery. The original station building has been converted to domestic use and painted white. *(Steve Turner)*

(below)Longford and Exhall station in the early 1900's, and it served a thinly populated area. The Hawkesbury Lane end of the station was the original station and the platform was constructed of brick and rubble, the station sign marks the southern limit of solid construction, here a wooden structure has been added to extend the platform for longer trains. The booking office is a small wooden building on the Coventry bound platform. A wooden waiting shed (with stove) and gentlemens toilets were provided on the Bedworth platform. Gas lamps provided the stations illumination. This station did not warrant the construction of a goods depot, however sidings were built on the northern side to provide extra capacity which this line lacked at its peak. *Lens of Sutton)*

Longford & Exhall

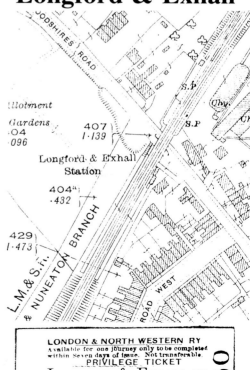

Bedlam Gates level crossing box is dwarfed by the towers of Foleshill Gas Works. This box controlled the gates and one signal each side protecting the crossing, and is about to be passed by a three car BRCW diesel multiple unit on a special passenger working between Coventry and Nuneaton on Sunday 23rd August 1981. These special train were common and connected in and out of the West Coast Main line when the direct line to Rugby or Birmingham was occupied by engineering work. This scene has been changed beyond all recognition, see the photograph below to see the change. *(Steve Turner)*

58017 propels empty MGR wagons of 11.26 from Garston Docks into the sidings at Three Spires Jn, on 11th April 1990. This scene has changed beyond all recognition with Bedlam Gates level crossing having disappeared under a new road scheme. The extensive crossovers and sidings have been rationalised, and the mechanical signalling is now just plain multi-aspect colour lights. *(Steve Turner)*

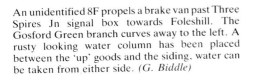

An unidentified 8F propels a brake van past Three Spires Jn signal box towards Foleshill. The Gosford Green branch curves away to the left. A rusty looking water column has been placed between the 'up' goods and the siding, water can be taken from either side. *(G. Biddle)*

(left)A Park Royal diesel multiple unit (MBS M50395 leading) comes to a halt in Foleshill station whilst working the 7.10 p.m. from Nuneaton (Trent Valley) - Leamington Spa (Avenue) local (the units blinds just show Leamington Spa, the original ones had the full station name on them). The station staff have whitewashed some bricks to spell the station name out in a little area given over to be a garden. The gentlemens toilets are a simple brick structure. A down line diverges just off the end of the Nuneaton platform. (Michael Mensing)

(centre)Foleshill station looking north on 8th April 1964. The station had few facilities, but had undergone alterations. A footbridge crossed the line at the southend of the station, a wooden building was located on the Nuneaton platform, it had two rooms, and had two fire buckets (on each platform). At a later date a long wooden shelter had been built on each platform, to accommodate the large number of workers that used the station from the areas engineering works. The station was still light by gaslamps. (D.T.Thompson)

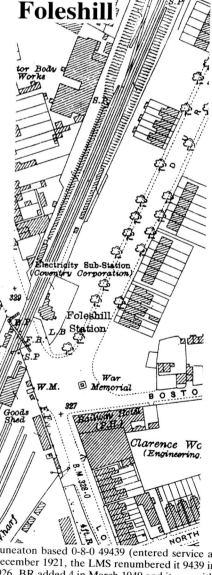

Foleshill

Nuneaton based 0-8-0 49439 (entered service as 36 in December 1921, the LMS renumbered it 9439 in April 1926, BR added 4 in March 1949 and it was withdrawn in December 1962) approaches Foleshill with a north-bound goods on 24th June 1961. The driver looks out of his cab to see what is going on. Here there is two goods lops as well as sidings serving the Whiteway Industrial Estate on the right. (Michael Mensing)

Daimler Halt

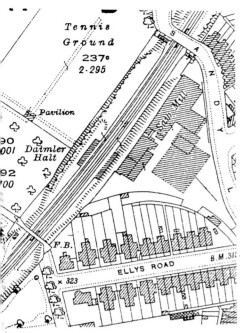

*(above)*Daimler Halt on a wet 1st June 1964, looked as though it had been closed, it retained the small booking shed at the base of the steps and the LMR maroon enamel station board, but nothing else. The only station to have been provided with good electric lighting, was reduced to three lamps placed at the top of the telegraph. Would you have forsaken the warm car or the bus to travel by rail from this station! *(D.T.Thompson)*

The 9.45 a.m. Euston - Birmingham (New Street) hauled by English Electric Type 4 D298 speeds north through the now closed Daimler Halt on Sunday 10th July 1966. Electrification engineering work saw this train diverted from Coventry to Nuneaton on its final leg to Birmingham. The road bridge sees a Coventry Corporation Atlantian bus passing over-.*(Michael Mensing)*

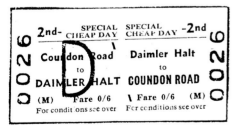

41226 departs from Daimler Halt with the 5.14 p.m. from Nuneaton (Trent Valley) three coach push and pull train (with two passengers alighting), and passes the six coach 5.28 p.m. from Coventry on 24th July 1957. The halt has two corrugated iron shelters and was light by electric lamps (non of the other station had such modern facility), with LMR maroon totems every two lamp posts. The Coventry platform was approached by a set of descending stairs, with two little cabins for issuing tickets. *(G.Biddle)*

Coundon Road station as viewed on a wet 1st June 1964. Colourlights had appeared on the Coventry platform. The station platforms had two different architectural designs, the oldest of the two was on the Nuneaton platform, it was a typical LNWR wooden structure with two rooms, with pitched slate roof, each room has as coal fires. A brick building with a flat roof is placed a little way along the platform for the gentlemens conveniences. While the Coventry platform has a modern looking slanted wooden roof. Because the station had low platforms a set of steps was provided for passengers who were unable to leap off or climb up onto the train. Gas lamps provide the lights as well as are used to attach the enamel totems. (D.T.Thompson)

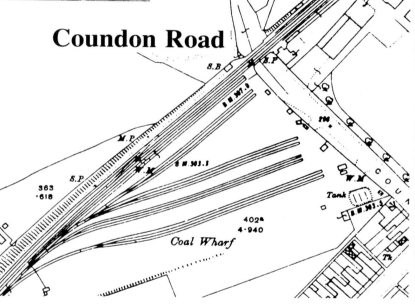

Coundon Road

(centre) Coundon Road Level crossing, coal yard and signal box as seen from the rear of a Met-cam dmu from Coventry - Nuneaton (Trent Valley) on 12th November 1960. (H.B. Priestley/G. Hurst Collection)

(left) A allover blue livery 3 car surburban dmu approaches Coundon Road Station signal box, with a shuttle from Coventry to Nuneaton on 12th September 1971 to connect in and out of diverted Euston - Birmingham trains. (Ron Kosys)

At about the turn of the century, a four 6 wheel LNWR passenger coaches have plunged down the embankment while shunting at Coventry and blocks Albany Road causing some interest to the locals. The brakedown train is in the process of rescuing the stock. *(Courtesy of Coventry City Libraries)*

Coventry

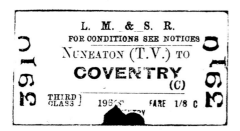

Black Five 45139 (2E) ambles through Platform 3 of Coventry station on 16th July 1962, the modernised station is now completely finished. A local dmu is standing in Platform 4 awaiting to depart to Birmingham (New Street). *(H.B. Priestley/G. Hurst Collection)*

Platform 4 of Coventry station on 22nd July 1961 is still in the throws of construction as Metro Cammell (DTC) 56344 arrives with the 1.15 p.m. from Leamington Spa (Avenue) to Nuneaton (Trent Valley), a man (in a cloth cap, arm band and horn) walks past the unit is acting as the watchman for the construction workers. He would blow the horn to warn staff of an approaching train. *(Michael Mensing)*

Brush Type 4 1842 comes off the Gosford Green branch and passes Three Spires Jn signal box with an empty cartic train to Linwood near Paisley on 4th August 1971. The headcode for the train was 4S32. *(Ron Kosys)*

*(centre top)*Bell Green signal box is boarded up out of use on 13th June 1966. This box controlled the avoider line as well as access into Bell Green goods depot. *(N.D.Mundy)*

*(below centre)*Ordnance Sidings signal box is derelict by 13th June 1966. The window frames have been destroyed and all the rodding has gone, but the frame is still in place. This box used to control the eastern access onto the Foleshill Railway. *(N.D.Mundy)*

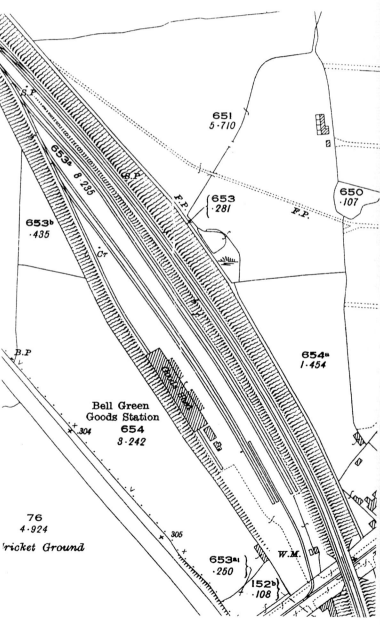

*(left)*Gosford Green Signal box is still in use on 13th June 1966, and controlled the line into the goods yard, and this was empty. *(N.D.Mundy)*

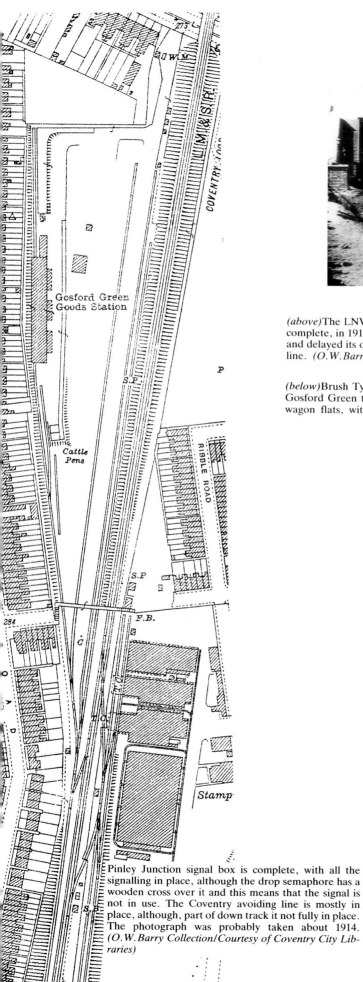

(above)The LNWR is still in the process of finishing Gosford Green Goods depot, it looks nearly complete, in 1914, but the outbreak of the First World War caused materials to be in short supply, and delayed its opening for three years. The footbridge carried the Humber Avenue path over the line. (O.W.Barry Collection/Courtesy of Coventry City Libraries)

(below)Brush Type 4 1958 arrives at Gosford Green light engine with headcode 0S32 to work a Gosford Green to Linwood car train. Gosford Green terminal is full of Hillman Hunter cars on wagon flats, with the container depot full of blue containers. (Ron Kosys)

Pinley Junction signal box is complete, with all the signalling in place, although the drop semaphore has a wooden cross over it and this means that the signal is not in use. The Coventry avoiding line is mostly in place, although, part of down track it not fully in place. The photograph was probably taken about 1914. (O.W.Barry Collection/Courtesy of Coventry City Libraries)

4. Coventry - Leamington Spa Ave.

In November 1839 plans were submitted by the Warwick and Leamington Union Railway for a railway from Coventry to Leamington. The plans were approved in the Warwick and Leamington Union Railway Act of 18th June 1842, and this allowed the railway company to construct a line from the London and Birmingham Railway at Coventry to communicate with the towns of Warwick and Leamington. The company to raise £130,000 in 25,200 £25 shares, and to be allowed to borrow £130,000. Company to erect bridges over the Glebe lands.

The railway to commence with a junction with London and Birmingham Railway in the Parish of St. Michael passing through the parishes John the Baptist; Strivehall; Stoneleigh; Kenilworth; Leek Wootton; Hill Wootton and Milverton and terminate at road between Warwick and Leamington in the Parish of Milverton. The railway processes no level crossings.

Railway to be constructed within 7 years. Milestones to be placed at ¼ mile intervals.

Power to lease to London and Birmingham Railway (L&B) and for the L&B to purchase the company.

That every steam locomotive engine to be used on the railway to consume its own smoke, if not, the company to forfeit £5 for each day this locomotive not used.

The London and Birmingham Railway used its options set out in the 1842 Act and sort to purchase the Warwick and Leamington Union Railway before it had been built. A meeting of shareholders was convened for 7th March 1843 and the members resolved that its authority be transferred to the London and Birmingham Railway. The Act of Parliament of 3rd April 1843 authorised the London and Birmingham Railways purchase of the Warwick Union Railway. It also authorised the raising of additional funds, raising of the maximum carriage weight limit from 4 tons to 8 tons. Plus the alteration of line levels.

On the 9th December 1844, the line between Coventry and Leamington was opened to passenger use. The 'Royal Leamington Spa Courier' gave the following description of the line - "The new branch road from this place, and just completed, is eight and three quarters in extent. The distance from the Leamington station to its approximating one at Kenilworth is about three miles and three quarters, hence to Coventry, five miles, a distance which, at an average rate of speed, is easily accomplished in less than 25 minutes, indeed the whole extent of the line to London, a distance of 120 miles, can now be effected in the short space of four hours and a half. The new branch is what is technically called 'a single line', and has cost in its construction £170,000 (although the original proposition for the execution it did not exceed £130,000); it has been completed thus far in the short space of eighteen months. When we look at the superior judgement, scientific skill, the beautiful gradients and easy curves that have been obtained.

Mr Stephenson has improved his predecessors (Mr Jackson Woodhouse) and by his plan brought us nearer to the ancient city of Coventry by 2 miles and a quater. The individuals who contracted for the execution of the work, were Mr Jackson, of London and Mr Cumming, of Birmingham, who fulfilled their engagements in a manner that reflects the highest credit upon them.

The station is about three quarters of a mile from Leamington, and a mile from Warwick. It is in the parish of Milverton, and borders close to the road leading to the County Town, and near to that spot well known to every octogenarian - the Gunnery Farm. The approach to it is good; and the yard, the right of which is planted with shrubs, is spacious, and well adapted for the reception of carriages, & etc. The main edifice, composed of blue brick, picked, and stone quoins, presents a very pleasing aspect. In the centre is a stone colonnade, supported by columns of the Roman Doric order of architecture. The interior is judiciously fitted up; there being, as usual, reception rooms for ladies and gentlemen, and officers for booking passengers and parcels, as well as, for the surveyor, superintendent, and engineer - all of them well adapted to their respective uses. The covered way at the back, which fronts the line of rail, is lofty and of sufficient width to afford every accommodation for passengers waiting for the arrival and departure of the trains. The house, at the edge of the yard, built after a similar style, is a residence of Mr Fowler, the Managing Clerk. The resident engineer, is Mr Docker.

The formal opening took place on Monday last, in consequence of the report made to the Board of Trade, by their Inspector of Railways, Major General Paisley, who had the previous week made an experimental trip throughout the new line, and pronounced it perfectly safe and satisfactory. As early as eight o'clock in the morning a large number of persons had assembled at the Station house, to witness the first train starting to Coventry;

and, although the thermometer stood many degrees below the freezing point, and a keen and cutting wind from the northeast together with a dense and gloomy sky, with every probability of a fall of snow, prevailed throughout the day, the crowd hourly increased; but the persons assembled seemed entirely absorbed in the important proceedings of the day, and to feel no discomfiture from the uptowardstate of the weather. The bustling scene around them received additional gaiety from the number of carriages, omnibuses, cars and various other sorts of vehicle that very minute or two came dashing up to the appointed place of rendezvous. During the day six trains passed to and from Coventry, consisting of six carriages. At twenty minutes past eight in the morning, one of those grim green and yellow monsters gave forth the preliminary warning note, which our friend, Sam Weller, describes - as two hundred and forty screams in one. And shortly afterwards the first train started and reached Coventry in twenty one minutes; whereas in times gone by it took an hour and half by posting. The bridges and embankments of the line were also crowded with spectators.

The branch line, which is of a singular construction, diverges by a steep curve out of the mainline at Coventry, and by means of a continued series of ascents, preserves an undulating surface to Leamington. The steepest gradient is about 176 feet, and that but a short length; the deepest cutting, not far distant from Gibbet hill, is 51 feet, and the highest embankment about 40 feet, near the line crossing the river Avon nigh Milverton. Leaving the Coventry station to the east, the traveller arrives at Stiviehall, the family mansion of the Gregories, long seated in this count, and then passing under two bridges, in the centre of which are conspicuously placed the family arms of the Leighs, neatly executed in large granite characters, the line progresses towards Kenilworth, where a view of that venerable and interesting monument of antiquity, the Castle - the pleasure of royalty -is obtained. Upon entering Kenilworth, there is a viaduct, beautifully situated, over the valley, and composed of seventeen arches of brick, faced with stone. The Kenilworth station house is a plain but substantial building, erected after the plan of some of those neat and cosy, but romantic domiciles, which are to be found in the wilds of Switzerland. Whilst the 'The Coventry Standard' describes Kenilworth station as - situated on the outskirts of the town, it is built of Kenilworth stone. The next prominent feature of the line is the viaduct over the river Avon, composed of nine arches, of 60 feet span, in the neighbourhood of the property of the Hon. C.B.Percy, and the 'Coventry Standard' describes it as beautiful! There is a timber bridge, of 50 feet span, uniting the roads of Leek and Hill Wootton, and Stoneleigh, with Guy's Cliffe.

Since commencement, no less than 2,500 persons have availed themselves of the great facilities which it presents.

The first timetable is given below -

Weekdays								Sunday	
		123	12	12	12	12	123	12	123
		a.m.	a.m.	p.m.	p.m.	p.m.	p.m.	a.m.	p.m.
Coventry	d	9.11	10.41	12.49	3. 0	4.44	7.19	9.45	12.55
Kenilworth	d	9.26	10.56	1.04	3.15	4.59	7.34	10. 5	1.10
Leamington	a	9.36	11.06	1.14	3.25	5. 9	7.44	10.15	1.20

Weekdays								Sunday	
		123	12	12	12	12	123	12	123
		a.m.	a.m.	a.m.	p.m.	p.m.	p.m.	a.m.	p.m.
Leamington	d	8.20	10.10	11.55	2.15	4.15	6.10	8.35	7. 0
Kenilworth	d	8.30	10.20	12. 5	2.25	4.25	6.20	8.45	7.10
Coventry	a	8.45	10.35	12.20	2.40	4.40	6.35	9. 0	7.25

Fares from Leamington

	Single	Day Tickets
First Class	2s.0d	3s.0d
Second Class	1s.6d	2s.0d
Third Class	0s.9d	None

Within one year the Leamington branch has spurned the company into more proposed railways as the Hudson railway mania reached its peak. Between 1845 and 1847, the company placed three lines for approval. The first was a 1 mile extension from Milverton to Leamington Priors (nearer Warwick than Leamington), and the Rugby and Leamington railway. Both lines were approved by the Acts of 27th July 1846 and 13th August 1846. The Leamington Priors railway allowed the company to raise £85,000 and build one level crossing at Leamington Priors. With five years to construct. This was soon followed by the widening of the line fronm Coventry to Milverton as well as a new line to Berkswell. This again was approved by parliament. The Act of 22nd July 1847 allowed the railway company to raise £230,000 to finance the necessary works and must be built within 5 years. The financial bubble burst and many authorised lines were abandoned in the more restrained times.

The line from Milverton to Rugby survived the collapse of confidence, construction costs were reduced and it opened to passenger use from 1st March 1851 (for more details see Chapter 5). Provision was made for a station to serve Leamington, but the residents of Leamington had to put up with passenger trains passing high overhead for nearly three years. But when the LNWR station eventually opened in February 1854 the local press ignored the event. Leamington suddenly appeared in the local press timetables and in Bradshaws. The first Leamington station was renamed for the first time as Warwick (Milverton). Leamington Spa opened to a weekday service of 10 arrivals and departures one of which was a mixed train. The service on Sunday was 3 arrivals and departures. The fare from Leamington to Kenilworth was 1s.0d *Express*; 10d *1st*; 6d *2nd* and 3½ *3rd* class and to Coventry 2s.0d *Express*; 1s.6d *1st*; 1s.0d *2nd* and 9d *3rd* class. Warwick (Milverton) was renamed to Warwick in July 1856 and reverted back in February 1857. However the public found that after October 1860 this station became Leamington Milverton.

On the morning of 17th June 1861 the line suffered a temporary closure when the bridge at Leek Wootton near Kenilworth collapsed.

It is minuted that the LNWR, proposed to erect a 2 road shed at Coventry in the fork of the Rugby and Leamington lines and was opened in 1866.

At Leamington the LNWR and GWR lines pass close to each other, and a connection was put in between the marshalling yards. It was a single line and came into use on 26th January 1864. During October 1875, Leamington Milverton was altered, deleting Leamington and the suffix - (Warwick) was added. This lasted until July 1876 when it became Milverton (for Warwick).

The LNWR placed plans before parliament in November 1880 for widening of London and Birmingham Railway between Milverton and Kenilworth and construction of a line from Kenilworth to Berkswell. Parliament approved the works in the LNWR New Railways Act 18th July 1881. "A Kenilworth to Berkswell Railway of 4 miles 47 chains 65 links in length. Commencing in Parish of Kenilworth by junction with Coventry - Leamington Railway to terminate in Parish of Berkswell terminating by junction with London and Birmingham Railway.

Milverton - Kenilworth widening. Commencing in Parish of Milverton - Leek Wootton to Parish of Kenilworth. Starting 500 yards north of road under railway in Parish of Milverton to 500 yards southwest of south end of Milburn Viaduct. All works to be completed in five years".

As part of the widening scheme the original London and Birmingham Railway station at Milverton (for Warwick) was closed on 13th October 1883. It was replaced by a new station just north of Warwick Road.

Milverton to Kenilworth widening was opened to all traffic on 2nd March 1884, and on the same day the Kenilworth Jn to Berkswell Jn opened to goods traffic. The 31st May edition of 'Royal Leamington Spa Courier' had a LNWR advertisement announcing the opening that the Leamington to Birmingham service would commence using the Berkswell line from 2nd June 1884. The advertisement is reproduced opposite. At the same time Milverton (for Warwick) was renamed to Warwick (Milverton) and this remained until 1952.

The LNWR decided to take advantage of the widening between Miverton and Kenilworth to erect a new motive power depot at Milverton, it was to be 6 road northlight type shed, and when opened it became a sub shed of Rugby with code 8W.

By the 1890's Coventry shed has been made into four roads, but this was not large enough to service the locomotives it was allocated. The LNWR doubled its size in 1897, using a shed that had been dismantled at Crewe and had a 42 foot turntable added.

On the 1st October 1910, the LNWR and Midland Railway started a joint passenger service from Nottingham to Leamington Spa Avenue, using both companies stock. It left Nottingham at 8.55 a.m and returned from Leamington at 3.20 p.m.

Leamington station was renamed Leamington Spa Avenue from 12th July

1913. The outbreak of the First World War brought home to the LNWR that the section of single line between Coventry and Kenilworth Jn was a bottle neck to vital war work. The company resolved to eliminate it. The provision of a signal box and a 245 yard long crossing loop at Gibbet Hill was brought into use in March 1916. In August 1918 the LNWR timetable changed Leamington Spa Avenue to become just Leamington Spa.

The LNWR was merged into the London Midland and Scottish Railway (LMSR) on 1st January 1923. By the 1930's the LMS had built new types of locomotives and these started to filter into this area, with the LMS version of the Midland 2P compound being one of the first.

The LMS introduced new shed codes in 1935 Coventry became 2F and Warwick 2E. In 1938 the LMSR agreed to improve facilities at Warwick and Coventry sheds. The 42 foot turntable at Coventry was replaced by a 57 foot one. At Warwick it was intended to erect a coaling tower, ashpits and add a new turntable, however only a 57 foot vacuum turntable was installed.

Nationalisation of the LMSR brought little change, with this line being brought under the London Midland Region (LMR). BR changed the codes of both Coventry and Warwick shed to 2D and 2C repectively. It was not until the 27th June 1951 that the LMR decided to add the suffix - Avenue to its station in Leamington, the Western Region having added - General to its station at the begining of the Winter 1950/1 timetable. Warwick (Milverton) was not renamed Leamington Spa Milverton until February 1952.

Work commenced in 1957, of rebuilding the roof of Coventry shed, the

LNWR roof was completely removed, and replaced by a new higher roof, to give better headroom. Whilst the shed under going this work only 5 engines could stable there, others were rehoused at Rugby or Nuneaton.

On 17th November 1958, British Railways decided to close both Coventry and Warwick sheds, although Coventry was retained as a signing on point. Coventry's allocation went to Rugby and Nuneaton whilst Warwicks went to the former GW shed at Leamington. Although closed, 2 diesel shunters were stabled inside Coventry shed at weekends during that winter. Both depots were used to stable withdrawn locomotives and stored diesel multiple units.

On 15th June 1959, passenger services ceased between Leamington and Rugby and with there demise saw the end of steam hauled passenger on the Nuneaton/Birmingham, Coventry and Leamington Spa services. They were replaced by Monument Lane and Ryecroft based Metropolitan Cammell; Birmingham Railway Carriage and Wagon Company (BRCW); Park Royal and initially Derby Lightweight diesel multiple units. Both Coventry and Warwick sheds closed and the engines were either condemned or transfered away. A few weeks later on Friday 3rd July saw the last SX 5. 9 p.m. Birmingham New Street to Leamington Spa Avenue over the direct line from Berkswell to Kenilworth. It was diverted to run via Coventry.

The electrification of the mainline from Rugby to Birmingham, required a diversionary route, and the Berkswell and Coventry to Leamington and Rugby lines were used regularly. The large steam engine, like Britannias, Royal Scots, Jubilees powered these trains as well as well the new diesel English Electric Type Fours.

Dr Beeching produced his infamous plan in 1963 for a rationalised British Railways and the Leamington, Coventry and Nuneaton line was listed to be closed. As a prelude the regular pattern Sunday service was withdrawn at the end of the Summer timetable on 8th September.

Soon followed by the closure of the public delivery depot at Leamington Spa Milverton on 11th November.

Closure notices appeared on all local stations stating that British Railways (London Midland Region) wished to withdraw passenger services from Leamington, to Berkswell, Coventry and Nuneaton. Soon objections had been received by the local TUCC. They instituted public meetings for the objectors to voice cases of hardship.

The local TUCC reported that it could not find that any hardship would be caused by the withdrawal of passenger services from Leamington Spa Avenue to Berkswell and Coventry. Final closure notices appeared stating that passenger services would be withdrawn from 14th November 1964. At the last minute, people objected to the Traffic Commissioners (who used to issue bus route licences) that the substitute bus timetable was not acceptable and the closure was temporarily withdrawn.

Substitute bus services were put in place in early 1965 and passenger services were withdrawn between Leamington Spa Avenue; Kenilworth to Berkswell and Coventry (Nuneaton) on 18th January 1965. See Table 3 for the final passenger service. This led to the closure of Leamington Spa Avenue; Leamington Spa Milverton and Kenilworth stations. The 'Royal Leamington Spa Courier' showed the last Leamington bound diesel multiple unit at Kenilworth Jn and said a few words on the end. Public goods facilities were withdrawn from Kenilworth two weeks earlier on 4th January.

Work commenced in November 1965 on a new connection between the former G.W.R and LNWR lines at Leamington, cutting over both companies goods yards at Leamington. This would enable freight trains onto the Coventry and Berkswell lines without having to reverse over the eastern connection at Leamington Spa General. On 15th May 1966 the new spur came into use and from that day the old eastern connection and the line through Leamington Spa Avenue could close. Parcels from Nuneaton and Coventry ran into Leamington Spa General station. Upon closure of Nuneaton shed, the thrice daily parcels train reverted back to being Leamington based, as well as changing to a Type 2 diesel. After September 1966, freight trains normally heading for Bordesley were diverted over the new spur and onto Bescot.

The daily Leamington to Nuneaton parcels was changed from locomotive hauled to a diesel parcels unit or if short a single car unit in December 1968. Work on demolishing Milverton and Kenilworth stations was advanced at the end of January 1969. At Milverton the timber platforms were being removed and the street level buildings gutted. Kenilworth station buildings were partially let to a building merchant, the platform mounds are being removed.

The Berkswell Loop was prematurely closed on 17th January 1969 by a derailment and it was found that Coventry to Kenilworth could operate without too much disruption to through freight. It was found that the Berkswell line was no longer required. The Berkswell end was severed on 16th March. It was found that freight could be diverted via Coventry without too much disruption. Public goods delivery continued at Leamington Spa Avenue until closure on 19th May 1969, however a private coal merchant continued to operate.

Lifting of the Berkswell loop was undertaken by George Cohen of Kettering and they commenced work in May 1970 using shunter 3983 (2A), stabling at night and weekends at Kenilworth Jn. During the weekend of 9th-10th December 1972, the line was extensively singled. Upon leaving Coventry the former double line to Gibbet Hill Signal box was reduced. Commencing adjacent to the end of the former carriage sidings. At Kenilworth Junction, the double line has been retained to form a crossing loop and ends approximately half a mile of Kenilworth station. From here to Milverton the line was singled. Signal boxes at Gibbet Hill, Kenilworth Jn and Milverton were closed. Probably one of the last L.N.W.R signals at Milverton was demolished. Coventry Power box operates the loop and the northern section whilst Leamington North controls the southern end of the line. By July 1973, all the redundant track as well as the remains of the Berkswell line were removed. The signal boxes at Gibbet Hill and Kenilworth Junction

Table 3

		B		SX		SX		SO						B
														SX
		a.m.	a.m.	a.m.	a.m.	a.m.	a.m.	a.m.	a.m.	p.m.	p.m.	p.m.	p.m.	p.m.
Nuneaton Trent Valley	d		6.37		7.20	7.40	8.10	9.20	11.10	12.36	1.10	3.10	4.20	
Coventry	d	3.22	7. 5	7.25	7.47	8.12	8.37	9.46	11.36	1. 2	1.36	3.36	4.48	5.19
Kenilworth	d		7.16	7.35	7.57	8.23	8.47	9.56	11.46	1.12	1.46	3.46	4.58	5.29
Leamington Spa Milverton	a		7.22		8. 3	8.29	8.53	10. 2	11.52	1.18	1.52	3.52	5. 4	5.35
Leamington Spa Avenue	a	3.44	7.25	7.43	8. 6	8.32	8.56	10. 5	11.55	1.21	1.55	3.56	5. 7	5.38

		FSX	FO			
		p.m.	p.m.	p.m.	p.m.	p.m.
Nuneaton Trent Valley	d	5. 0	5.10	5.20	6.10	7.10
Coventry	d	5.31	5.37	5.54	6.38	7.37
Kenilworth	d	5.41	5.47	6. 4	6.48	7.47
Leamington Spa Milverton*	a	5.47	5.53	6.10	6.54	7.53
Leamington Spa Avenue	a	5.50	5.56	6.13	6.57	7.56

B To of from Birmingham (New Street)

		B		B SO	SX	B SO	B SX					SO		FX	FO	B SX	SX	SO	B
		a.m.	a.m.	a.m.	a.m.	a.m.	a.m.	a.m.	a.m.	a.m.	p.m.	p.m.	p.m.	p.m.	p.m.	p.m.	p.m.	p.m.	p.m.
Leamington Spa Avenue	d	6.40	7. 7	7.45	7.45	7.57	7.59	8.10	9.15	10.15	12.15	1.35	2.15	4.15	5.28	5.33	6. 0	7.15	7.15	8.47
Leamington Spa Milverton	d	6.42	7. 9	7.47	7.47	8. 0	8. 1	8.12	9.17	10.17	12.17	1.37	2.17	4.17	5.30	5.35	6. 2	7.17	7.17	8.49
Kenilworth	d	6.50	7.17	7.55	7.55	8. 8	8. 9	8.20	9.25	10.25	12.25	1.45	2.25	4.25	5.38	5.43	6.10	7.25	7.25	
Coventry	a	7. 1	7.30	8. 6	8. 6			8.31	9.36	10.36	12.36	1.56	2.36	4.36	5.49	5.54	6.21	7.36	7.36	9. 6
Nuneaton Trent Valley	a	7.29		8.31	8.33			9. 2		11. 2	1. 2	2.21	3. 1	5. 7	6.23	6.23		8. 1	8. 5	

were demolished.

Coventry to Leamington reopened to passenger services on 12th May 1977. When Inter City diverted most of it Birmingham to Oxford, Paddington and South Coast trains over this route. The new route served two important passenger growth centres of Coventry and Birmingham International Airport. These trains now linked the area with Glasgow, Leeds and Newcastle to the north and Oxford, Reading, Paddington and the South Coast resorts. The site of Leamington Spa Avenue station was levelling in August 1977 to make way for redevelopment of the site into a garage.

The mainstay of passenger services was the Brush Class 47 and later in the 1980's the Class 50 worked alot of the Paddington trains. The Fifties disappeared in 1990, followed by the introduction of HST's on the Newcastle to Poole service in May 1991 and sixth months later on the Glasgow to Poole train. The ageing 47/8's now work the other passenger trains.

Freight traffic over this route has dwindled down to a handful of trains, the major traffic from Coventry Colliery to Didcot ceased in the autumn of 1991. Today only a Coatbridge to Southampton freightliner traverses this route on a Monday morning and it is used by MGRs diverted away from Saltley and Solihull line.

Regional railways proposed to extend the Lincoln to Coventry service through to Leamington and Stratford upon Avon. Rail privatisation seems to have shelved this project, which would have probably enabled Kenilworth station to rebuilt and reopened to passenger traffic.

LNWR 2-4-2T 46654 (entered LNWR service as 2130 in June 1893, and was renumbered by LMS to 6654, BR added the suffix '4' in December 1948, and was withdrawn in September 1953) comes to rest on Platform 1 at Coventry, having just arrived with a two coach push-pull stopper from Leamington Spa Avenue on 27th August 1953. *(Alec Ford)*

Rebuilding work is progressing at Coventry as Park Royal DMU, passes the base of the wall for the new Platform 2, with 2.10 p.m. Nuneaton to Leamington Spa (Avenue) on 25th February 1961. *(Michael Mensing)*

Coventry

On 19th April 1958, Ivatt Tank 41320 (2E) pulls away from Platform 1 of Coventry station with the 1.20 p.m. Nuneaton (Trent Valley) - Leamington Spa (Avenue) 2 coach push-pull local. A young train spotter records his observation in his book. At the same time a railwayman walks along the platform carrying his tea caddy and shoulder bag. A sight you do not see now. *(Michael Mensing)*

Banbury based WD 90148 passes through Coventry station on the middle road on a short coal train (made up of old wooden and newer metal wagons) on 19th April 1958. The signal attached to the overbridge has given the road onto the Kenilworth line, probably heading for the Western Region. *(Michael Mensing)*

Light engine 3545 has just come off the Leamington line into Coventry station in July 1948. The up platform extends east towards Coventry No.1 Signal box. *(G.Coltas)*

Coventry No. 1 signal box controlled the eastern end of Coventry station and the line to Kenilworth. By 22nd April 1958 the former LNWR signals had been replaced by more modern semaphores. The rebuilt Coventry shed was located behind the signal box and is a hive of activity. The LMS 57 foot turntable is hidden behind the box. (H.C.Casserley)

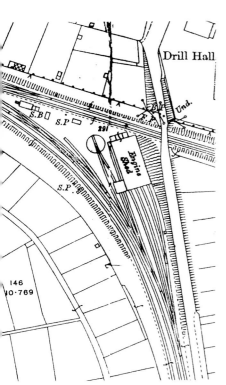

(centre) In 1953 the four road shed at Coventry is host to a variety of locomotives, the only number that can be seen is 42585 Stanier 2 cylinder 2-6-4T visible, other engines stabled here are a two ex LNWR 7Fs and a Cauliflower. Five empty coal wagons sit next to the shed, one wagon still has 'Firbeck' visible on the side, the colliery was located between Worksop and Doncaster. Rebuilding work commenced in 1957, with the old LNWR roof being replaced by a lighter and much higher structure. (G.Coltas)

BR rebuilt the 1897 shed with a brick walls and replaced the roof, On 22nd April 1958, the former LNWR locomotives have been replaced by an Ivatt Class 2 2-6-0, LMS 4F, 8Fs. The Ivatt Class 2 is being coaled using the conveyor located above the tender. Next to this locomotive is the water column and two enginemen are talking to each other. The rails of the LMS 57 foot turntable can be seen on the left. This depot was closed later this year on 7th November. H.C.Casserley

Inter City reopened the Coventry to Leamington Spa line to passengers on 2nd May 1977. Diverting most of its Birmingham to Paddington and South Coast trains this way. On 28th May, 47484 'ISAMBARD KINGDOM BRUNEL' climbs away from Coventry with the 16.38 Birmingham (New Street) Paddington train, composed of six Mark 2 coaches and 1 Mark 1 Buffet, and it is about to pass under A444 roadbridge. *(Michael Mensing)*

(above) This fine stone railway bridge is called 'The Coat of Arms Bridge' and is located just south of Coventry. A coat of arms has been carved in the stone, and is believed to belong to the Gregory family. *(H.C. Casserley)*

(left) Nearing its journeys end, Black 5 44771 excellerates away from under Stoneleigh Road bridge with a Summer Saturday Llandudno - Leamington Spa (Avenue) train on 17th August 1963. *(Michael Mensing)*

On Sunday 29th April 1962, the signalman returns to Kenilworth Jn signal box having passed to the driver of 8F 48559 (2A) the token for the single line to Gibbet Hill. The engineers train having been just propelled off the Berkswell line. *(Michael Mensing)*

An ex LNWR 18" Goods (better known as Cauliflowers) 0-6-0 8450 (Entered LNWR service as 1476 in March 1898 and withdrawn as 58381 in June 1952) on a train from the Coventry to Leamington Spa (Avenue) enters the double track section at Kenilworth Jn, the fireman looks back at the box after handing the token for the single line section from Gibbet Hill to the signalman. (R.S. Carpenter)

English Electric Type 4 D255 with narrow yellow warning panel, excellerates away from Kenilworth Jn with the diverted 10.13 a.m. Birmingham (New Street) - Euston express on Sunday 6th December 1964. The train consists of BR Mark 1 coaches except the first carriage is an ex LNER Gresley BG. The Berkswell branch diverges left and was regularly used at night to stable Royal trains on visits to the Midlands. (Michael Mensing)

(below) Rebuilt Royal Scot 46158 'THE LOYAL REGIMENT' (21C) is working hard as it pulls the 9.40 a.m. Wolverhampton (High Level) - Euston away from Berkswell along the Kenilworth Jn. This train was diverted on Sunday 4th September 1960 away from the Coventry area because of electrification work. (Michael Mensing)

A 4F 4360 lets off its whistle as it eases a coal train round the curve at Kenilworth Jn on the Berkswell line in the 1930's. The front wagon belongs to the LNER (Letters NE used) and other private owners wagons include the Beeston Coal Company. (R.S. Carpenter)

A pair of Cauliflowers leave Kenilworth with a seven coach local train to Nuneaton in the late 1930's. The exhaust smoke from the engines shows that the rear engine crew are working hard and providing most of the power. The loop line connects into the goods depot and is protected by a ground frame. Whitemoor brick works is on the left (today it is covered by a 1960's housing development. (G.Coltas)

LMS 4F 4350 passes a tall LNWR co-actor semaphore (for drivers to get a long distance view of a signal) as it approaches Kenilworth station with a southbound Target 49 coaltrain in 1938. All the wagons are private owner and appear to be from different places. The siding to the right serves Whitemoor brickworks. (G.Coltas)

A pair of light engines 8459 (withdrawn April 1937) and an unidentified 4F head north through Kenilworth station in 1937. The Cauliflower has a metal box perched on the tender The down platform still has its gas lamps all in tact, however this not the case on up platform. Two wagons are stabled in the goods yard, both lines are very well used. Kenilworth box was unique in the area, having being built above the station canopy to enable the signalman a clear view in either direction. R.S.Carpenter)

Kenilworth

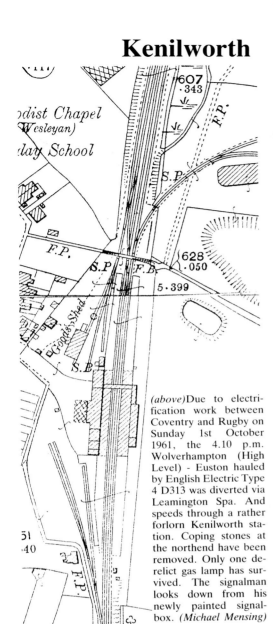

(above)Due to electri-fication work between Coventry and Rugby on Sunday 1st October 1961, the 4.10 p.m. Wolverhampton (High Level) - Euston hauled by English Electric Type 4 D313 was diverted via Leamington Spa. And speeds through a rather forlorn Kenilworth sta-tion. Coping stones at the northend have been removed. Only one de-relict gas lamp has sur-vived. The signalman looks down from his newly painted signal-box. (Michael Mensing)

(centre)A derelict Kenilworth station is about to be passed by no heat 47355 on 1521 Liverpool (Lime Street) - Poole train on 29th July 1978. Only part of the up platform has been removed, and surprisingly the foot-bridge remained. The station buildings and goods yard have been let to a builders merchant. (Michael Mensing)

A pristine LMS 3 cylinder compound 1113 (2A) has just arrived at Kenilworth with a late evening stopping train to Leamington Spa (Avenue) on 28th August 1936. The station roof is covered with asbestos sheets, with a few roof lights on the Coventry bound platform. Beneath which a barrow is piled high with parcels. (G. Coltas)

(above) On 1st April 1990, 50036 'Victorious' haules the Sundays only 1513 Paddington - Wolverhampton train over the River Avon viaduct at Hill Wootton (between Leamington Spa and Kenilworth). This class could be seen working any Paddington - Birmingham trains from May 1976 until July 1991, when they were transfered away from Old Oak Common depot. (Steve Turner)

Old Milverton is passed by 0-6-2T 6890 (entered service as 16 in November 1899, and the LMS renumbered it in June 1927, withdrawn in December 1945) pilots 0-6-0 8430 north, with a seven coach stopper in 1938. (G Coltas)

A pair of original 2 car Derby Lightweight diesel multiple units climb away from the Avon viaduct between Kenilworth (church tower visible above line on horizon) and Old Milverton on Sunday 11th May 1958 whilst working 5.22 p.m. Nuneaton (Trent Valley) - Leamington Spa (Avenue) service. These units were used on fillin turns away from there usual routes. (Michael Mensing)

8F 8111 and 'Cauliflower' 8450 work hard to bring their train up the climb to Old Milverton with a late afternoon 8 coach Leamington to Nuneaton stopper in the summer of 1938. The tall distant co-actor built to be visible by the driver of an 'up' train, before he reached the summit of the climb from the River Avon viaduct. *(G. Coltas)*

The LMS tried out experimental railcars from various manufacturers and here Railcar No. 1 passes Old Milverton with a northbound late afternoon local passenger in 1936. Passengers entered the railcar through the central sliding doors. A footpath crosses the line by means of an underbridge. *(G. Coltas)*

The original stationmasters house at Milverton (built in 1844) is now used for non railway domestic use. The railway is located behind the wall. *(Bryan Hicks)*

An ex Midland Railway 4-4-0 2P 40413 comes onto Warwick shed and is passing the unusual shaped tank on a sunny June 1951 evening. In the background the top of the ex LNWR Warwick signal box is visible. *(G.Coltas)*

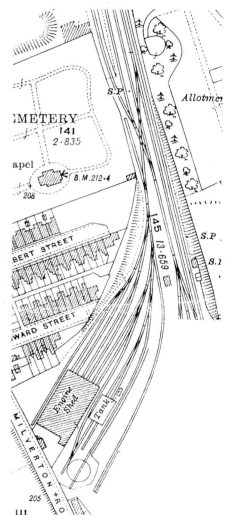

(centre) Warwick depot was a standard north-light shed and was built with six roads to house at least 12 engines. In May 1948 a grimy LMS Fowler 2-6-2T 44 (later BR 40044) sits outside the depot, with the number only visible after its has been partly cleaned. Letters LMS can only just be seen. Two engines just appear out of the gloom, probably a Webb tank and a 7F 0-8-0. *(G.Coltas)*

BR Standard 4-6-0 73003 is standing outside Warwick Shed on Sunday 29th April 1956. The LMS provided a 60 foot vacuum operated turntable Some coal wagons are stabled beneath the large water tank. Two sets of push-pull stock are stabled on the mainline line side of the depot.*(Michael Mensing)*

Leamington Spa
(Milverton)

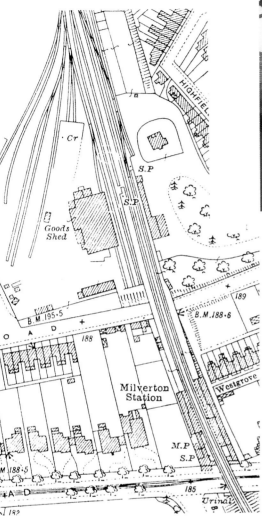

(above) 8556 0-8-0 passes through Warwick Milverton with a southbound coal train in 1937, made up of local colliery wagons. The LNWR constructed this station 200 yards to the south of the original, and used wood for all buildings except for the booking hall at road level. *(G Coltas)*

(centre) Former LNWR G2 9409 heads north through Warwick Milverton station in 1937. The bridge marks the boundary between the first (flagstone) and second (wood) station platforms. Note the curve on which the second station was erected and the bi-directional signal at the south end. *(G. Coltas)*

Milverton station was approached by a road level booking office, and by 1st October 1967 (over two and a half years after closure), the BR sign had been removed from above the booking hall entrance. Midland Red has its bus timetable attached to the corner of the building. The platform canopy still survives as do the enamel totems. *(T.J.Edgington)*

A pair of Cauliflowers 8450 and 8513 (withdrawn as 58381 in June 1952 and 28513 in March 1950) climb away from Leamington Spa over the Princes Avenue Viaduct with at least seven coaches. On a local passenger train to Nuneaton (Trent Valley) in late 1937. *(G. Coltas)*

2nd—SINGLE SINGLE—2nd
Leamington Spa Avenue to
Leamington Spa A   Leamington Spa A
Leamington Spa M   Leamington Spa M
LEAMINGTON SPA MILVERTON
(W)   3d. Fare 3d.   (W)
For conditions see over   For conditions see over
0208   0208

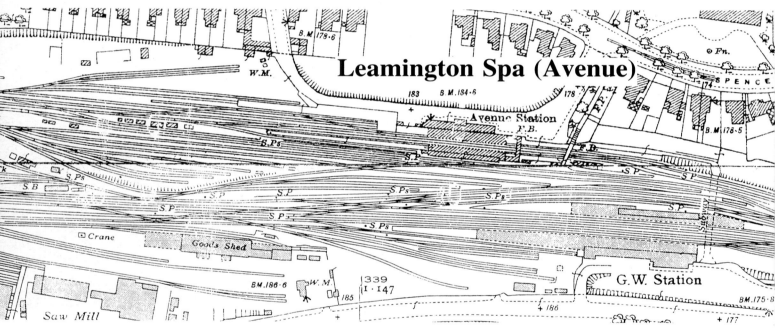

Leamington Spa (Avenue)

The western end of Leamington Spa (Avenue) station is a hive of activity with Belpaire boilered G1 0-8-0 8922 (started LNWR service as 1051 in November 1902, rebuilt to a G1 in September 1926 and a G2A in September 1945. The LMS renumbered it in September 1926. BR withdrew the loco in May 1959) acts as station pilot in the late 1930's. *(R. S. Carpenter)*

An end of an era as Ivatt Tank 41227 sits in Leamington Spa (Avenue) having brought the last passenger train - 7.54 p.m. from Rugby (Midland) on Saturday 13th June 1959. A group of passengers and well wishes mill around waiting for the departure to Leamington Spa (Milverton). A group of students can be seen carrying a coffin to mark the lines death. In the bay platform a Metrocammell diesel unit awaits its next service. From Monday 15th June the remaining passenger service to Coventry and Nuneaton (Trent Valley) will be taken over by the diesel units. Ending 115 years of regular passenger steam trains into this station. *(Michael Mensing)*

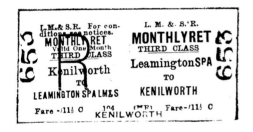

A green BRCW two car unit propells into the westbound platform, to form the 4.15 p.m. departure to Nuneaton (Trent Valley), on 24th June 1961. The western end of the platform has been extended using wood. A group of passengers are waiting to join the train as soon as it arrives. Note that the station is still being light by gas lamps and that the Gentlemens toilets are suffering from a structural defect. *(Michael Mensing)*

Leamington Spa (Avenue) station buildings (built of light coloured bricks) remains intact on 8th April 1967, after over two years of being closed to passengers. The entrance to the booking hall was protected by a small canopy. *(T.J. Edgington)*

5. Leamington Spa Ave. - Rugby Midland

The Rugby and Leamington Railway company submitted plans for a railway linking the towns of Rugby and Leamington Spa in November 1845, this was to give a direct link from London to the Spa town. Work was sanctioned in the Act of 13th August 1846. - "Authorised the building of a line from the London & Birmingham Railway, commencing in the Parish of Rugby and terminating in the Parish of Leamington.

The company to raise the sum of £360,000 by the sale of 22,500 - £16 shares. To commence in Rugby, in field 17 and end in field 117 in the Parish of St Mary Leamington.

The railway to be constructed by the London and Birmingham Railway, to be leased to London and Birmingham Railway at a rent of 4%, with power to sell to London and Birmingham Railway.

Company not to obstruct more than half of High Street or continue any obstruction more than 12 weeks. Company to make proper approaches and avenues to proposed Leamington Station, approach road at same width of streets. Company to obtain consent of Commissioners of the Township of Leamington, 14 days notice to be placed in two Leamington newspapers.

The London and Birmingham Railway to provide locomotives and stock and raise £36,000, company allowed interest of 5%. Five years to complete."

Work did not commence straight away as the London and Birmingham Railway did not have sufficient funds for the work. The first timetables appeared in the December 1850 editions of the 'Rugby Advertiser' newspaper, three months prematurely, as the LNWR was expecting it to open by then.

In February 1851, the LNWR wrote to the Commissioners of Railways requesting an inspection to enable them open the line to passengers. Captain G. Wynne inspected the Rugby and Leamington branch railway on 18th February, and reported - "That it was 15 miles chains in length. The line was incomplete, inasmuch as the junction had not been made with the mainline. He therefore refused to allow the line to open." The company secretary Mr Charles Stewart, wrote back to the commissioners on 20th February and informed them that the junction with the mainline will be completed on Monday 24th February and will be ready for inspection the on Tuesday, the following day. The Directors are anxious to open the line to the public on the 1st March.

Captain G. Wynne reinspected the line on the 25th February 1851 and gave his report -"I have reinspected the Rugby and Leamington branch of the LNWR, the junction has been completed and I am of the opinion that the line may be opened with safety and for the conveyance of passengers.

Deviations have been made in constructing the line beyond the limits allowed by Parliament". He then listed seven alterations in the planned gradients. While at 9 miles 53 chains (from Rugby) an open cutting of 10 chains had been substituted for a tunnel.

The line is laid single throughout, except at the Rugby junction, where it is double for about half a mile. The works have constructed to carry double line of rails. The company to work the line with one engine only".

The company replied, that the unauthorised deviations of the line levels were necessary to pass over and under certain bridges. The explanation seems to have accepted, as the Railway Commissioners took no action.

The 'Royal Leamington Spa Courier' of 22nd February 1851 gave the following extensive description of the new line from Rugby to Leamington (Milverton) - "The line was examined by Capt. Wynne, the Government Inspector, on Tuesday Last. The new line which branches from the London and North Western trunk at Rugby, and joins the Coventry and Leamington branch at Leamington, is fifteen miles eight chains in length. The steepest inclinations, or gradients are 1:100; they occur, at first at about eight miles and a half from Rugby, from Marton to Hunningham Hill, secondly from Offchurch to the Radford Cuttings, and thirdly, from the projected new station at Leamington, to the Station already in existence. The cuttings and embankments contained the following - Hunningham Hill 247,260 cubic yards; Offchurch Hill 211,254 cubic yards; the soil of the former being very hard red marl, and the latter of the like material, with sand. The total quantity of earth excavated has been computed at 1,230,596 cubic yards. The character of the soil throughout is principally red marl, with the exception of between the second and sixth mile from Rugby, where the portion of the excavations made through strata of blue lias, blue and yellow, and yellow lias, and rock and clay.

The number of bridges on the line is thirty five, of which fourteen, are occupation bridges. Of these structures thirteen are formed of brick set in motor; nine brick set in cement; six of cast iron; two of wood; one of wood; and iron; three of boiler plates; and one of wrought iron lattice. There are five viaducts, respectively named - the Birdingbury, Ichene, Offchurch, Leamington and Leam containing in the whole sixty seven arches. The most prominent and interesting features of these various structures are the following :-

The Birdingbury viaduct is composed of five elliptical arches, each sixty feet span, for carrying the railway over the public road from Franton to Birbury, the river Leam, and the eel ponds upon the estate of Sir Theophilus Biddulph, Bart. At Hunningham, there has been constructed a wrought Iron lattice Bridge, for carrying the public road from Bascote, over the extensive cutting already described. It is 150 feet span remarkable for the lightness of its appearance, being an open network of slight bars, and rises to an elevation of fifty four feet above the railway. The bridge was erected by Messrs. Smith, Smith and James, of Leamington. The total cost of the bridge has been about £3,500; including brickwork, masonry approach roads and fencing.

The viaduct at Offchurch is opposite the entrance into Lord Guernsey's park. It is a well proportioned structure, consisting of five elliptical arches, each of sixty feet span, by means of which the railway is carried over the brook and the Warwick and Napton Canal. It is formed of blue Staffordshire bricks; the centre arch crosses the canal obliquely, at an angle of forty degrees, and faced with Derbyshire stone. In conformity with an agreement made with Lord Guernsey by the Company, this viaduct is of an ornamental character, and, from its great height, has a very striking effect.

The viaduct through the town of Leamington consists of forty one arches; the span over principle streets possessing considerable engineering interest. Those over Court street and Althorpe street are wrought iron tubular girders of forty two and sixty feet span respectively, showing much novelty in their details, especially in the mode employed of suspending the platforms, which is so arranged as to give the greatest possible amount of roadway with the least practical elevation of the line. They were tested by the Government Inspector, by placing two engines upon each, when the deflection was scarcely appreciable.

We now come to the most important feature of the line, namely, the Wooden Lattice Bridge, constructed across the main road in High street, Leamington, from the corner of Clemens street, where Copps's Royal Hotel originally stood, to the southern extremity of Bath street. This works exhibits consummate engineering skill, its design belongs to Mr Dockray, the resident engineer of the London and Birmingham Railway. Its strength had been thoroughly tested by laying upon it nearly three times (1,240 tons) the weight to which it was calculated it would every be subjected. The bridge, which is composed of two wooden lattice girders, running parallel to each other to an extent of 150 feet, is 17 feet in depth and 26 inch wide. The girders rest upon two massive piers, constructed of Derbyshire stone, which rise to an elevation of 22 feet above the level of the street, the clear distance between the buttresses being 138 feet 9 inches, - a span which is greater than that of any similar structure in the kingdom".

The Rugby and Leamington line opened to all traffic from 1st March 1851 and the first timetable has reproduced in Table 1 below -:

Table 1

Weekdays		a.m.	p.m.	p.m.	p.m.	p.m.
Leamington Spa	d.	8.45	12.10	3.15	6. 5	8. 0
Rugby	a.	9.20	12.50	3.50	6.35	8.30

Weekdays		a.m.	a.m.	p.m.	p.m.	p.m.
Rugby	d.	7.45	9.40	1.30	4. 0	7.10
Leamington Spa	a.	8.20	10.15	2. 0	4.30	7.40

Intermediate stations between Leamington and Rugby opened with little or no local press announcements. Each station suddenly appeared in the railway timetables published by the local press and were altered at the beginning of each month. Marton made its first appearance in the 1st January 1852 edition of the 'Rugby Advertiser', with a weekday service of 5 trains each way, taking 18 minutes to Leamington and 20 minutes to Rugby. Birdingbury appeared to open on 1st February 1853, with served by 5 trains to Rugby and 4 to Leamington. The new station in Leamington Spa possibly opened on 1st February 1854, appearing in Bradshaws and both Leamington and Rugby newspapers, the first station for Leamington was renamed Milverton. No ceremony was reported in any of the local papers. It was nearly twenty years, before a station was opened to serve Dunchurch, and appeared on 2nd October 1871, it was served by 7 trains each way on a weekdays and 2 on a Sunday to Leamington, with only 1 to Rugby. The Sunday service did not last long and had disappeared by 1883.

Traffic between Leamington and Rugby did not grow fast enough to warrant the doubling of the line until the 1880's. The first section to be doubled was from Rugby to Dunchurch and opened on 22nd March 1882. The 'Rugby Advertiser' newspaper of 17th February 1883 stated - ""That work had commenced on doubling Leamington to Marton and was expected to be completed by August." However that appeared to be optimistic as it did not open until 28th January 1884.

In the 1870's the LNWR provided a siding with two lines for Nelsons Lime Works of Napton, and it was located where the road between Marton to Birdingbury road passes beneath the railway. It disappeared off RCH maps by 1905, it would have closed as soon as the Weedon line opened.

Goods trains were exchanged between the LNWR and GWR at Leamington using a single line connection. This arrangement could not cope with the traffic, and the LNWR and GWR sanctioned works for a double track connection (facing Rugby) at the eastern end of Leamington Spa Avenue station. Goods trains commenced using the new spur from 10th July 1908. Trains had to reverse over the connection.

On 1st January 1923 the LNWR was absorbed into the London Midland and Scottish Railway (LMSR). This did not affect the locomotives working this line with 2-4-2T and 4-6-2T remaining on passenger and 7F's on goods. It was not until the 1930's that the dominance of LNWR engines was challenged by the introduction of the Fowler 2-6-2T on passenger work. In the 1930's a large number of Webb 2-4-2T were fitted for push pull (motor) operation. Various railcars were used in the 1930's on Rugby - Leamington - Coventry locals. All LNWR Precursor 4-6-2T's had been withdrawn by late 1941.

The line passed from LMSR control onto the London Midland Region of British Railways on Nationalisation and the motive power remained with motor fitted ex LNWR 2-4-2T and Fowler tank engines. Birdingbury was the first to lose its public delivery facilities from 3rd August 1953. From 1958 the push-pull workings passed into the hands of Ivatt 2-6-2T's.

As part of British Railways West Coast electrification plans it was proposed to electrify the line between Rugby, Leamington and Coventry. However due to financial stringency BR axed this proposal.

After the withdrawal of passenger services over the Daventry line, local rumour said that the Leamington to Rugby service was next, BR did not try to introduce a dmu service to cut costs, and in December 1958 the inevitable happened, the closure notices appeared. The local TUCC held a public enquiry in Rugby on 10th March 1959, and heard that Leamington Council objected on the grounds that it would affect its livelihood as a health resort, and British Thompson Houston in Rugby voiced fears about being able to recruit people from Leamington to work in Rugby. British Railways claimed that the line cost just under £16,000 per annum to run and receipts were only £4,600. B.R. would subsidize an additional bus service by some £3,000 per year and it would still save £8,000. The proposals were put back for further discussion. This did not prolong the life of the passenger service for much longer.

The Winter 1958-1959 timetable has been reproduced in Table 2 below -:

Table 2

down mainline and the bay at Rugby Midland station. There was an air of expectancy, a little sadness and much good humour on Saturday night, when British Railways - with the acquiescence of the Central Transport Users' Consultative Committee - ran their last passenger train over the direct line from Rugby to Leamington.

Cameras clicked and history conscious passengers hung from the carriage windows. A studious young gentlemen asked if he could right an inscription on the engine. "Yes", said the Authority. "So long as it isn't rude."

Somebody had a piece of chalk, and suddenly appeared the epithet "OH, SIR BRIAN".

The last train from Rugby was hauled by Ivatt Class 2 tank 41227 with shedplate (2C). Two push-pull sets, four carriages in all made up Driver C.Wright and Fireman G.Cooknell busily autograph books with commendable legibility from their cab aloft.

'The Leamington' received the right of way under an avalanche of cheering and waving. There was a long, rather plaintive wail on the whistle, two or three soft throated chuffs, and then a series of sharp explosions as 63 tons of engine made short shrift of the salute of six fog signal detonators. With more whistle - wailing and friendly waves from the signalman and his mate in Rugby No.5 box, which looked very London and North Western in the evening sunlight, we threaded our way through the maze of points to the neatness of the double tracked well - aligned and evenly graded line to Leamington. Then into the 50 m.p.h. run, with no slowdown for Dunchurch, where a little knot of people waived.

At Birdingbury, where there were a dozen or so waited, there were more photographs, and even the T.V. cameraman stepped down from his first class compartment. The guard waived his green flag. A woman waived a Red Ensign. More detonations under the wheels sent a heard of cows scampering to the corner of the field.

To the goodly crowd at Marton, where the station carpark accommodated five cars and a motor scooter, "Oh, Sir Brian" was barely discernible. Children and others posing for the innumerable photos on the buffer beam rubbed most of it away.

Everybody - except a dignified policeman - waved as the train chuffed off. From his window the T.V. man lunged over the loading gauge and made a photographic sweep at Marton outlined in faded London Midland Region maroon on the opposite platform.

Marton junction loomed up, with the Weedon line bearing away to the left, and a 50 m.p.h. speed limit sign. Talk on the train said this section had just been laid with the new British Railways standard flat bottomed rail.

Platform celebrations continued at Leamington Avenue. But the purists travelled onto Milverton, which was after all the terminal station for the Rugby service. They alighted at Milverton, held a brief inquest on the wooden platform and the carriages were shunted into the siding.

The last train from Leamington Milverton left at 7.35 p.m. hauled by fellow Ivatt Tank No.41285 and passed the last Rugby near Dunchurch. This engine returned light to Leamington."

Due to the electrification of the Rugby, Coventry and Birmingham line, regular occupation of the line was required by the engineers. From 1960 to 1965 trains from Birmingham to Rugby and Euston were diverted from

Weekdays				N								B
				SO	SX	SO	SO	WO		SX	SO	
		a.m.	a.m.	a.m.	a.m.	a.m.	p.m.	p.m.	p.m.	p.m.	p.m.	p.m.
Leamington Spa (Milverton)	d	7.0	7.47	10.25	10.32	11.50	1.0	1.38	4.30	6.20	6.36	7.43
Leamington Spa Avenue	d	7.5	7.53	10.30	10.37	11.56	1.5	1.42	4.35	6.24	6.44	7.50
Marton	d	7.17	8.5	10.42	10.49	12.8	1.17	1.54	4.47	6.37	6.56	8.2
Birdingbury	d	7.21	8.9	10.46	10.53	12.12	1.21	1.58	4.51	6.42	7.0	8.6
Dunchurch	d	7.27	8.15	10.52	10.59	12.18	1.27		4.57			
Rugby Midland	a	7.37	8.25	11.2	11.11	12.28	1.38	2.15	5.15	7.0	7.16	8.21

Weekdays						C				
				SO	WO	SO	SO	SX		
		a.m.	a.m.	p.m.	p.m.	p.m.	p.m.	p.m.	p.m.	p.m.
Rugby Midland	d	8.13	10.24	12.16	12.49	1.19	2.40	2.45	5.35	7.54
Dunchurch	d	8.21	10.32	12.24	12.57	1.27	2.48	2.53	5x43	
Birdingbury	d	8.26	10.37	12.29	1.2	1.32	2.53	2.58	5.51	8.9
Marton	d	8.30	10.41	12.33	1.6	1.36	2.57	3.2	5.57	8.15
Leamington Spa Avenue	a	8.42	10.53	12.45	1.18	1.48	3.9	3.14	6.9	8.27
Leamington Spa (Milverton)	a	8.49	10.57	12.49	1.22	1.52	3.13	3.18	6.13	8.31

B   From Birmingham New St. dep. 6.26 p.m.
C   To Coventry arr. 2.14 p.m.
N   To Northampton Castle arr. 8.58 p.m.
x   Saturdays Excepted

In the early 1960's the major source of freight was the Rugby Cement Works at Bilton, it received three or four chalk trains worked in as trips from Rugby line and returned empty to either Leighton Buzzard or Rugby. The only through freight was Boston to Cardiff; Willesden to Birmingham Curzon Street, in the early hours of the morning as well as a 8.55 a.m. Welham to Leamington. A local pickup ran between Rugby and Leamington serving intermediate public delivery sidings.

Rationalisation of wagon load traffic meant that most public delivery sidings were to close. Marton closed on 3rd July 1961, followed by Dunchurch on 2nd November 1964 and lastly New Bilton Wharf on 25th June 1966. By late 1964 the only traffic between Bilton Sidings and Marton Jn was a daily Rugby - Leamington trip and light engine movements. Coal trains for Rugby Cement Works at Southam was now the main source of traffic between Leamington and Marton Jn, but from 4th April 1966 it was closed to all traffic. Coal trains for Southam now ran via Rugby, however a full length train could not be runround by a locomotive at Marton Jn. Trains had to split at Rugby and worked in two portions, one in the morning and this returned with engine and brake, for the afternoon portion (except on Saturday).

Marton Jn signal box was closed on 4th July 1967 and track lifting between Marton Jn and Leamington began in early November, and by the 25th, all track had been removed. By 1968, Marton station had been levelled with only the platform edge being kept as a retaining wall. Both Birdingbury and Dunchurch stations survived as private homes, fenced off from the track.

On 3rd March 1968, the LNWR bridge over Leamington High Street was demolished and the girders removed for scrap. Three other bridges in Leamington suffered the same fate. The only remains of Leamington Spa Avenue was the subway and a footbridge. During October 1968 work commenced on singling the line between Rugby to Marton Junction, a crossover was installed at Bilton Sidings, and this severed the up line. Lifting of redundant track between Rugby and Marton Junction commenced in May 1969.

Coal trains to Rugby Cement at Southam was the only traffic west of Bilton Sidings. However this traffic had ceased by June 1985. The last train to Marton Jn was Fisons weedkilling train on 20th June haul by Bescot based 31247. Redland Tiles at New Bilton Works was the last source of traffic on the line, a 08 trip was worked from Rugby, but this traffic was sparse and ended with the demise of Speedlink in July 1991. The line remains insitu and is occasionally used by railtours.

Fowler design 2-6-2T 17 stands in Leamington Spa Avenue awaiting to depart with an afternoon local service to Rugby just before the Second World War. It consists of two coaches, with one compartment and one corridor carriage. The LMS target sign says it is just Leamington Spa. The wooden fencing had a number of enamel signs advertising Virol (a childrens tonic) and Camp Coffee (still available). (G. Coltas)

Exhaust and steam partially envelop 41227 (with British Railways painted on side of the loco) departs away from Leamington Spa (Avenue) past LNWR drop semaphore signals, with an eastward push-pull local in July 1951. The rear of General station with a locomotive partly visible. The former GWR Leamington Spa South signal box controlled the eastern connection between the GWR and LNWR lines. (G. Coltas)

(right) Precursor Tank 4-4-2T 6824 (entered LNWR service as 1523 with 3 ft 3 inch wheels, and was renumbered to by the LMS in February 1924 and was withdrawn in February 1940. It was one of the last two engines of this class) passes Radford Semele on a three coach Rugby to Coventry local via Leamington Spa in 1932. This class was introduced in 1906 for heavy suburban and branch line working, but was found to be too heavy for most branches. (R.S. Carpenter)

(above) Nuneaton based 8F 48504 throws up plenty of smoke as it works hard to climb up Offchurch bank with a coaltrain to Southam Rugby Cement Works from Nuneaton on 12th March 1966, during the final weeks of operation as a through line. (Bryan Hicks)

The Fisons weedkiller train is approaching Marton Jn hauled by 31247 on 20th June 1985, having trundled down the line from Rugby Leamington Jn, at a line maximum speed of 30 m.p.h. Here the engine will round the train by using the loop line on the left, and then continue to Southam. This was the last train to use either line. (Ron Kosys)

Marton

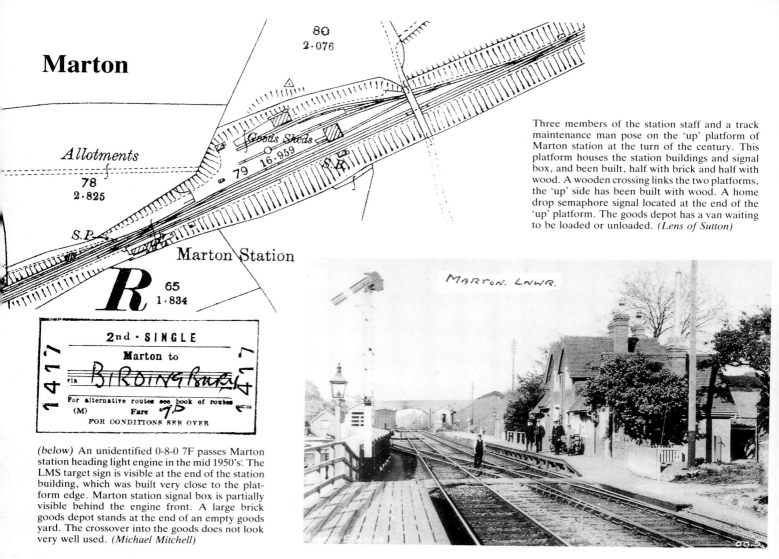

Allotments

78
2.825

80
2.076

Goods Sheds

79 16.959

S.P.

Marton Station

R 65
1.834

2nd · SINGLE

Marton to

via BIRDINGBURY

For alternative routes see book of routes
(M)   Fare 7D

FOR CONDITIONS SEE OVER

1417   1417

Three members of the station staff and a track maintenance man pose on the 'up' platform of Marton station at the turn of the century. This platform houses the station buildings and signal box, and been built, half with brick and half with wood. A wooden crossing links the two platforms, the 'up' side has been built with wood. A home drop semaphore signal located at the end of the 'up' platform. The goods depot has a van waiting to be loaded or unloaded. *(Lens of Sutton)*

MARTON. LNWR.

(below) An unidentified 0-8-0 7F passes Marton station heading light engine in the mid 1950's. The LMS target sign is visible at the end of the station building, which was built very close to the platform edge. Marton station signal box is partially visible behind the engine front. A large brick goods depot stands at the end of an empty goods yard. The crossover into the goods does not look very well used. *(Michael Mitchell)*

Birdingbury station and goods yard taken just before the First World War. Two members of staff and two members of the general public pose for this view. A junior porter sits on the once piece of essential station equipment a barrow. A wooden waiting shelter is perched on silts on the up platform. The signal box built with a brick base and wooden body is placed at the Rugby end of the platform. The goods yard has one van and one wagon visible. The goods depot has basic facilities of a brick office and a small wooden shed, the LNWR did not provide a lifting crane. (T.J.Edgington Collection)

Birdingbury

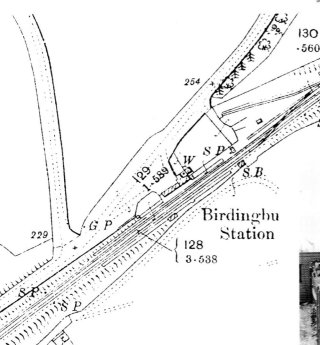

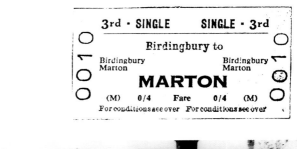

(centre) A push-pull train (with an unidentified LNWR tank propelling two passenger carriages and dragging a four wheeled van) enters Birdingbury station with an afternoon train from Leamington to Rugby. Two passengers are about to join this train, one apparently carrying a coal scuttle. The station building is uniquely different from its fellow branch stations. Platforms are illuminated by paraffin lamps, and have well attended gardens. Passengers cross the line by a crossing in the middle of the platforms. (D.T.Thompson)

The 7.54 p.m. from Rugby (Midland) to Leamington Spa (Milverton) is the last 'down' passenger train to stop at Birdingbury. It arrived ahead of time after a spirited run. The train has been was strengthened from the normal 2 coaches to four to cater for the increased demand on the last day. A group of people wait for the last westbound departure, a lady is waving the ensign and is holding a bunch of flowers. The engine hooter was liberally pulled as the train departed west into the sunset. (Michael Mensing)

(above) On the last day of passenger service, Ivatt 2-6-2T 41227 (2E) propels the 4.30 p.m. Leamington Spa (Milverton) to Rugby (Midland) away from Dunchurch station, retaining its original lamps till the end. Dunchurch signal box just pops out from the undergrowth. This station closed after the departure of this train. The fireman and passengers hang out to be photographed. (Michael Mensing)

Dunchurch

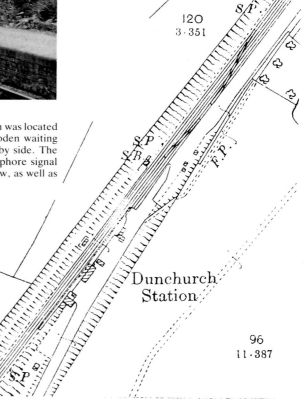

120
3·351

Dunchurch
Station

96
11·387

Dunchurch station at the turn of the century looking west towards Birdingbury. The station was located someway from the village, in the country. Both platforms are built of brick, small wooden waiting sheds have been provided on each platform, a set of steps has been placed on the Rugby side. The main station buildings are only partially visible on the 'down' side. A home drop semaphore signal indicates the approach of a train. The the platform is loaded with parcels and a full barrow, as well as a pipe smoking man looking towards the photographer. (Lens of Sutton)

Ivatt tank 41321 and two compartment coaches makes a spirited departure from Rugby (Midland) past Bilton Sidings Signal box on Whit Monday 26th May 1958 with 5.35 p.m. to Leamington Spa (Milverton). The gradient board indicates that it is about to begin a climb of 1:127. *(Michael Mensing)*

Unnamed Britannia 70047 leaves Rugby (Midland) and passes Bilton Sidings signal box with on Sunday 26th June 1960 with 10.30 a.m. Euston - Wolverhampton (High Level). This train was diverted over the Leamington line due to pre-electrification works between Rugby and Coventry. *(Michael Mensing)*

Metro-Cammell two car diesel multiple unit passes New Bilton Wharf Public Siding (on the left) with wagon visible, on a diverted 12.35 p.m. Birmingham (New Street) - Rugby (Midland) train on Sunday 26th June 1960. In the background a grain silo has two sidings which have wagons in them. *(Michael Mensing)*

Rugby (Midland)

LNWR Webb 46654 2-4-2T passes Rugby No.7 signal box with an evening departure from Rugby (Midland) to Leamington Spa Avenue on 4th April 1953, and an unidentified 0-8-0 7F, waits in the loop to proceed behind the passenger with a goods train. In the background you can just glimpse the rear of a goods heading towards Rugby along the former Midland Railway line to Leicester. *(Alec Ford)*

LMS 2-4-2T 6669 (withdrawn in September 1949 based at 8B) sits at the end of the western bay platforms at Rugby on 3rd July 1948, waiting to depart with a train to Leamington Spa. Rugby No.4 signal box controlled this end of Rugby station, with its original LNWR signals visible. The box was wiped away with electrification. *(H.C.Casserley)*

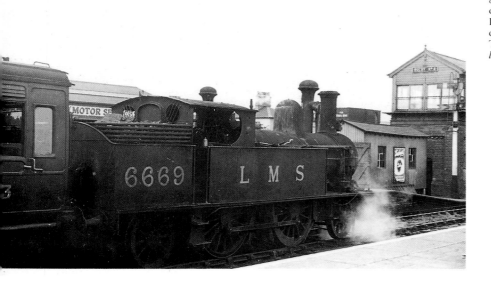

The time is approaching 2.40 p.m. and the Ivatt tank 41321 (2C) is getting steamed up ready to depart from Platform 6 at Rugby (Midland) with the 2.45 p.m. push-pull train to Leamington Spa (Avenue) on 29th April 1958. Behind the train on platform 5, a newly introduced dmu is stabled awaiting its next departure, probably to Leicester (London Road). Platform 1 has all the railway paraphernalia - barrows, bicycles, mail and piles of parcels that used to be found on are main stations. *(Michael Mensing)*

6. Marton Jn - Daventry - Weedon

A group of Daventry businessmen lead by Richard Hattersley; William Gaskell; George Fred Gwyn; Ben Nowell; Sam Druce and William Yates Freebody, formed the Daventry Railway Company to promote the construction of a railway to serve the town. The company placed its plans before parliament in November 1861 and it was sanctioned by the 'Daventry Railway Act' of 30th June 1862.

"The company to raise £30,000 in 3,000 £10 shares. The six promoters were made directors. Construction of a railway was authorised - commencing in a field called Ford Field in the Parish of Daventry in occupation of Hill Edwards near public pound in Daventry. Terminating by junction with LNWR at point signal staff 3 furlongs north of Daventry Turnpike near Weedon station passing through parishes of Daventry; Newnham; Norton and Dodford. To be built within 3 years."

The Daventry Railway company was not successful in raising sufficient funds to build the line, in the time stipulated by parliament. It did not receive approval by parliament for an extension of time, thus the scheme folded. Daventry had to wait another 24 years for its railway.

In November 1884 the LNWR presented its plans for a short branch from Weedon to Daventry, roughly following the first proposed line. This line was approved by parliament in the 'Weedon and Daventry Railway Act' of 16th July 1885. "This enabled the LNWR to construct a line of 4 miles 3 chains and 5 links in length. Commencing in Parish of Dodford, westside of the companies London to Birmingham Railway, at or near a bridge carrying the public road from Daventry to Northampton over the railway at Weedon station. Terminating on southside of the road from Daventry to Long Buckby, 250 yards north east of Daventry Church.

At Weedon the company to build - "A deviation to alter 55 chains and 20 links in Parish of Weedon Beck to Dodford of companies London and Birmingham Railway, southend of Weedon Viaduct at a point 280 yards northwest of bridge carrying road for Daventry to Northampton over that railway at Weedon. Abandon and discontinue so much of London and Birmingham Railway necessary by such deviation. To be constructed within five years."

The line from Weedon to Daventry was opened to all traffic on Thursday 1st March 1888. The 'Northampton Mercury' gave the following report on the opening - "The work was commenced by the London and North-Western Railway Company and the contract was given to Messrs. Naylor Bros. of Derby Dale, Huddersfield.

Colonel Rich was sent down by the Board of Trade on Monday to make the necessary examination of the line before it could be passed; and he commenced his tour of inspection at Weedon shortly after ten. He arrived at Weedon in a special train from Euston; and he was accompanied by Mr R. Turnbull (Assistant Traffic Superintendent, L and N.W.R.); Mr J. Groome (District Superintendent); Mr W. Hurst (Resident Engineer): Mr H.B. Thornhill (Assistant Chief Engineer); Mr James Angus (Divisional Engineer); Mr A.M.Thompson (Superintendent Signal Department); Mr W.T. Tunbridge (Telegraph Superintendent); Mr A.M. Mumford (Locomotive Superintendent); and Inspectors of various departments. Mr Marshall, Mr Butcher, Mr Smith, Mr Acock, and others.

The construction of the new line was adopted by the Railway Company as the opportunity of effecting some much needed improvements at Weedon. The station there was no doubt all very well sixty years ago, when passengers sat on the top of the railway coaches, with the guard behind, keeping a watch on them and the parcels; but for years it has been a positive disgrace. Probably it has had the lowest platform on the whole system: probably the worst paved. Now all that has been done away with, and a brand new station, with two modern platforms, has been erected. The alterations commence some distance from Blisworth and the London side of the old station. Nearly opposite to Weedon Church the old line is discarded, and the new one takes its place, gradually rising right through the station. Under the high road to Daventry a large girder bridge has been built; and the station platforms abut upon this, on the opposite side of the road to the old station. The booking office is placed on the bridge connecting the two platforms, the waiting rooms, and so on, some of which - those on the Daventry platform are already erected, will be at platform level. The down platform, is about 400 yards in length; the Daventry trains start from the left side; the Rugby trains from the right. A hundred yards or so beyond the station, a large signal box Weedon No. 2 has been built, controlling all the points of the junction.

From this point the Daventry line, which is a single one, has a rather steep rise: indeed for three-fourths of the distance, the line takes a steep gradient which is almost uniformly one in 80. After running parallel with the old line for 600 or 700 yards, all the time getting higher, the new railway diverges to the left, and runs along the valley of Dodford Brook. This little

stream flows at the bottom of the table land which, commencing at Weedon, stretches almost to Daventry. The main road runs, first in the centre of this upland, and then along its northern brow. The stream and the railway run below and the embankments can be plainly seen at several points from the road. The railway passes just to the right of Dodford Vicarage, almost going through the incumbents garden. The church is farther to the left. Thence, still rising, the railway passes close to the base of Borough Hill, which is on the right, and ends at the Norton-road, exactly in front of the east end of Daventry parish station. As the line is a single one all the way, Daventry Station has only one platform, and upon this the east and north east wind plays with all its fury. On the cold day like Monday, with the snow a foot deep on all the country side, there is probably not a colder station in all the Midlands. The new railway is laid with steel rails, steel sleepers, and steel keys. The rails are long ones, but not so heavy as those usually employed for main lines. They weigh 80lbs. to the yard. Six road bridges and several of the minor size had been made, two of the larger are skew bridges, a kind of erection always of more a less trouble to engineers and architects. There are no level crossings.

There is every facility for the proper conduct of the line, both at Weedon and Daventry. At the latter place there are plenty of sidings, stabling for half a dozen horses, cart sheds, goods shed, and the stationmasters residence. The new stationmaster at Daventry is Mr Joseph Izzard, until recently booking clerk at Weedon. Mr Allmitt, the careful and respected stationmaster at Weedon, will have charge of the enlarged station. The two stations were built for the contractors by Messrs. Parnell & Son of Rugby.

Colonel Rich minutely inspected the alterations at Weedon, and paid most particular attention to the signalling department and the levers for moving the points. Then he proceeded in a small train to Daventry, accompanied by most of the officials above mentioned, stopping at various places on the road to examine the bridges, arches and embankments. At Daventry Station there was another searching investigation. This concluded, the party re entered the train and the return journey, nearly all down hill to Weedon, was accomplished in less than ten minutes. Colonel Rich appeared thoroughly satisfied with what he saw; and though his inspection may necessitate a few trifling alterations.

The first train to run was a goods train, which left Weedon soon after seven. It conveyed a large quantity of coals and several empty passenger carriages. At Daventry the engine, was attached to these carriages, without the coal wagons, and formed the first passenger train. About 80 passengers were conveyed in it. The bookings were to various parts of the North Western system, but most were 'returns to Weedon' - fare 8d, a considerable number of Daventry people experiencing an ardent desire to take a train trip on the day of opening. A large number of people assembled to see the train off, and a cheer was raised as the engine puffed out of the station. Large numbers awaited its return, and the train departing a second time the number of passengers was more than doubled. People kept about the station the whole day long and the crowds seemed to get thicker every hour.

The Corporation decided to mark the event by proceeding together over the new line. They met by invitation of the Mayor at the Moot Hall, thence proceeding to the station, entering a saloon carriage attached to the 12.35 p.m. train from Daventry. They returned in less than an hour and headed off to a typical Victorian celebration of a meal, drinks and speeches."

The table below shows the first timetable between Weedon and Daventry :-

Table 1

Weekdays		a.m.	a.m.	p.m.	p.m.	p.m.	p.m.
Weedon	d	9.15	11.10	1. 0	5.15	6.45	7.25
Daventry	a	9.25	11.20	1.10	5.25	6.55	7.35

Weekdays		a.m.	a.m.	p.m.	p.m.	p.m.	p.m.
Daventry	d	8.25	9.55	12.35	4.35	5.30	7. 5
Weedon	a	8.35	10.05	12.45	4.45	5.40	7.15

Company engineer Mr F.Stevenson presented plans to parliament in November 1889 to extend the line from Daventry to join the Rugby to Leamington line near Marton. It would be 14 miles and 6 chains in length.

Parliament sanctioned this work as part of the LNWR Further Powers Act of 4th August 1890. "The Daventry to Leamington Railway was to be 14 miles 47 chains and 60 links in length. Commencing near the northern terminus of the present line, to terminate in the Parish of Hunningham by a junction with the Rugby to Leamington line at or near a bridge carrying Ridgeway Lane over that railway. To be constructed within 5 years."

The LNWR submitted plans in November 1892 to build a new railway and alter the levels at Weedon and on the extension. This work was sanctioned in the Act of 27th July 1893. "New Railway and deviation. A junction at Weedon 36 chains 15 links long wholly in the Parish of Dodford commencing by junction with LNWR companies railway and terminating by junction with Weedon and Daventry railway. A deviation and alteration 1 mile 51 chains 11 links in length in levels of construction authorised in 1890 act, as lies between points 2 miles 61 chains and 4 miles 31 chains shown on the plans. Alter road No.3 at Braunston to inclines of slopes to 1:9."

This act enabled the company to construct the terminating platform at Weedon and reduce some of the gradients between Daventry and Flecknoe. The railway opened to all traffic on Monday 1st August 1895. The timetable is given in Table 2 below.

Table 2

Weekdays		a.m.	a.m.	a.m.	p.m.	p.m.	p.m.	p.m.
Warwick	d	7.20		9.55		3.35		6.30
Leamington	d	7.25		10. 0		3.40		6.35
Southam & Long Itchington	d	7.37		10.12		3.52		6.47
Napton & Stockton	d	7.44		10.18		3.58		6.53
Flecknoe	d	7.54		10.26		4. 6		7. 1
Braunston	d	8. 2		10.32		4.12		7. 7
Daventry	d	8.10	10. 0	10.40	2.20	4.20	5.40	7.16
Weedon	a	8.25	10.10	10.50	2.30	4.30	5.50	7.25

Weekdays		a.m.	a.m.	a.m.	p.m.	p.m.	p.m.	p.m.
Weedon	d	9.12	9.44	11.51	1.42	5.10		7.30
Daventry	d	9.23	9.54	12. 0	1.52	5.20		7.40
Braunston	d	9.31		12. 8		5.28		7.48
Flecknoe	d	9.37		12.14		5.35		7.55
Napton & Stockton	d	9.46		12.22		5.43		8. 3
Southam & Long Itchington	d	9.50		12.28		5.49		8. 9
Leamington	a	10. 5		12.40		6. 5		8.25
Warwick	a	10.10		12.44		6. 9		8.30

Press coverage of the opening of the extension was patchy with the local Leamington newspapers ignoring it, however the 'Rugby Advertiser' reported thus :- "Early September 1892, the first sod in the construction of the new extension line from Daventry to Leamington was cut. The main object of the railway, which is a few chains under 14 miles long, is to relieve the traffic from the north at Rugby station, and give a direct communication between the mainline of the L and N W Railway Company at Weedon, via Leamington, to Birmingham, but it has also had the effect of opening up a district, the residents of which have a long time felt keenly the want of such accommodation. The contract of Messrs. Walter Scott and Co. of Newcastle upon Tyne, was accepted for the construction of the railway, and aided by exceptionally fine weather, they were enabled to push on with the operations very rapidly, the result being that by October last they had completed the earth works and bridges, and practically all that was required to finish the line was the laying down of the top ballast and rails, which the L&NW Company undertook themselves. From an engineering point of view was not very great, though the ground to be traversed was decidedly rough and hilly, especially at the Daventry end, and some 26 cuttings, ranging up to 40 or 50 feet deep, and necessitating the removal of quite a million cubic yards of soil, had to be made; and a similar number of embankments had to be tipped. The notion appears to be prevailing in some quarters that the railway company would utilise the new line by which Kilsby Tunnel would be avoided - for their express traffic, but this hardly seems likely, as, not-withstanding the many cuttings and embankments, the length is anything but level and includes several steep gradients. It was hoped originally that the line would be opened earlier this year, but was delayed by various causes. It was not until Thursday, the 1st of August, that the railway, having been inspected and passed two days earlier by Col. Yorke - an officer sent down by the Board of Trade - was first used by the public.

The men upon whom devolved the honour of conducting the first passenger train up the line from Leamington to Daventry and thence to Weedon were John Clarke and William Aiken, both Leamington guards and the driver of the engine (David Russell) hailed from the same town. The train left Leamington without any ceremony at 7.25 a.m., and the passengers totalled 60 to 70, of whom, perhaps, a third booked from Southam, where a crowd of nearly 100 people had assembled, and as the engine steamed into the station a ringing cheer broke from them. Nothing of special interest occurred in the journey, though at each station there were several passengers to pick up, and the villagers along the route turned out to see the first train. The train later returned a little later, leaving Daventry at 9.25 a.m, and among the number who took seats in the coaches were Mr Groome (superintendent of the district), Mr Hurst (resident engineer of the line) and several other officials.

On quitting Daventry, where a new platform, with waiting rooms and the usual offices, have been built, and the line is spanned by a light bridge, a salute was fired by the explosion of a score of fog signals, which had been

placed on the line before the engine, and as the train got into the open it was greeted by a flourish of trumpets, which came from the direction of Mr Burton's garden.

After crossing the Norton and Welton Roads - the latter at the brow of the hill which overlooks the reservoir a little more than half a mile from Daventry - the railway intersects the Ashby St. Ledgers Road, and cuts the end of the old Middlemoor reservoir about a mile and a half from the town. Then passing near the tunnel and alongside the canal, it runs close by the southern side of Braunston, and through the wharf near the Ship Inn, where five or six houses, which stood in the way, have had to come down. Here, at a point three miles from Daventry, the first station has been built, and a very pretty and convenient structure it is. From end to end the platforms measure 100 yards, and the centre is covered in by a wooden awning. For the convenience of general passengers a commodious waiting room and booking office has been provided. Its dimensions are 24 ft by 10ft. Adjoining is a smaller waiting room for ladies only, furnished, and measuring 15ft by

10 ft. In addition there are the usual lavatories and stationmaster's offices. a good horse dock, a milk landing, and shortly cattle pens will be provided on the down side, where already suitable goods shed has been built. The shed is 58 ft. long by 27ft. wide. Amongst other necessaries in the shed are two large hand cranes, each capable of lifting 30 cwt., and a patent weighing machine by Pooley and Sons.

The entrance to the station is 100 yards from the highway; the platforms are reached by two flights of steps, each with a corrugated iron roof, and there is a subway for passengers to cross from the up to the down side. Owing to the depth of the bank, the station has been erected on piles, and the view from the platform is worth seeing. That the residents of this populous village appreciate their new station was proved by the large number who booked during the first day the line was open. In the forenoon, the courteous stationmaster, Mr Alfred Morgan, issues tickets to considerably over 100 persons, a good number of whom took a trip to Daventry or Leamington, just for the fun of the thing.

Leaving Braunston, the line was carried by a heavy girder bridge, supported by strong buttresses and three massive steel stanchions, over the road to the wharf, and through the parish of Wolfhampcote. The church, a very old and dilapidated looking structure, stands within a stone's throw of the line, and a quarter of a miles farther on the M. S. & L. Railway will cross over the track - the buttresses to support the ironwork having already been built. After crossing by a girder bridge the Oxford Canal for the only time, to the north of Nethercote, Flecknoe Station - built in the angle of the four roads leading from Shuckburgh to Sawbridge, and Grandborough to Flecknoe - is reached. The building here is very small, unassuming in character, and there is only a single platform on the down side. To give some idea of the size of the waiting room and the offices we may say they were built by the Railway Company at Crewe, and conveyed in three sections - on trucks of the 'crocodile' pattern - to their destination. Netherthless, Mr Kirk, the stationmaster, booked during Thursday morning about twenty passengers to various places. Proceeding towards Leamington, the line passes Tomlow Spinney, and crosses the Warwick and Napton Canal for the first time at a spot 8½ from Daventry. A mile farther on Stockton station is reached. This, like Flecknoe, is a pitch pine box-like structure, but differs from the former in that it possesses a double platform. Mr Law, the stationmaster, booked about 40 passengers by the first four trains. Continuing, the railway comes on through the limestone works of Messrs Nelson & Co. and crosses an arm of the canal. Facilities, in the form of three sidings, have been given here for the easy transport of lime and cement. Immediately after leaving these works the line is taken under the Southam and Rugby road, on past the limeworks of Messrs. Griffin, Graves, and Kaye and Co. - each of whom has a siding - and gliding beneath the road from Southam to Long Itchington, another commodious station, resembling closely that at Braunston is found. This is almost midway between Southam and Itchington, and instead of running to Marton as heretofore, the omnibus will only travel between Southam and the new station in future. Mr Arthur Mason's (stationmaster) first bookings were :- 7.35 a.m. train, *31*; 9.52 a.m., *10*; 10.10 a.m., *18*; 12.29, *21*. There is also a goods yard and shed and the usual conveniences. From here the line crosses the River Itchin, the Warwick and Napton canal for the second time, and a mile and a half from the junction with the Leamington and Rugby line at Hunningham Hill cross the Itchen river twice.

It is partly single line, and the mode of signalling is what is known as the electric staff system, patented by F.W. Webb and A.W. Thompson. The principle on which it works was aptly described recently by an official as "the three ones", which meant that the object was to ensure that one train was in the section at one time. The line is divided up into sections, the dividing stations being Weedon, Daventry, Braunston, Stockton, Southam and Marton Junction, and here mechanical appliances have been provided. The system is pronounced to be an excellent one, and if properly carried out, cannot but secure for the passengers the greatest possible safety. Before starting alone the line, the driver is supplied with a staff - a rod of steel a foot and a half long - taken by the stationmaster from the ingenious machine or "box," in which ten such staves are fixed. An intimation is given to the official at the other end of the section to the effect that this has been done, and the latter thereupon locks the machine. On entering the second section, the driver is given another staff, which he again exchanges for a third at the next stopping place and so on throughout the whole length of the line. In addition to this arrangement, the ordinary signals are used. At present arrangements have been made for the running of four passenger trains daily each way, and two goods trains, and on Thursday everything passed off most satisfactorily.

It may be mentioned that the third class fare from Rugby to all stations on the line is a uniform one of 1s 8½d., and the passenger may travel either by way of Leamington or Weedon.

At Daventry the extension of the line to Leamington was not meet by the same enthusiasm as the opening from Weedon. A few persons found their way to the station to watch the first arrival from Leamington at 8.10 a.m., and saw about 50 passengers alight. Some Daventry people walked to Braunston so that they may ride on the first train over the new line.

It may be mentioned that the third class fare from Rugby to all stations on the line is a uniform one of 1s 8½d., and the passenger may travel either by way of Leamington or Weedon.

At Daventry the extension of the line to Leamington was not meet by the same enthusiasm as the opening from Weedon. A few persons found their way to the station to watch the first arrival from Leamington at 8.10 a.m., and saw about 50 passengers alight. Some Daventry people walked to Braunston so that they may ride on the first train over the new line.

For a short while the LNWR tried dropping a slip coach for Leamington at Weedon, this experiment did not last long. On 1st May 1910 the LNWR commenced using a composite motor set (formed of two coaches and a tank engine) on the Weedon to Leamington and Warwick Milverton service. Flecknoe The commencement of the First World War in August 1914, did not initially effect the passenger service, major cuts were experienced in January 1917, Flecknoe was closed to passengers from 1st August and was not reopened until 1st March 1919.

After grouping of the LNWR into the LMSR in 1923, the motive power

remained ex LNWR 4-6-2T and 2-4-2T locomotives. In the 1930's the Fowler design 2-6-2T engine appeared and started working local passenger duties on the Weedon line. Between 1922 and 1928, The LMSR provided a siding at Storton (1 mile 39 chains from Weedon No.2 SB). It had disappeared from the RCH 1956 handbook.

The passenger service did change much through the 1930's, it was not until May 1939 that the LMSR made any major alterations and introduced an emergency timetable in anticipation of war. The service was reduced to eastbound trains leaving Warwick (Milverton) at 6.55 a.m. to Weedon; 7.33 a.m.; 12.44 p.m. SO to Napton & Stockton; 3.33 p.m. to Weedon; 4.26 p.m. to Napton & Stockton and 6.45 p.m. from Leamington Spa Avenue to Weedon. Westbound services all terminated at Warwick (Milverton) and left at 8.12 a.m. from Napton & Stockton; 9.12 a.m. from Weedon; 1.36 p.m. SO; 5.18 p.m. from Napton & Stockton; 5.28 p.m.:9. 9 p.m. from Weedon. This timetable withdrew all the Weedon to Daventry shuttles. In July 1939 the pre-emergency timetable with a few alterations was resumed. The outbreak of war on 3rd September brought the reintroduction of the May emergency timetable.

The prewar timetable was never fully reintroduced and the Weedon to Leamington and Warwick Milverton service ran in a reduced form, with an additional through train on Saturday.

The line passed from the ownership of the LMS to British Railways on 1st January 1948, and came under the control of the London Midland Region. On 1st July 1950 the Railway Executive added the suffix "London Road" to the former LMSR station at Braunston. Flecknoe station was the first station to close to passengers on 3rd November 1952, however the staff were kept at the public delivery siding until October 1956. Braunston London Road was built with two platforms but by 1956 the up platform had been removed, the crossing loop remained for goods traffic.

Warwick shed was the home to the last two LMR Webb 2-4-2T 46604/16, and by June 1955, 46604 had been reduced to one passenger duty the 7.30 a.m. Leamington Spa - Napton & Stockton and 8. 7 a.m. Napton & Stockton - Leamington service, then it shunted at Milverton and returned to shed. However by late August it had been withdrawn and was soon replaced by a LMS motor fitted 0-4-4T 41909 which had arrived at Warwick from Watford. It was soon found at work on the Weedon and Northampton trains. These engines were well liked by the drivers and firemen.

A report appeared in the 'Railway Observer' of a journey on the 9. 0 a.m. from Weedon to Leamington on 27th April 1956, it left Weedon punctually with 40157 (2C) on a single brake third M5850M and four passengers. The locomotive had no problem in coping with the 1 in 80 climb from Weedon to Daventry. The stations had been recently been repainted and were in a good state of repair. A number of passengers entrained at Southam and Napton.

The poor passenger service was not conducive for passengers to travel by rail, and with a more frequent local bus services, serving the centre of villages and towns, the railway could not compete. Passenger trains between Weedon and Leamington Spa (Milverton) were withdrawn and Weedon and intermediate stations at Daventry; Braunston; Napton & Stockton and Southam & Long Itchington were closed at the end of the Summer timetable on 15th September 1958. With no Sunday service, the last passenger train ran on Saturday 13th.

Table 3

Weekdays		2		C SO	N SX	N SO	E	B SX	SO
		a.m.	a.m.	p.m.	p.m.	p.m.	p.m.	p.m.	p.m.
Leamington Spa (Milverton)	d	7.10		12.49	2.37	2.50	4. 7	5.55	
Leamington Spa Avenue	d	7.16	7.30	12.55	2.43	2.58	4.20	6. 0	6.30
Southam & Long Itchington	d	7.31	7.45	1.10	2.58	3.13	4.35	6.15	6.45
Napton & Stockton	d	7.37	7.51	1.17	3. 4	3.19	4.41	6.21	6.51
Braunston	d	7.50			1.30	3.17	3.32		
Daventry	d	8. 0			1.42	3.27	3.42		
Weedon	a	8. 8			1.50	3.35	3.52		

2   Second Class Only
E   To Nuneaton Trent Valley a. 6.58 p.m. (SX) 6.50 p.m. (SO)
N   From Northampton (Castle) d. 6.14 p.m.

Weekdays		2		SO		E	N SX	N SO
			SO					
		a.m.	a.m.	p.m.	p.m.	p.m.	p.m.	p.m.
Weedon	d		9. 0		2.30		6.41	6.46
Daventry	d		9.13		2.42		6.53	6.58
Braunston	d		9.21		2.50		7. 0	7. 5
Napton & Stockton	d	8. 9	9.33		3. 3	4.55	7.12	7.17
Southam & Long Itchington	d	8.15	9.39	1.50	3.14	5. 0	7.18	7.23
Leamington Spa Avenue	a	8.32	9.56	2. 6	3.31	5.20	7.35	7.40
Leamington Spa (Milverton)	a	8.35	10. 1	2.10		5.50		

2   Second Class Only
B   From Birmingham (New Street) d. 5. 8 p.m.
C   From Coventry d. 12.23 p.m
E   From Nuneaton Trent Valley d. 3.12 p.m.
N   To Northampton (Castle) a. 4. 1 (SX) 4.12 (SO)

The demise of the Weedon Flyer was described by the 'Rugby Advertiser' and 'Leamington Spa Courier' and reported - "The last passenger train left Northampton Castle station at 6.14 p.m. on Saturday, arrived at Daventry station at 7.10 p.m. with six coaches (1 L&Y BCK, 1 LNW SO, 1 LNW, 1 MR and 2 LMS non corridor coaches) and carrying at least 100 passengers. Normally, the train has had two coaches, with an average of half a dozen passengers a day on the whole of the journey.

From the train at Daventry alighted the Mayor and Mayoress of Daventry (Alderman and Mrs G. Williams) and Mr William Henry James (80) of Market Square, Daventry. He was taken by his mother on the first public train from Weedon to Daventry on 1st March 1888. They joined the train at Weedon.The single fare from Weedon to Daventry on the last day was 8d, the fare had only doubled in 70 years.

Sixty or seventy of the passengers went through to Leamington. Souvenir hunters have been travelling from station to station by car and bicycle and buying tickets at the various booking offices to add to their collections.

At Napton and Stockton, where a dozen press photographers were present, gathered on the platform were several people who watched the last train go through. Long Itchington station platform was packed. At 7.50 p.m. they heard their last passenger engine's whistle, followed by twelve bangs from the detonators placed on the track.

The station staff reported a record sale of tickets - singles to Stockton and Leamington and tickets for bicycles, prams and even dogs, September 13th, 1958 may well be an unlucky day for people who have prams, omnibuses do not take them."

Whilst the 'Leamington Spa Courier' gave the following report :-"Never did the Weedon Flyer have a reception like the one it got on Saturday night, when it rolled into Leamington Spa Avenue station for the last time. There was an air of gala expectancy, albeit in a small and intimate way as we waited on the gaslit platform.

Why, the Leamington station master himself, Mr Alfred Winter, had made a special point of turning up (though in a brown trilby hat) for the occasion!

As we waited, he explained that the train had been given four extra coaches, for the benefit of extra passengers who were expected to make the last sentimental journey. Mr Winter further announced that an 'up' train (to Rugby) would be held on the opposite platform, regardless of timetables, to whisk passengers from the flyer back eastwards. The closure of the line would save British Railways £11,000 per year.

At 7.47 p.m. the up train pulled in, paused, moved forward a few yards as if anxious to be off. The last flyer should have arrived at 7.43 p.m. Then 25 minutes overdue, the Flyer began to come in. Foreman Jack Morris leapt nimbly across the rails with his lamp and prepared to greet an important visitor.

We ran forward and cheered back at those who cheered as they hung from the windows. Then, with a doomful snort, the Flyer stood still and disgorged her two score of history conscious passengers.

Many of them scurried across the bridge to catch the up train back to Rugby and the bus back to Daventry. But for about 30 the fun was not over yet. In a cheerful jumble they surged forward to the engine. The Ivatt Class

2 tank no. 41228 was driven by Alfred Smith from Dickens Road, Warwick.

The driver was handed a glass beer mug containing a retirement card from an 'old railway collegue'. Mystified, he stoutly denied that he was retiring for least three years. He shook many hands amid the popping flashbulbs, he admitted "I've never known anything like it in 20 years of engine driving". Whilst his fireman Derek Malin, of Chesford Crescent, Warwick could only muster a sooty firemans grin."

Two sets of converted electrification coaches were stored in Daventry goods yard for over twelve months from June 1960. The 1961 working timetable showed a healthy freight traffic between Weedon and Southam. The goods depots were served by two daily pickups, 10.07 a.m. (SX) Leamington Spa - Weedon and 07.50 a.m. (SX) Blisworth - Leamington. Four or five chalk trains ran to Rugby Cement Works at Southam & Long Itchington. Coming from either Grove Siding, Leighton Buzzard (ex Tottenhoe) or Blisworth. Coal was worked in by Nuneaton engines.

Napton to Southam (Rugby Cement) lost it regular through freight on 5th November 1962. British Railways withdrew all public goods facilities from Daventry; Braunston; Flecknoe and Napton on on 2nd December 1963, with no other traffic the line between Weedon and Southam (Rugby Cement Works) was effectively closed. The three mile stub to Rugby Cement and the goods depot at Southam & Long Itchington survived and was served as required by the daily Rugby - Leamington pickup goods. Track lifting commenced on 7th April 1964 at Daventry and 8F 48349 was noted at Napton & Stockton on a demolition train. Lifting was completed between Napton and Weedon No.2 by early May and the mainline connection was taken out of use on Sunday 10th May.

Rugby Cement had decided that the chalk from Tottenhoe would arrive at Long Itchington & Southam by newly constructed pipeline and came into use in 1965. This ended the most lucrative traffic on the line. The last public goods at Southam & Long Itchington was closed from 5th July 1965. Coal had now become the only reason for the retention of this spur line from Marton Jn. Until the closure of the Leamington to Marton line April 1966, Nuneaton 8F's would bring East Midlands coal from Nuneaton to the cement works. The operating practice changed and the coal train was broken into two portions and to enable easier runround at Marton Jn. Steam ended in 1966 with the closure of Nuneaton shed and the freight was worked by BR/Sulzer Type 2's (later Class 25's) until the end.

The traffic for Rugby Cement at Southam came from Rugby and required a reversal at Marton Junction. The signal box still controlled the line until 4th July 1967 when the line from Rugby to Southam became single line throughout, operated as one engine in steam.

By January 1968 the station at Daventry had been demolished and the goods yard levelled and the line to the south being used as part of an industrial estate. The line is now part of the Daventry bypass. Southam & Long Itchington station was flattened and the bank graded by July 1968.

Coal traffic to Southam had ceased by Summer 1985, the last train to traverse the line was on 31247 on 20th June when a weedkilling train ran to the buffer stops to the east of Southam. On 1st August the line was officially closed to all traffic, thus ending 90 years of usefulness.

Bunker first 41231 is working hard to climb away from Marton Jn with its train from Leamington to Weedon in 1956. Normally a two coach push-pull set, today is composed of three maroon non corridor passenger coaches and one blood and custard brake. *(G.Coltas)*

Southam & Long Itchington

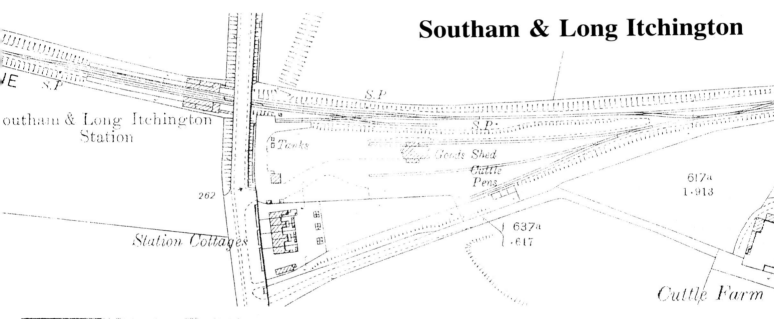

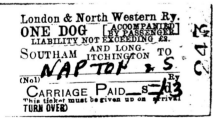

The 2.37 p.m. from Leamington Spa (Avenue) to Northampton (Castle) was the last train of the day to depart from Leamington Spa (Avenue) for stations east of Napton & Stockton. Here Ivatt 2-6-2T 41228 comes off the single line section from Marton Jn into Southam & Long Itchington on a wet 18th January 1958. This train ran along the West Coast mainline from Weedon to Blisworth before reversing for Northampton. *(Michael Mensing)*

Push-pull propelled by 41227 comes to a stand at Southam & Long Itchington on the 6.14 p.m. Northampton (Castle) - Leamington Spa (Avenue) local on 20th May 1958. All the station buildings are housed in one block on the 'down' (Leamington) platform. The gents toilet is located at the western end and where the vents appear in the slate roof. A corrugated iron roof protects passengers as they descend the steps to the booking office and the platform. Whilst the up platform is now bare. (*T.J.Edgington*)

An unidentified 8F is seen leaving Southam & Long Itchington with a train of empty chalk wagons. The goods depot is laid out on the southside of the line, it has a wooden goods shed, and the yard has a line of empty wagons stabled in it. In the background Southam Lime Works looms large, it was a large stack of coal as well as two lines of wagons in its sidings. (*Michael Mitchell*)

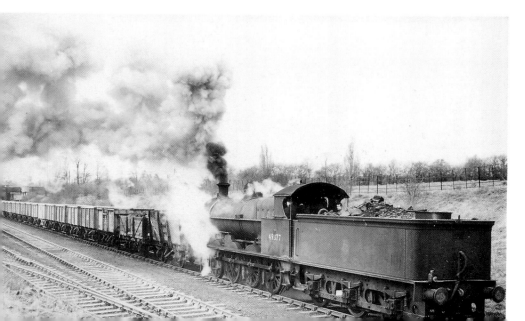

A 0-8-0 49377 (Entered traffic in November 1902 as LNWR 1055, was rebuilt twice to G1 in March 1922 and to G2a in June 1940. Withdrawn in October 1962) pulls away from Southam & Long Itchington on 8th April 1958 with an eastbound goods train. The leading two wagons are loaded with coal, whilst the others are empty chalk wagons. The track that leads to the left goes into the public goods depot. (*R.C.Riley*)

Weedkiller train hauled by 31247 (BS) has reached the stop block just to the east of Southam Cement Works on 20th June 1985. Trains were only allowed to travel at a maximum speed of 20 m.p.h. over the branch from Marton Jn. This was the last train to traverse this line. *(Ron Kosys)*

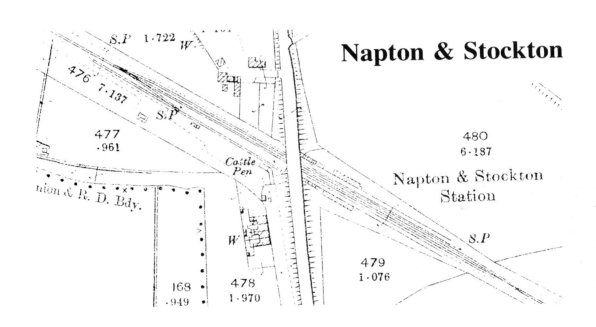

Napton & Stockton

The main buildings on Napton & Stockton station were placed on the down platform, from where the majority of the customers would depart. This view was taken just before the First World War. A member of staff stands by booking office door, the station clock is on his right. The walls are covered in enamel plaque advertisements extolling New Hudson bicycles and Tower Tea. The LNWR has its own noticeboards giving the local timetable and an unidentifiable poster. A well dressed gentlemen sits on the named station seat. The platform is festooned in flower pots, tubs and window boxes, once typical of the country station. Its goods depot is visible through the bridge arch (with bridge plate 42 attached) and is full of vans and loaded wagons, one of which is owned by the Midland Railway. The station was located just under a mile from the village of Stockton and about 2 miles from the village of Napton on the Hill. *(Lens of Sutton)*

On 20th May 1958, Class 4 42566 2-6-4T has arrived at Napton & Stockton with 5. 8 p.m. from Birmingham (New Street) composed of a LMS BG M20997M and non corridor compartment coach. This train has been given the road to proceed and to propell into the down platform and return to Leamington A simple wooden platform has been built on the 'up' platform. A 8F is stood at the down home signal, and will follow the Class 4 to Southam. (T.J.Edgington)

On 20th May 1958, 8F 48131 enters Napton & Stockton station with 18 wagons loaded with chalk for Southam Cement Works. This train has to wait for the proceeding passenger to arrive at the next section at Southam & Long Itchington station. The pine box station building holds the booking office, staff rooms and toilets, one window and one door have been blocked up since opening. The British Railways timetable is posted on the wall, as well as the bus companies timetable. (T.J.Edgington)

The Stanier Black 5 44833 was the sixth engine to work the RCTS 'Grafton Railtour' on Sunday 9th August 1959. Originated from Kings Cross with a rake of Gresley coaches and passed through Hitchin; Bedford; Northampton (Bridge St.); Blisworth; Woodford Halse; Calvert; Verney Jn; Banbury before reaching Leamington. This locomotive took over in the exchange sidings, and ran to Berkswell, here due to capacity problems on the mainline the loco had to run to Kenilworth Jn before it could run round. Here it is seen heading east, away from Napton & Stockton on the return leg to Kings Cross. It will work the train as far as Luton (Bute Street), before being relieved by North British Type 2 D6101. (Michael Mensing)

Flecknoe

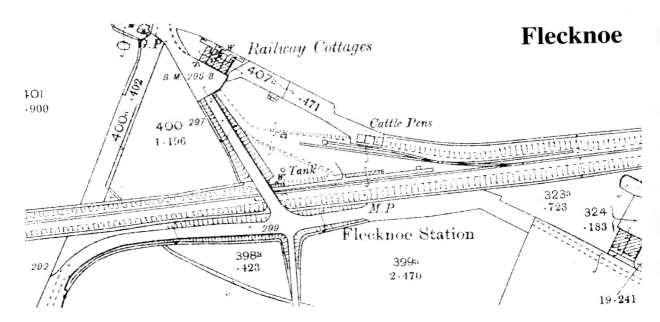

The stationmaster of Flecknoe poses for this photograph on the step to his office with pipe in hand, note that the seat has been positioned to show the stations name. The station was a simple wooden platform, light by paraffin lamps. A barrow has a churn shaped object waiting to be put on the approaching train which has blown its whistle to warn the station of its approach. The goods depot siding leads off behind the station. This line was built with a double track formation, but was never required. Flecknoe station was located in a sparsely populated area and served the surrounding hamlets of Flecknoe (1½ miles); Lower Shuckburgh (1½ miles) and Grandborough (3 miles). *(Lens of Sutton)*

(below) In May 1966, this was the view of the site of Flecknoe station, looking west towards Napton & Stockton. All that remains is a small wooden shed and a sectioned concrete building. *(Michael Mitchell)*

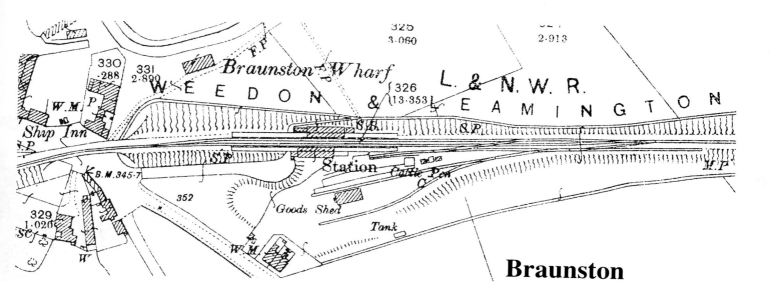

Braunston

Looking along the 'down' platform at Braunston towards Flecknoe, you can see a small wooden structure with a Braunston wooden sign on its front, this was the second signal box to be erected here. The crossing loop here was bi-directional, and was probably altered upon the demise of the 'up' platform. The station canopy extends to cover part of the platform. A water column and shute are to be found at the end of this platform. Station lighting was paraffin lamps. *(D. T. Thompson)*

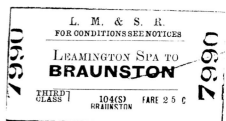

Five days after the line closed to all traffic Braunston (London Road) station has been stripped of its signalling. The view is looking east towards Weedon, the water column and leather shute are still in situ. Once a double platformed station, the up platform was approached by a subway and this was a unique feature on this line. The down platform is partially solid with a modern concrete base for half of the way, with the rest being wood on concrete piles. The station was light by paraffin lamps. The brick goods depot is partially visible behind the wooden fence. *(G. Biddle)*

Daventry

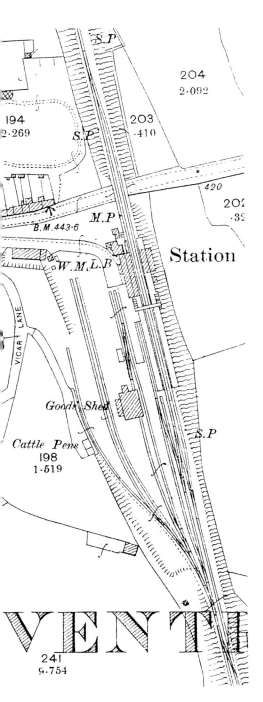

A deserted Daventry station on 10th June 1957, looking north from near the footbridge, on the 'down' side the ornate wood fretwork canopy covered this part of the wooden platform. The sign says - Booking cloak room and parcels office. At the end of the platform notices on either side tell you to cross the line only by the footbridge. An open door on a wooden slate tiled hut with 'DAVENTRY' on the front is in fact the station signal box. Rodding disappears both north and south along the track. *(H.B.Priestley/G.Hurst Collection)*

(centre) The main station building at Daventry station was constructed from wood and the entrance was through the doors covered by a short canopy. A United bus company timetable is placed by the entrance door. Although closed the offices are still in use, when this photograph was taken on 28th July 1959. *(H.C.Casserley)*

(right) Saturdays only 2.50 p.m. Leamington Spa (Milverton) - Northampton (Castle) push-pull is eased away from by 2-6-2T 41285 (2C) with a standard two coach rake on 6th September 1958. One week later this train would be the last through train Northampton from the Daventry line. The station is still being light by gas lamps. Daventry station was the only one on this line to have a footbridge. *(C.Riddle)*

Weedon

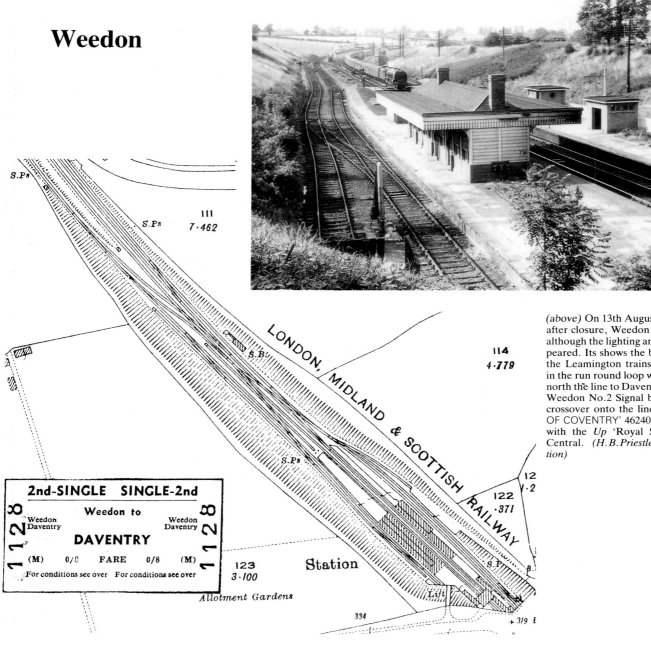

LONDON, MIDLAND & SCOTTISH RAILWAY

S.Ps

111
7·462

S.Ps

S.B.

S.Ps

S.Ps

114
4·779

12
·2

122
·371

S.P.

B.

123
3·100

Station

Allotment Gardens

334

+ 319 E

Lift

(above) On 13th August 1959, nearly a year after closure, Weedon station is still intact, although the lighting and totems have disappeared. Its shows the bay platform used by the Leamington trains. The water column in the run round loop was still insitu. To the north the line to Daventry climbs away from Weedon No.2 Signal box and is shows the crossover onto the line is well used. 'CITY OF COVENTRY' 46240 (1A) is approaching with the *Up* 'Royal Scot' from Glasgow Central. *(H.B.Priestley/ G.Hurst Collection)*

A clean Warwick based Ivatt 2-6-2T 41227 is waiting in the back platform of Weedon station to propel its two coach motor set on the 2.27 p.m. departure to Leamington Spa (Avenue) on 18th January 1958. A youngster is looking out of the locomotive. The water column is situated next to the locomotive and note the large wheel for turning on the water supply. *(Michael Mensing)*